★★★★★★★★★★★
AMERICAN
GUERRILLA
★★★★★★★★★★

Also by Roger Hilsman

★ ★

Strategic Intelligence and National Decisions (1956)

*To Move a Nation: The Politics of Foreign Policy in the
Administration of John F. Kennedy* (1967)

The Politics of Policy Making in Defense and Foreign Affairs (1971)

*The Crouching Future: International Politics and
U.S. Foreign Policy* (1975)

To Govern America (1979)

The Politics of Governing America (1985)

*The Politics of Policy Making in Defense and Foreign Affairs:
Conceptual Models and Bureaucratic Politics* (1987)

★★★★★★★★★★★★★★★★★★★★★★★★
AMERICAN
GUERRILLA
★★★★★★★★ ★★★★★★★★★★★★★★

My War Behind Japanese Lines

ROGER HILSMAN

Brassey's (US), Inc.

Washington • New York • London • Oxford
Beijing • Frankfurt • São Paulo • Sydney • Tokyo • Toronto

Brassey's (US), Inc.

Editorial Offices　　　　　　　　　*Order Department*
Brassey's (US), Inc.　　　　　　　　Macmillan Publishing Co.
8000 Westpark Drive, 4th Floor　　　Front and Brown Streets
McLean, VA 22102　　　　　　　　　Riverside, NJ 08075

Library of Congress Cataloging-in-Publication Data

Hilsman, Roger.
　American guerrilla : my war behind Japanese lines / Roger Hilsman.
　　　p.　cm. — (An AUSA book)
　　ISBN 0-08-037436-0
　　1. World War, 1939–1945—Underground movements—Burma.
　2. Hilsman, Roger.　3. World War, 1939–1945—Personal narratives,
　American.　4. Guerrillas—United States—Biography.　5. Guerrillas-
　-Burma—Biography.　6. Burma—History—Japanese occupation,
　1942–1945.　I. Title.　II. Series: AUSA Institute of Land Warfare
　book.
　D802.B8H5　1990
　940.53′591′092—dc20　　　　　　　　　　　　　　　　89-25261
　[B]　　　　　　　　　　　　　　　　　　　　　　　　　CIP

British Library Cataloguing in Publication Data

Hilsman, Roger
　American guerrilla: my war behind Japanese lines. - (An Ausa book)
　1. World War 2. Far Eastern campaign. Anti-Japanese espionage. United
　States, Office of Strategic Services. Biographies
　I. Title
　940.54′25′0924

ISBN 0-08-037436-0

Published in the United States of America

★★★★★★★★★★★★★★★★★★★★★★★★★★★
Contents

★ Contents ★

MAPS

★ ★ ★ ★ ★ ★ ★ ★ ★ ★ ★ ★ ★ ★ ★ ★ ★ ★ ★ ★

AN AUSA INSTITUTE
OF LAND WARFARE BOOK

The Association of the United States Army, or AUSA, was founded in 1950 as a not-for-profit organization dedicated to education concerning the role of the U.S. Army, to providing material for military professional development, and to the promotion of proper recognition and appreciation of the profession of arms. Its constituencies include those who serve in the Army today, including Army National Guard, Army Reserve, and Army civilians, and the retirees and veterans who have served in the past, and all their families. A large number of public-minded citizens and business leaders are also an important constituency. The Association seeks to educate the public, elected and appointed officials, and leaders of defense industry on crucial issues involving the adequacy of our national defense, particularly those issues affecting land warfare.

In 1988 AUSA established within its existing organization a new entity known as the Institute of Land Warfare. Its purpose is to extend the educational work of AUSA by sponsoring scholarly publications, to include books, monographs, and essays on key defense issues, as well as workshops and symposia. Among the volumes chosen for designation as "An AUSA Institute of Land Warfare Book" are both new texts and reprints of titles of enduring value that are no longer in print. Topics include history, policy issues, strategy, and tactics. Publication as an AUSA Book does not indicate that the Association of the United States Army and the publisher agree with everything in the book, but does suggest that the AUSA and the publisher believe this book will stimulate the thinking of AUSA members and others concerned about important issues.

To the memory of the many with whom
I served who never made it back—
    in the West Point class of June 1943,
    in Merrill's Marauders, and
    in OSS Detachment 101.

PREFACE

The members of my generation were born immediately during and after World War I and came to adulthood just in time to fight as ordinary soldiers and junior officers in World War II. Our casualties were high. My class at West Point, which graduated in June 1943, suffered more casualties than any other class at the academy, before or since.

But this was only the beginning. Looking back, my generation can say that they have often been frightened, but seldom bored. Not only did we fight in the most extensive war in history, but at the end of that war we witnessed the first nuclear fireballs. Many of us were called back to serve again during the Korean War—a war made necessary, we were told, by the imperative of meeting Communist aggression. We watched the world change from a battlefield to cold-war tension and political maneuvering. We learned to live with the ever-present threat of still another world war, one that would be overshadowed by a mushroom cloud. In 1962 we lived through the first—and so far the only—nuclear confrontation in history, the Cuban missile crisis.

John F. Kennedy was a member of this generation, and when he became president a number of us were appointed to high office in his administration. In this capacity we were involved in the decisions about whether the United States should intervene with military force in Laos and later in Vietnam. On both occasions, the decision was against such intervention. Shortly after Kennedy was killed, the decision was reversed.

This book concerns World War II. No one person could have participated in all the events of a war that encompassed the globe. Neither could the experience of an individual who participated in one particular event provide an exhaustive view of that event. The experience of one ordinary soldier who landed at Normandy would provide only a sketchy understanding of the battle as a whole. The experience of the commanding general at Normandy, Dwight D. Eisenhower, would give him an understanding of the battle as a whole, but only a dim awareness of the myriad of individual experiences. And neither Eisenhower nor that soldier could understand events in the Pacific theater except through what they read and were told. Still, an attempt to understand the war in the light of a particular individual's experiences might offer some insights that are different from those of either today's historians or tomorrow's. This book is such an attempt.

I was born in 1919. An Army brat, I decided to go to West Point, and shortly after graduating, served with Merrill's Marauders as a platoon leader in Burma. Ninety-five percent of the enlisted men in my company were either killed or wounded. So were all of the original six officers, six replacements for the original officers, and six replacements for the second six—a total of eighteen officers, or 300 percent, either killed or wounded. I was lucky; I was wounded and lived to tell about it.

After getting out of the hospital, I served for a time as the Office of Strategic Services (OSS) intelligence liaison officer to headquarters, British Fourteenth Army. Then I commanded an OSS guerrilla battalion operating behind enemy lines. Later I was in China with the OSS, and at the end of the war, I was assigned to the OSS prisoner-of-war rescue mission sent to Mukden, Manchuria. There among the POWs I found my own father, who had been taken prisoner when the American forces in the Philippines surrendered in 1942.

The OSS mission to Mukden witnessed some of the earliest signs of the Cold War. We watched the Soviets systematically strip Manchuria of machinery, tools, and many other things that would have been useful in rebuilding China. This pillaging violated the Potsdam and Yalta agreements, and it fell to us— three young officers of the OSS mission and the only Americans in the country other than POWs—to present the American protests to the Soviet high command and to receive their brusque rejections.

Shortly afterward, I returned to what we fondly called the "zone of the interior," and it is at this point that this book ends.

Thus the bulk of this book relates my experiences as an American guerrilla in Burma. However, I have added an epilogue that deals with a period when things were turned around, when Americans were fighting *against* guerrillas—in Vietnam. When John F. Kennedy was elected president, he appointed me director of the Bureau of Intelligence and Research in the Department of State. Later, I replaced W. Averell Harriman as assistant secretary of state for Far Eastern affairs. In both jobs, Vietnam was one of my principal responsibilities. It seems obvious that the OSS experiences in Burma with guerrrillas operating behind Japanese lines had lessons for Vietnam on the questions of whether the United States should become involved in Vietnam with combat forces and, if it did, which military strategies and tactics would be effective in fighting communist guerrillas. The epilogue details the struggle over the United States's policy toward Vietnam from Kennedy's inauguration to President Johnson's decision to bomb North Vietnam and send American ground forces to South Vietnam. Essentially, it is the story of how those of us with World War II experience as guerrillas tried to persuade the top officials of the American government, both civilian and military, that those experiences were relevant to Vietnam—and how we failed in that attempt.

For various reasons, a few of the names of people have been changed.

For help in researching facts, dates, names of people, and places and locating pictures, I am grateful to Bill Brough, Pierce Ellis, Jim Ward, Dean Brelis, Joe Ziino, Eleanor Hilsman, Dr. Charles G. Hutter, Dan J. Barnwell, Joseph Lazarsky, and Daniel Mudrinich. Eleanor Hilsman, Bill Brough, Hoyt Hilsman, Amy Kastely, Ashby Hilsman, Sarah Hilsman, Alan Platt, and W.H. Royce read the manuscript and offered valuable suggestions. Eleanor Hilsman prepared the index.

My thanks to Vicki Chamlee, Connie Buchanan Leyden, Don McKeon, Jr., and Patrick Roach for contributing their editorial expertise to *American Guerrilla*.

Roger Hilsman
Hamburg Cove   Morningside Heights
Lyme, Connecticut   New York City, New York

1

Portents of WWII

World War II was the central experience in the maturing of most people in my generation. The war dominated the years of our young adulthood, and in terms of both public issues and private emotions, it colored our later lives. Unlike Vietnam— the war that dominated our children's lives—World War II was a "good" war. Hitler was a maniacal monster, and young as we were, we saw this and understood its implications. My father was an army officer, which undoubtedly inclined me toward West Point and a military career. But my mother's father and grandfather had been lawyers and judges. Relatives often remarked that I looked and talked like my maternal grandfather, and I thought that what talents I had were more suitable to a legal career than a military one. Politics and social affairs attracted my attention more than art, music, or even sports. My grades were good at school, and I was active in high-school public speaking. Later my roommates at West Point wrote in our yearbook that I was happiest when arguing; that I was willing to argue at any time, at any place, on any subject; and—they added maliciously—that I was willing to take either side.

I thought hard about going to Stanford and then on to law school. But even a high-school student could see the evil of Hitler and his vaunting ambition for world domination. Although his "Final Solution," the Holocaust, lay in the future, he made no secret of his insane hatred of the Jews. For a time in high school I flirted with the idea of joining the Loyalists in Spain. But if a high-school student could see that Hitler was evil, he could also see that Hitler was bent on having a war, a big war, and that nothing would really stop him short of total defeat. Going to Spain

1

would be noble, but it would also be futile. I decided that if my generation was going to have to fight a war anyway, I might as well do it right, go to West Point, and become a soldier.

After the war was over and I had seen combat, I began to realize that behind my decision to go to West Point lay deeper, essentially psychological motives. But I must confess that I had some pretty frivolous motives for going to West Point as well. At Sacramento Senior High School boys had to take gym or ROTC, and since my father was an army officer I took ROTC. There I rose to be a cadet officer, then a company commander, and then the cadet colonel. So I thought maybe I could follow my father in an army career. In the final year, when seniors began asking each other what they were going to do next, I answered that I might go to West Point. West Point was far from Sacramento. It was a romantic place. Girls would ooh and aah, and their reaction no doubt encouraged me as much as the menace of Hitler.

Even so, the war was on all our minds. As I recall the mood of those times, Chamberlain's "Peace of Munich" did not shake our conviction that a war with Hitler was inevitable—at least, did not shake it for very long.

★ ★
A European *Wanderjahr*

I graduated from high school in 1937 and went off to a school in Washington, D.C., whose purpose was to prepare students for the competitive examinations for West Point. After a year of cramming, I did well in the mental exams, but in the physical exam I failed the eye test. The doctors thought the eye trouble was temporary, due to excessive studying, and it seemed almost certain that the Point would accept me the following year. So I had a year to kill. In early October, days after the signing of the Peace of Munich, at the age of eighteen, I set sail for Europe. It was to be a classic *wanderjahr*.

When I arrived in London the parks were still a patchwork of air-raid trenches and piles of raw earth. Though people were echoing Chamberlain's jubilant cry for peace in our time, in the youth hostels, where I stayed, young people gathered around the fire each evening, a mug of hot tea in one hand and a wholesome British biscuit in the other, and argued about Munich. The consensus was pessimistic. Munich and the policy of appeasement had bought a year or two of peace, we agreed, but war would finally come. As the year wore on and I wandered from country to country, the mood in the hostels darkened.

On the boat going over I had made friends with another American, Howard Hall Bristol, who was on his way to study French at the Sorbonne in preparation for the American Foreign Service exam. We arranged to meet in Paris and see the sights. As it turned out, we spent more time talking about the coming war than sightseeing. Bristol was a serious-minded New Englander, a prototype of the blue-blood Yankee WASP. I don't remember him ever telling a joke or even responding to one with anything more than a smile. He was the interpreter in our arguments about the war with French-speaking students, and his French was very good.

I remember only once when it failed. Like most of the youths bumming around Europe, we were lacking for money. We tried to order meals that were filling and cheap. One day, when we were particularly hungry and near the end of our month's budget, we went to a restaurant that didn't offer our usual spaghetti. It did have a cheap entree called *moules*. The word was not yet in Bristol's vocabulary, so Bristol asked the waiter what it was. My friend didn't understand the answer. "It is some sort of fish dish," he reported to me, "and it comes in a great big bowl." That sounded great. *Moules* turned out to be mussels in their shells. A great big bowl of them was no more than an appetizer.

Our economizing proved more disastrous when we met in Florence during Bristol's Christmas holidays. Our plan was to travel to Greece and back to Milan and Switzerland. Toward the end of the trip, just before we left Italy, we tried to be more economical than usual and to use all of our lira. The cheapest food we could find were dried figs—a few lira bought a huge quantity. We didn't know about the laxative effects of figs, so we ate nothing else the whole day. That evening we were watching the sunset with two English-speaking girls we had met at the pension when suddenly a look of utter distress came over

3

Bristol's face and with only a mumbled apology, he went dashing into the bushes beside the road. The rest of the evening, he kept his distance from us all.[1]

Even when we were sightseeing, the war was not far from our minds. Late one afternoon in Paris we climbed one of the twin spires of Notre-Dame to the roof at the top. Paris was a lovely sight. It was a crisp autumn day. Fires were lit, and up from the chimney pots curled a wispy smoke tinged a charming pink by the setting sun. As the Seine flowed serenely, lights began to flicker on all over the city. We sat on a gargoyle, enchanted. But not for long. One or the other of us began to wonder aloud what would be the smart thing to do if you were caught in Paris in an air raid. We felt it was a serious and immediate problem. One alternative was to take shelter in the Paris underground. The deepest part was nearby, where the tunnel went under the Seine to reach the Île de la Cité. We finally decided the best solution was to sit on this gargoyle on the top of Notre-Dame, where we could watch Paris burning. After all, we reasoned, even Hitler might want to preserve one of the architectural treasures of the world.

We were naive. Later in my travels I came to believe that the old city of Rotterdam was one of the most charming in Europe. It was filled with architectural treasures. After the war, in 1950, my wife and I were driving through Rotterdam with our two young children, and as we approached the outskirts I described what a charming city it was. About that time we saw a sign saying "Centrum" with an arrow, obviously pointing to the city center. After a while we came to a sort of open field. There were weeds everywhere but not much else. Then we saw another Centrum sign, this time with the arrow pointing in the opposite direction. Somehow we had missed the city center. We turned around and again saw nothing until we were back at the original sign. Suddenly I remembered—Rotterdam had been the first victim of German saturation bombing. The open field of weeds *was* the Centrum.

By October of 1938 I was in Rome at the ancient Forum,

---

[1]The records of the Foreign Service do not list Bristol as having entered it, and I have never been able to discover what happened to him.

and in my prewar mood of foreboding what impressed me almost as much as the Forum itself was a mosaic that Mussolini had had placed on the wall between the Via Imperiale and the main Forum. The mosaic was a series of maps and dates depicting the city-state of Rome, Rome after it had conquered most of Italy, and finally, Rome at the height of its empire. The purpose may have been merely to inform tourists of the history of ancient Rome, but in the atmosphere of the time, what seemed to me portentous and sinister was the large vacant space at the end of the mosaic—as if to imply that Rome was waiting for conquests yet to come.

Toward evening that same day, I had supper at a little *trattoria* perched above Trajan's Forum looking right across to the top of his column. Some nineteen-year-old lieutenants in the Italian army, all of them members of Mussolini's Fascist party, were at the next table. We struck up a conversation, and I was tempted to mention the mosaic. It soon became clear that they also had the coming war on their minds. What we talked about was not whether there would be a war, but how it would be fought. Would it be a repetition of the trench stalemate of World War I, or would it be a war of movement along the lines of the new doctrine of tanks, blitzkrieg, and air power that both the British and the German military were espousing?

From Rome, I went to Florence and Venice; by ship to Athens; by rail to Belgrade, over to Milan, to Switzerland, and through the Low Countries on my way to Germany. I stayed at youth hostels and pensions, all of them crowded with young people from every country, and the conversation always turned to the threat of war. War was coming, most of us concluded, and it was best to make ourselves ready.

★ ★

Nazi Germany

If I had any doubts about Hitler, two weeks in Nazi Germany settled them. My first stop, a sentimental visit, had been Koblenz. My father had been in the army of occupation after

World War I and commanded a battalion stationed in one of the Rhine castles near Koblenz, Ehrenbreitstein, which was actually a fortress. Bright and early the morning after I arrived, I trudged up to the fort and stood on a parapet towering over the river below. What I didn't know—and wouldn't have realized the significance of if I had—was that the SS was using Ehrenbreitstein as some sort of training school. In a burst of adolescent high spirits, I turned to two black-shirted youths beside me on the parapet and tried to explain in phrase-book German that my father had commanded American troops there. Their hostility was intense. I suddenly realized that this was because I was an American, not because they understood anything I was trying to say. I beat a quick retreat.

My bad German had probably saved me from a beating, and I began to understand I had not only been naive about Nazi Germany but I might also be running some risk. Foolishly, I was carrying two books around in my backpack that wouldn't have been palatable to Germans, John Gunther's *Inside Europe* and another paperback recounting Hitler's rise to power in equally disapproving terms. After it got dark, I found a trashcan in one of Koblenz's back alleys, and when I was sure no one was looking, I dumped both volumes.

Everywhere I went in Germany that early spring of 1939 I met with the same hostility. News headlines were blazing with propaganda against Jews and Americans. I remember one in particular referring to the American president Franklin "Rosengelt." One night in Berlin I was turned away from half a dozen little pensions, the only kind of hotel I could afford, although it was obvious none of them was full. Finally I persuaded an old man that since Hilsman was a German name I should be entitled to friendlier treatment.

Even the one occasion when I was treated warmly turned out to be frightening. In Berlin, in the neighborhood of Unter den Linden, I asked two young men for directions. To my delight they spoke English and not only supplied the directions but invited me to join them for a cup of tea. They led me to what seemed a rather elegant antique shop in a sort of courtyard off a nearby street. Another young man was apparently in charge, but there were no customers. We had tea, and one of my hosts pulled out a case full of silk ties and said he traveled all over the country selling them. I'm certain they weren't Jewish, but gradually it became clear that they were very anti-Nazi. They spoke freely against Hitler in a joking and lighthearted way. When I got ready to leave, they became serious. "You're a nice young American," they said, "but very naive. You must be careful in this country. You shouldn't accept invitations to tea. And you shouldn't wander away from the tourist spots and hotels." They, too, spoke of the coming war.

The hostility, the fear, the constant propaganda—all of it began to get to me. I still had four weeks left in Germany before my ship sailed, but I lost heart. The next day I went to the American Express office and exchanged my tickets to get on a ship that left two weeks earlier.

The ship departed from Hamburg, and as soon as it cleared the dock I went to the ship's library and found a copy of Sinclair Lewis's *It Can't Happen Here*. I read it straight through, until about three in the morning, with the ship pitching and rolling in the North Sea. The theme of the book was, of course, that it *could* happen "here," in America. When I finally went to bed, the idea of going to West Point wasn't just an idle adolescent notion, it was an all-consuming ambition.

I entered West Point as a plebe on 1 July 1939, exactly two months to the day before the German army invaded Poland and World War II began.

★ ★

West Point

Going to West Point seemed to me to be the ultimate in preparing for war, but most of the time I spent there was not nearly so relevant as I had thought it would be. Perhaps the service academies should be postgraduate schools that teach nothing but military subjects. From the beginning, West Point and the other academies provided an undergraduate education first and military training second. Very little of a cadet's time in the pre–World War II period was spent studying military subjects. West Point cadets, like ROTC students in civilian colleges, had classes in "military science and tactics" two or three times a week. Here they learned the basic skills of the soldier: close-order drill, how to assemble and disassemble hand weapons, how to shoot them with some degree of accuracy, and the rudiments of squad and platoon tactics. Unlike his counterpart in ROTC, the West Pointer also spent three of his four summers in military training. Cadets got only one summer vacation in the entire four years.

What made the military training even less relevant was the American army of 1939, as well as the armies of most of the Allies, was training for World War I. Throughout 1939 and early 1940, the period of the "Phony War," what fighting there was recalled World War I. Two sides would look at each other from their trenches and fortifications. But on 10 May 1940 the Germans unleashed their armored Panzer divisions. By 4 June the British were desperately trying to save what troops they could from Dunkirk, and by the thirteenth the Germans had occupied Paris. At West Point, all this had yet to have an impact.

Not even a year later, in the summer of 1941, had the impact been felt there. The training program, as it had for many years, culminated in maneuvers that lasted about a week. The corps of cadets would make long marches, bivouacking each night in tents pitched in orderly rows that looked like pictures of the soldier's life in the Spanish-American War. Our uniforms were about the same vintage—wide-brimmed, Stetson campaign hats, riding britches, and leggings. Teddy Roosevelt would have felt perfectly at home.

The mock military exercise toward which the whole of training had been aimed was a nighttime replacement of one unit by another in a set of trenches copied from World War I. However, it is only fair to say that even the army did not think very highly of the military training at West Point. In the infantry, before a graduate of either West Point or an ROTC program was given an actual command, he was required to go through the officer's basic course at Fort Benning, Georgia, where he got three months of intensive training that was much more up to date.

If most of the West Point experience did little to prepare cadets for war, one part of it was crucially relevant, although I didn't realize it until after I had been in combat and the training saved my life. Paradoxically, this part came out of the "plebe system," which, at the time I was at West Point, seemed to me both anachronistic and dehumanizing.

A cadet enters West Point on 1 July and spends the whole summer in "Beast Barracks." From the moment the raw recruit sets foot on the reservation, the military establishment comes down with its whole weight, stamping him in its mold. He is immediately given a close-cropped haircut, exactly like all the other recruits. He takes a bath and is issued a new set of clothes, his uniform. He is called a plebe, the Latin word for the lowest class in ancient Rome. He must say sir to every upperclassman who addresses him, and he must answer all questions in a crisp, military manner while standing at attention and looking straight ahead. Even in the mess hall he must sit at attention, eating a "square" meal—that is, making righthand corners with his fork as he raises it to his mouth. Everywhere a plebe goes, he must move at the "double," a military dog trot. At any seeming infraction of several thousand rules, he is "braced," or forced to stand in an exaggerated form of attention while an upperclassman yells in his ear to get his shoulders further back and suck his stomach further in.

The plebe is required to memorize all sorts of useless litanies: the number of names on Battle Monument, the number of gallons of water in the reservoir, the definition of time, and Colonel Fishbein's "fixed opinion" ("I give it as my fixed opinion that there are more horse's asses in the army than there are horses"). Almost fifty years later, I can still recite the definition of leather:

> Sir! If the fresh skin of an animal, cleaned and divested of all hair, fat, and other extraneous matter, be immersed in a dilute solution of tannic acid, a chemical combination ensues. The gelatinous tissue of the skin is converted into a non-putrescible substance, impervious to and insoluble in water. This, sir, is leather.

If a plebe makes a mistake in any of these litanies or in carrying out any of the orders with which he is deluged, if he is fresh in any way ("B.J." or "bold before June," when he will become an upperclassman), or even worse, if he appears indifferent, exerting anything less than all he has—if he is guilty of any of these misdemeanors, he will be punished in various fiendish ways that go under the rubric of hazing.

In the nineteenth century and up to the time of World War I, hazing included physical beatings of one sort or another. During World War I these were outlawed, and after that an upperclass cadet was not allowed to touch a plebe. What he can do, however, is order the plebe to perform a variety of tasks that in fact bring physical pain. The plebe, for example, may be required to "sit up" at a meal—sit braced and not eat at all. Missing a meal is more torture for a cadet than one might think. The physical demands on all cadets are high, and cadets are always ravenous. Sitting up is one of the milder forms of punishment, since most plebes find ways to hide chocolate bars and other goodies in the barracks. For a more serious infraction, a plebe might be required to report to an upperclassman's room at reveille in full field equipment to do pushups or other calisthenics.

In my day, the favorite punishment for serious infractions was the "clothing formation." On a Sunday afternoon, when luckier plebes were free, those to be punished were assembled in the basement of one of the barracks, called the sinks because in the older barracks the basement was where the toilets and showers were located. Here the plebes were braced and dressed down by a drill sergeant's tirade. The upperclassman in charge then issued instructions: "You have three and one-half minutes to report back here in full dress!"

Plebes lived on the top floor of the fourth-floor barracks, and there were no elevators. Up the stairs they had to dash, change into full-dress uniform with all the proper accoutrements, and get back to the basement in exactly three and a half minutes. Anything missing from the prescribed list of equipment, a belt awry, a button unbuttoned, brought on massive abuse all out of proportion to the failure.

Then came new instructions—this time, say, full field equipment, including rifle, bayonet, helmet, gas mask, and canteen. Up the stairs once more. Frantically change clothes. Back down again. The time allowed was too short; the orders were impossible to carry out. Yet the plebe was expected to make a heroic effort.

10

All armies have some sort of boot camp in which the new recruit is forced to behave like an automaton, being subjected to various kinds of humiliation and submitting to authority in ritualistic and often painful ways. The difference is that boot camp lasts at most only a few weeks; cadets must endure the plebe system for a whole year.

The fact that hazing is so widespread, that it has been performed in so many different cultures throughout history, suggests it has some practical utility and is not just tradition. To the sociologist it suggests the rites of puberty or the tribal initiation ceremony. Hazing may well serve some of the same psychological functions. Going through a difficult initiation ritual does produce a sense of belonging, of being a member of the in-group, and this is as useful to armies as it is to primitive tribes.

But the orthodox and classical explanation offered by the military is different: Hazing inculcates discipline. War, the argument goes, requires automatic and unquestioning obedience at times of enormous physical and mental stress. I never wondered about this explanation as a cadet. Even today, I don't doubt that hazing began in the days of the Greek phalanx when soldiers were more successful if their actions were coordinated, if their shields covered each other and their spears were thrust at their comrades' opponents as well as their own. But after I had been in combat myself and was wounded, I began to think the reason that all armies have some form of hazing was quite different. We will return to this subject later, when the story tells of combat.

Even today West Point and the other military academies provide an undergraduate education similar to that of civilian colleges. The reason goes back to the way wars were fought in 1803, when West Point was founded. Even though American colonials had tried to teach Braddock's men to fight Indian fashion—taking cover behind trees or whatever else offered protection rather than firing volleys from close-order drill formations—they knew that to hold a position against an enemy with artillery required fortifications. Building fortifications required a knowledge of engineering, and U.S. schools did not teach engineering. Harvard, Yale, Columbia (then King's College), Princeton, and the College of William and Mary were

11

really not much more than divinity schools with an emphasis on liberal arts. The few Americans who qualified as engineers had been trained in Europe. It was this scarcity of trained engineers that made the contributions of Lafayette and the Polish officer Kosciuszko so important to the American Revolution. So West Point was established to provide the U.S. Army not with combat officers and generals, but engineers. It was no accident that both the railroads and the Erie and Panama canals were built by graduates of West Point.

At West Point in the 1940s, academic courses for the cadet's first two years concentrated on algebra, geometry, calculus, and mechanical drawing on the one hand, and on the other, English grammar, composition, and literature; European history; and French, German, or Spanish. The last two years were devoted to chemistry, physics, electrical engineering, and civil engineering, as well as economics, law, and more history. The fact that the curriculum was not entirely math, science, and engineering and offered as much language, history, and economics as it did was due mainly to the efforts of Colonel Herman Beukema, professor of economics, government, and history, who campaigned hard for such courses in the 1930s and 1940s.

The economics and history courses gave an eager student some idea of larger political issues, but nothing else. The only course that had any direct relevance to war was taught in the first-class, or senior, year. A year-long course in military history, it consisted of a step-by-step analysis of battles and campaigns. "Gentlemen," the instructor said on the opening day, "welcome to military history. Until today you have dealt with squads and platoons. Here you will deal with nothing smaller than a division!" I was delighted! This was why I had come to West Point.

As I was to learn only much later, the course was not concerned with strategy in its true sense. Strategy is really the area where politics and military force meet, where military force is used to achieve political ends. This was not studied at West Point, nor indeed was it systematically studied at any of the nation's higher institutions for military education, the war colleges. I didn't learn anything about strategy until I studied international politics at Yale.

What we studied was battlefield tactics, how the great generals had moved their divisions, corps, and armies around on battlefields, the circumstances in which they decided on flanking movements; and when and how they committed their reserves. We cadets thought it heady stuff, but in fact it had little to do with the kind of war we would have to fight. Most of the class ended up as lieutenants and captains commanding platoons and companies. There was little of relevance for those of us who played larger roles in the federal government later on.

The only person I knew at the time who could have put this kind of knowledge to practical use was the instructor. He was a lieutenant colonel named Max S. Johnson, and he was that rare creature, a military intellectual. He knew his military history. He had thought about it deeply. And he longed to put his knowledge into practice. He hoped to be assigned as chief of staff to a division, which would have been only one step up in rank. In that job, he felt, he could use his knowledge and perhaps before the war was over be promoted to command a division himself. But he was stuck at West Point. On occasion his sense of outrage at the cruelty of fate overwhelmed him. Once when a not-too-bright cadet was doggedly repeating, "But I still don't see how you know when to commit your reserves," it was too much for Colonel Johnson. He hurled the textbook, a thick copy of Napoleon's campaigns, clear across the room where it thudded against the blackboard on the other side. "How the hell do I know? I've never been in battle. I spend all my life preparing for war, and when it comes I end up trying to teach a bunch of thick-headed cadets."[2]

---

[2]Colonel Johnson did get to be chief of staff of a division in 1944–45, but he never commanded a division. He became an assistant division commander in Korea in 1953. His last post was, fittingly for a military intellectual, commandant of the Army War College. He retired in 1959 as a major general.

2

★ ★

The Onslaught of War

Two months after I arrived at West Point in 1939, Germany invaded Poland, and the war began. To cadets, it all seemed far away. And I had a personal problem that distracted me from thoughts of war. In the middle of my first summer, in Beast Barracks, I caught cold and was sent to the hospital. In the military there is no such thing as being a little sick and staying in your room. Either you are fit for full duty or you are in the hospital. When I recovered from the cold, I still had a low-grade fever that would rise a degree or so each day toward evening. I felt fine, but the military treats any increase in temperature at all as a sign of serious illness. When classes started in the fall I was allowed to attend them, but the doctors kept me in the hospital and ran me through every conceivable test. One doctor was convinced that I had contracted undulant fever from drinking goat's milk when I was traveling in Greece. It was a medical problem that gave zest to his usual dull routine of blisters, sunburn, insect bites, colds, and flu, the infirmities that plague cadets. It took weeks before the tests finally convinced him that what I probably had was low-grade, chronic sinusitis. In disgust, he sent me back to the barracks.

After so many weeks of idleness, I was in poor shape to face the rigors of plebe life, and it overwhelmed me. Within a fortnight I was back in the hospital with a raging case of double pneumonia. Looking back, I have to confess that I helped to bring it on, probably half consciously. Coming back to my room in a heavy sweat from a hazing session. I had thrown myself in a chair and sat there in a fit of depression, ignoring the open window. The doctors sent for my parents, but the new sulfa drugs pulled me through. I got out just in time for final exams, and having missed two of the three months of classes, I failed. In the jargon of West Point, I had become a "foundling" because I had "been found deficient in academic subjects." However, the authorities recognized the special circumstances and turned me back to the class below.

My father was stationed at Fort Howard, Maryland, just outside Baltimore on the Chesapeake Bay, and I dragged home to face eight months of idleness. This was the period of the "phony war" in Europe. The Allies sat in their bunkers on one side of the border, and on the other, the Germans sat in theirs. After my initial discouragement with the academy's education program, I realized that I could at least turn this time into an opportunity to build on all the stimuli of my year in Europe. Systematically, I read my way through the Great Books series—the University of Chicago's newly unveiled secret in true education.

The year was not totally monastic. Another officer's son, Donald Rehm, was stuck at Fort Howard that year, too, and he had gotten himself introduced to what his diligent research revealed were the only two pretty girls in the entire twenty miles from Fort Howard to Baltimore. One of them was Eleanor Hoyt, the other Posy Callahan. He was already dating Eleanor, so I dated Posy. My relationship with Posy was episodic, but Eleanor and I became "buddies." Eleanor was sixteen, like Posy of Irish descent, a bright, pert, slightly built girl about five feet two, with a warm disposition, chestnut hair, and a pug nose. The overall effect was terrific. Many years later, Eleanor was introduced to President Kennedy on the occasion of African Independence Day. Looking first at her face and then at the emerald-green dress she was wearing, he chuckled, "This should be Irish Independence Day!"

At Franklin D. Roosevelt's 1941 inauguration, two companies of the West Point corps of cadets marched in the parade and I arranged for Eleanor and my fellow cadet and friend, Tommy Farrell, to have a date following the parade. It seemed natural. His family was Irish Catholic from Albany, New York. Eleanor's mother was Irish and her father had grown up in New York State, in Port Leyden near the Canadian border.

Tom was a golden boy. A handsome redhead with as warm and happy a personality as the world has ever seen, he was near the top of his class academically and in football came close to making All-American. Eleanor liked him very much. His father was in Washington working as deputy to General Groves in the Manhattan Project. The two families got to know each other rather well. Tommy was killed in action in 1944 at Anzio.

★ ★

Return to West Point

I reported back to West Point when classes began in September 1940. Within a few weeks I decided that I did not like West Point at all. In fairness, I must also say that West Point did not particularly like me. Part of the problem, I now realize, was that my political biases were too liberal for the West Point of that day. I resented the indignities to which the system subjected plebes. I rebelled at the pressure toward conformity. When I became an upperclassman, with both the right and duty to haze plebes, I didn't do so and neither did some of my friends. This marked us, perhaps not as rebels but certainly as nonconformists.

And it was not just the plebe system that repelled me. The ultimate punishment at West Point for breaking the honor code was placing the offending cadet in "Coventry"—that is, subjecting him to silence. No one could speak to a cadet who had been silenced except in the discharge of official duties. Any cadet who did speak to a silenced cadet was himself silenced. Silencing could and did follow the offender into the army and affect him for the duration of his service career.

Only one cadet was silenced for actually violating the honor code in my time, and no one dared go against the ban. But racially prejudiced cadets succeeded in silencing the only two black West Pointers. Both of these men were in another part of the corps, and I did not go out of my way to become a martyr and befriend them. But when I met one of these two by happenstance, I spoke to him. Enough other cadets also spoke to them to make it impossible to extend the silence to us. But we were marked again as nonconformists.

17

What bothered me most of all was the regimented predict-ability of life at the Point. As a plebe, or a yearling, I knew exactly what I would be doing at any given moment of either my junior or senior year. If you wanted to know what you would be doing at 1417 hours on 18 October two years hence, you could look it up in the catalog. Every moment was scheduled.

All these dislikes seemed to stem, as I said, from my bias toward liberalism. Years later I realized that there were other, more fundamental reasons for them. After the war I discovered, to my surprise, especially considering the course my life had taken up to that point, that the source of my greatest satisfaction in life was reflection as opposed to action. To say that satisfaction came from things of the mind is too vague. To say that I discovered I was an intellectual would be pretentious. By reflection I mean something in between—problem-solving, analysis, learning, and the excitement in acquiring knowledge. There is an action side to my personality, as well as a reflective, analytic side, and I have probably been happiest when both could be fulfilled. But I ended up spending most of my working life as a professor, doing research, writing, lecturing, and teaching, and this has been my true calling.

West Point and the military—and rightly so—do not value this kind of ability highly, no matter what name you give to it. Almost every great military leader, as well as most military historians, has from time to time tried to set down the qualities of the successful general. Intellectual ability has never been higher than fifth place on any list. Decisiveness, determination, will—such qualities are obviously more important to generalship than theoretical analysis, curiosity, objectivity, or reflectiveness. In fact, keeping alternative hypotheses constantly in mind, vital to the intellectual, can lead to the fatal flaw of indecisiveness in a general.

Take, for example, the most brilliant general on either side in World War I, Ludendorff. He was a good example of why the military prize decisiveness and will power over intellectual brilliance. He agonized over his plans, trying to perfect them up to the very last minute even after troops had begun to move into position for the attack. The military say a bad plan vigorously pursued is better than a brilliant one pursued only lackadaisically. Worse is zigzagging from one plan to another. The solution the Germans adopted was to put Ludendorff under the direct command of the stolid, somewhat thick-headed, but iron-willed Hindenburg, who refused to make any changes whatsoever in a plan once he had approved it.

This is not to say that the military do not value intelligence. Most of the "star men" at West Point—those who are in the top 5 percent of their class—get to be generals. Alfred M. Gruenther is an example. He was the number-three man in his class and was so interested in things of the mind that his fellow cadets called him The Brain. The nickname stuck all his life and with good reason. He became an instructor at West Point. He earned money on the side as the chief referee in world-champion bridge matches and actually wrote a book on the game. He was one of Eisenhower's chief planners in World War II and his chief of staff when Eisenhower was head of NATO after the war. And he retired as a four-star general. But it indicates something of the attitude of the military that Gruenther's first command was his last post, that of Supreme Allied Commander, Europe. He never commanded a platoon, company, battalion, or division; he was always on the staff.

The most common criticism of the military is that they are simplistic, do-it-by-the-book bureaucrats who are at the same time excessively conservative, nationalistic, aggressive, and power oriented. The criticism is summed up in the phrase "the military mind." "Isn't it risky, even foolhardy," critics ask, "to let people with chauvinistic military minds, who tend to meet every problem by resorting to crude force, have important roles in the complex and delicate problems of diplomacy?" At the same time, the leaders of a modern nation could not deal with the problems of foreign affairs without constant advice from top military men. What keeps the military "on tap rather than on top" in modern nation-states is the principle of civilian supremacy.

Success in maintaining this principle depends on the military as much as on civilians—on whether they are loyal and conscientious public servants and, most important, on whether they are woven into the fabric of national life or stand apart from it. That the military in the United States are as deeply committed to the principles of civilian supremacy as any other segment of society seems beyond question. To anyone who knows the American military, books such as *Seven Days in May* that raise the specter of a military coup d'état are simply not believable.[1] For every flamboyant and charismatic Douglas MacArthur, there is a Matthew Ridgway, the West Pointer who more than any other single person kept the United States from going into Vietnam in 1954; a James Gavin, who led protest demonstrations against the Vietnam war in the 1960s; and a George Marshall, who served as secretary of state and of defense and whose farseeing statesmanship not only gave us the Marshall Plan that helped rebuild Europe but also kept us out of the greatest quagmire of all, China. Curtis Lemay, George Patton, and Douglas MacArthur were great military leaders, but their swashbuckling style and seemingly perfunctory commitment to civilian supremacy are not typical of the American military's ideal self-image. If any such general tried to lead a coup, the military would be the first to blow the whistle.

In fact, historical evidence shows that the military recently had a principal role in forestalling what some people thought was at least a potential coup. During the Watergate scandal, just after the House Judiciary Committee voted to recommend that Richard M. Nixon be impeached, fears arose that someone in the White House might telephone lower-ranking officers commanding troops stationed in and around Washington and order them, say, to occupy the Capitol and the congressional office buildings. Most officers at that level, it was reasoned, would automatically obey an order they thought was coming from the commander in chief, with no questions asked. Accordingly, the secretary of defense and the military chiefs of staff quietly issued instructions that no order from the White House was to be obeyed unless it came through channels—which meant to a military man that the order had to come from the president to the secretary of defense, to the Joint Chiefs of Staff, to the chief of staff of a particular military service, and so on down to the

---

[1] Fletcher Knebel and Charles W. Bailey, *Seven Days in May* (New York: Harper & Row, 1962).

20

commanding officer of the division, regiment, battalion, or company that was to carry it out.[2]

People also assume the military are trained to think of violence as the solution to every problem. But historically generals, with the exception of general-politicians, such as Napoleon, have been reluctant to go to war. One reason is probably that soldiers know better than most people the horrors war brings. Another is generals never feel they are quite ready. They always want another thousand tanks or aircraft, another million men!

But the military do inevitably develop a mind-set that is in some ways different from that of ordinary people. War demands teamwork, and the military must of necessity be organization men. It is also true that they focus their attention—as they should—on threats to American security and the use of violence in meeting threats. During the Cuban missile crisis of 1962, Robert Kennedy was upset that the Joint Chiefs gave so little consideration to the political implications of the military steps they recommended to the president. President Kennedy, also disturbed, nonetheless pointed out the military spent their lives training for war, and civilians should probably be more concerned if the military were consistently opposed to using arms or military means of intervention. If the military were not willing to fight, who would be?[3]

No matter how hard the military try to avoid it, their world is more isolated and narrow than the general population's. Members of the profession of arms must work hard to maintain their competency, especially in an era of high technology. This preoccupation tends to insulate the military and makes them more conservative than some other segments of society. The work of engineers, scientists, and doctors leads to similar results. Consider the position taken by the American Medical Association during the three or four decades that federal health legislation was a central issue. To say that the AMA's position during those years was Victorian is to be charitable,

---

[2]Theodore H. White, *Breach of Faith: The Fall of Richard Nixon* (New York: Athenaeum, 1975), pp. 22–23 and personal interviews.

[3]Robert F. Kennedy, *Thirteen Days: A Memoir of the Cuban Missile Crisis* (New York: Norton, 1971), pp. 14, 96, 97.

although it should also be said that part of its motivation was to maintain high incomes for doctors and that the AMA's views have changed considerably since that time. But the isolation of the military is greater than of other professionals simply because their work takes them to remote places. They spend a lot of time abroad, and their posts at home are usually on military reservations that are far enough away from population centers to give them room for training maneuvers.

How different are soldiers from engineers or industrialists or business executives? Modern warfare calls for the orchestration of a wide range of specialized functions. Men and women must be trained. Supplies, ammunition, and equipment must be provided for and transported great distances according to intricate schedules. War is a large-scale enterprise, and like other large-scale enterprises, it has become bureaucratized. The skills of officers are those of executives and administrators in any large organization, public or private, who must plan and coordinate the efforts of specialist teams. If officers have the skills of executives, they can be expected to have their bureaucratic rigidities as well—and there is no question that business executives have bureaucratic rigidities. After all, a businessman and not a soldier served as the model for the organization man.[4]

Remember, it was a general, Matthew B. Ridgway, who in effect vetoed the proposal to turn the Vietnam conflict into an American war in 1954. And it was not the military who were urging American intervention in 1965. The military were, in general, opposed to any limited war. In the years following Korea, old hands in Washington derisively called the Joint Chiefs of Staff the Never Again Club because of their frequent assertion that never again should the United States fight a limited land war on the mainland of Asia. Of course, once the United States had entered the Vietnam war, the military pressed hard for a policy of victory; but it was the "militarists" in civilian clothes who got us into the war in the first place.

In short, the stereotype of the rigid, archconservative militarist has little validity when applied to the American military.

---

[4]See William H. Whyte, Jr., *The Organization Man* (New York: Simon and Schuster, 1956).

And the concept of the military mind is more confusing than helpful. Anyone, civilian or military, who is given responsibility for a nation's security will become preoccupied with the power aspects of policy problems. Civilian secretaries of defense, if they do the job they are given to do, quickly develop military minds.

★ ★
Personal Predilections

I still disliked West Point. The academy duly took note of this attitude, and my senior year I was a sergeant, as low in rank as a senior could be unless he had been reduced to private as a result of disciplinary action. I might have lost myself in academics, but few of the courses seemed to offer any real intellectual challenge. In my day, the emphasis was more on learning by rote than by analysis, more on factual knowledge than theoretical. Competition was fierce for one of the top ten academic slots in our class of 514, and I had no stomach for beating enough facts and formulas into my head to play that game. Enough of the courses, however, included the theoretical and analytical work I liked, and it cost me no real effort to stay among the top 10 percent. There I lolled.

By and large I merely existed. I have sometimes wondered if I would have stuck it out until graduation if the war had not come along. After December 1941, of course, anyone who resigned from the Point promptly got drafted. I think the answer is, war or no war, I would probably have stayed. This was partly because of my relationship with my father, which I began to understand only later, at the end of the war. And partly it was because few cadets really liked life at West Point, and to quit before you graduated was to admit to yourself that you couldn't cope with the pressure. So even those who hated the place most still tried to stick it out.

As it turned out, my junior and senior years weren't too bad. I was one of a group uninterested in hazing plebes or adhering to the spit-and-polish side of life at West Point. With some I

23

shared a sort of barroom camaraderie, at least on the few occasions, such as football games, when we were able to get away from the academy. Johnny Mattfeldt, a fellow army brat from San Antonio, and I developed a repertoire of slightly ribald songs, and we had great times together. I also found a fellow "intellectual," and we spent a lot of our spare time talking and arguing. His name was Argonne Call Dixon, a renegade Mormon from Utah. We shared a love of reading and a lot of romantic notions. We had a game in which one of us would quote the first two lines of one of the quatrains from Omar Khayyam's *Rubaiyat*, and the other would have to reply with the concluding two. We both wrote what we fancied was poetry.

When I was a junior, the editor in chief of the cadet magazine *The Pointer* recruited me to the writing staff, and there I did find an interest. My senior year, 1943, I became the editor.

★ ★
Family Affairs

To backtrack a few years, when I was at Fort Howard as a turnback in 1940 was the period of the "phony war" in Europe. The war, which had seemed far away, got closer as spring wore on. And then, the British began evacuating Dunkirk and France fell. In the winter of 1940–41, after I had re-entered West Point, the Germans started their bombing campaign in the Battle of Britain. War seemed closer to home than ever, only to recede again in June 1941 when the Germans attacked Russia, and the place names of battles were so strange to American ears. In the fall of 1941 the United States was strengthening its forces in the Philippines, and General MacArthur had requested by name a number of colonels to become division commanders. My father was one of them. He had served for three years in the Philippines during the 1920s, when I was from eight to eleven years old, as commandant of cadets at the Ateneo de Manila, a prestigious Catholic military academy where the sons of educated Filipinos often went. Most of the graduates from my father's day held reserve commissions in the army; this reflected well on him, so it was natural that he was one of the commanders Mac-Arthur chose. In October, as my father was en route to the port of embarkation for the Philippines, he came to West Point to say goodbye.

My father had been a distant parent. He saw himself as a soldier, and he had been stern with his men, with himself, and with me. I never addressed him without saying "sir."

He had been born and raised in Texas, went to the College of William and Mary for one year, and then got a job as a salesman with the Burroughs Adding Machine Company. There is no doubt that he had the salesman's gift for enthusiasm. Anything that he bought for himself, whether a suit or an automobile, became the very best product of its kind. At times he would get carried away and make promises he couldn't keep or talk big about his connections and what he would do to help someone. When I first learned the word *braggadocio*, I thought of my father. He was also completely self-centered without being aware of it. This could result in a form of mild cruelty. I remember him saying more than once, when he was expostulating about some public figure of whom he disapproved, "Why, that so and so has no more idea of what is going on in the world than—than—young Roger Jr. here!"

Some of the qualities that made him a successful salesman and a charming friend were obstacles to a military career rather than assets. One was that he could not tell the difference between his good reasons and his real reasons. Another was that he tended to focus on short-range goals and then rationalize his actions with skillful, though convoluted logic. To give an example that illustrates both qualities, he knew enough about business practice from his time with the Burroughs Company to recognize when he was stationed at Fort Sam Houston that the post exchange was badly run. The job of post exchange officer carried a lot of special perks, but it was troop command and staff positions that furthered a military career, not being a post exchange officer. Yet my father sought the job, persuading himself that making the post exchange a success would be a giant step to promotion.

But he was very able, and he did make the post exchange a success. He actually turned it into such a large-scale enterprise that it attracted the attention of the Department of the

Army, although the attention was as much worry about the political effects of the store's competition with local merchants as it was pride in the accomplishment. He demonstrated his enthusiasm and ability in his next assignment as well. As commandant of cadets at St. Thomas Military Academy in Minneapolis, he so inspired the cadets that they won the Pershing Trophy for the best high-school cadet corps in the nation.

But in spite of his enthusiasm and ability, he was prone to self-delusion. He had had only one year of college and showed his lack of education. He could never rid himself of saying, "They was. . . ." But he was by nature extraordinarily intelligent. The problem was that he used his intelligence to convince himself that some wishful hope was a goal within his reach. In his spare time in Minneapolis, for example, when radio was in its infancy, he designed a home model. Thousands of other people had done the same thing, but my father convinced himself that his would become the standard, the one that Montgomery Ward would adopt and sell in the millions. But he was also resilient. When he finally realized that his radio design was no better than hundreds of others, it took him only a week or two to shake off the disappointment and go on to a new project.

His new project was making motion pictures. At Christmas, only a few weeks after his hopes about radio collapsed, my parents gave me a toy, hand-cranked movie projector with a film of one of the early animated cartoons. Within a few months my father was deep into motion-picture photography, still in his spare time. Another present that Christmas had been a set of circus animals with movable joints to create a variety of positions. My father used the animals to make an animated film, laboriously taking pictures of the animals one frame at a time so that they appeared to walk, stand on their heads, and do all sorts of wonderful things.

He was so good at motion-picture photography that when he was posted to the Philippines in 1927 as a company commander, the army commissioned him to make a sort of documentary film following an army recruit on his voyage from the recruiting station to his assignment in the Philippines. His film was so well received that the Philippine government persuaded the U.S. Army to give him leave to make another documentary about the leper colony at Culion. The film featured a leper who hid himself in the jungle, decided to give himself up, arrived at the leper colony, and was cured. The Philippine government rigged up buses with projectors and showed the film all over the islands to persuade more lepers to come in for treatment.

In the meantime, the leaders of the Ateneo de Manila asked the War Department to assign my father as commandant of their academy. They offered him something like $100 a month extra pay, a fantastic bonus for a captain at the time. He took the job, but only on the condition that he receive a summer's leave for what I have always thought was his most extraordinary act of creativity. He took his cameras and went on an expedition to film the "Wild Tribes of Northern Luzon" about the Bontoc Igorots and the Ifagao, who had been headhunters less than a generation earlier. After his death, the films he took on that trip became a valued item in the film collections of the Smithsonian Institution and the national museum of the Philippines.

With all this intelligence and creativity, and with the kind of enthusiasm that could be turned into charismatic leadership, why had my father not had greater success and more recognition?

One reason, I thought, was that he tended to concentrate totally on whatever it was that interested him at the time. After the war, for example, his last assignment was at the Presidio of San Francisco. He became interested in high-fidelity phonographs and records and became so engrossed that he asked for early retirement and bought the local phonograph and record shop. Then, a year later, when my parents bought a house, he couldn't wait to sell the record shop in order to spend every waking moment fixing it up! Other people might have seen these changing devotions as the flaw of a hobbyist.

I never heard my father say a bitter word about either of his parents. But his father was a traveling salesman who was rarely home, and his mother was a self-centered Southern belle who could have been the prototype for Scarlet O'Hara in *Gone with the Wind*. His childhood was lonely and unloved. His diary, written when he was about fourteen, mentions his father only once in passing and his mother not at all.

The decisive event in my father's childhood took place

when he finished grammar school in Tyler, Texas. His older sister was admitted to a sorority at the University of Kansas. The sorority was one with which his mother had connections, and she was offered the job of house mother. She put my father in a boarding house, packed up his younger sister, and went to live at the sorority with her two daughters. For the next year or two, my father worked as a delivery boy and lived alone in the boarding house. Then his father entered him in the College of William and Mary in Williamsburg, Virginia. But the money lasted only a year, so at the age of 18 or 19 my father was on his own, looking for a job.

My father's job as salesman with the Burroughs Adding Machine Company required him to travel as his father did. He married my mother in 1914. To eke out his earnings, my father joined the Texas National Guard and rose to lieutenant. The guard was put on active duty during the Mexican-border troubles of 1915, and about a year later he had a chance to become a regular officer and took it.

An incident that occurred many years later, when I was a teenager, is what makes me feel that these events were decisive in shaping my father's personality. By this time, he had held the rank of major in the regular army, and we were visiting Texas on our way to a new station in California. One day he asked my mother if she would mind if he paid a visit, by himself, to Tyler, the town where he had lived as a child. American army officers rarely wear their uniforms when they are off duty and never when they are on leave. But he dressed up in his uniform and ribbons and went to Tyler to call on all the people he and his family had known when he was a boy. He had to prove something to them.

My father's neglected childhood probably explains why he was a distant parent. Although he didn't mean to be so, he was also a domineering one. This was not intentional, but the result of the combination of intelligence, creativity, egocentricity, and the rest. I have no doubt he loved his only child, but his love for anyone had to be screened through his self-centeredness. Love for anyone else could not for him be unselfish love; his love had to be in terms of himself.

So I had come to understand very young—perhaps as early

as five or six—that I had to resist or be overwhelmed. So I resisted. When he commanded me to do something, I had no choice. But when he voiced an opinion that seemed to me arbitrary, I argued. Sometimes the argument ended by his ordering me to my room. But since ordering me to my room was to admit defeat, he did it less often than I probably deserved.

The tension between my father and me was released in silly ways. After I had been turned back to the next class at West Point, my family drove cross-country to spend our vacation in Sacramento, California, where my father had served as head of the army reserve of northern California, and I had gone to both junior high school and high school. He and I shared the driving, two hours on and two hours off. I was 21 years old, still a romantic adolescent. By slightly shortening or lengthening my stints of driving, I contrived for it to be my turn at the wheel when we entered Sacramento. It was a childish wish, but my father had exactly the same childish wish—and he had the power—to drive into our old hometown. So he kept the wheel when we got to Sacramento even though it was my turn to drive.

I couldn't say anything on such occasions, but I seethed and showed my anger in every way possible. His preoccupation with himself made him immune to my behavior. He wasn't even aware that I was resentful.

As for my mother, being in the middle between what amounted to two children constantly bickering must have been hell. Throughout my childhood she tried to be an honest broker between us. But she was also independent-minded and strong-willed. I later learned that when I was two years old, she had taken me to live in another town and enrolled in teacher training. My father was diligent in trying to persuade her of his love, and after a few months she returned.

My mother did not openly take sides between us, and I have no idea how she managed her relationship with my father, although I think I always knew that she both loved and resented him. Her resentments were spoken aloud only in her last years. I was aware of her love for him not so much by what she said as by an occasional act. For example, when I first went off to West Point, she clearly recognized that this marked the end of childhood and that never again would I be at home any longer than a few days. But she put on a brave face as they took me to the train and said goodbye, shedding not even a single tear. We waved, the train pulled out, and I turned to go to my seat. For some reason, I turned again and looked back. She did not see me, but I will never forget the agony on her face and the fact that she had turned to my father for comfort.

The way my mother managed her relationship with me was not by taking my side, even in private, but by being a sympathetic listener to every concern and passing thought that a child might have—except for the tension with my father.

Obviously because of our tense relationship, I was touched that my father made a special trip to West Point to see me before he sailed for the Philippines that autumn of 1941. When the visit was over and we said goodbye, he gave me as a farewell gift an aluminum cigarette case, the size and shape of a packet of cigarettes. I carried it throughout the war.

A few weeks later, my mother came to the Point to see me. If my father had been distant, she had been close. Given her family background, the fact that she was a warm parent was remarkable. Her family, the Prendergasts, were staunch Scotch-Irish Presbyterians, as Calvinist as could be. The family had settled in Texas when it was still a province of Mexico and remained there ever since. Her grandfather had graduated from the University of East Tennessee in 1841, and on returning to Mexia, Texas, he "read" the law under a local judge, passing the bar examination in 1845. "During those four years," his obituary read, "besides studying law, he had taught school and hunted Indians." I have no doubt that that was exactly what he did.

No alcohol was permitted in the Prendergast house. (My mother's grandfather, the hunter of Indians, had twice been the Prohibitionist candidate for governor of Texas, and her grandmother was a leader of the Women's Christian Temperance Union.) Playing cards or dancing on a Sunday was forbidden.

For the rest, they seemed to have shared the mores and prejudices of their time and place. But there is evidence that they were part of the tiny Texas group that didn't approve of the general prejudice against blacks—or, as they would have said, negroes. My mother used to say people in the South loved the

30

individual and feared the race. Certainly the Prendergasts loved the individual, and the love was returned. I was wounded in 1944, and the local newspaper in San Antonio carried the story. The next day my mother heard a knock at the door. When she opened it a large black woman was standing there weeping. "My baby's been hurt!" she cried. It was my nursemaid. The two of them hugged, kissed, and had a cry together.

There is evidence that the Prendergasts didn't fear blacks as a race either. My mother was the youngest of five children who reached adulthood. The oldest, Lillian, was for many years the head of the YWCA of Waco, and in the 1930s she succeeded in integrating it, even to the extent of having black and white girls share hotel rooms on trips. She wouldn't have succeeded had she not been both the daughter and granddaughter of judges, but she wouldn't have tried if the family had not had some views about racial segregation that were unusual for their time.

My mother's mother's role was wife, mother, and social leader. What distinguished her was that she had gone to college, rare for a woman born in 1859. She was also something of a tyrant and had the true Calvinist's nose for sin. To repeat one of my mother's oft-told tales, when revivalist preachers came to town, as they did regularly, they often stayed with the Prendergasts. One my mother found particularly odious. Self-righteous and bigoted, he was unkempt, with long flying hair and bright dark eyes that kept stealing glances at you sideways. He spit as he talked. He must have sensed her dislike, for one night from the pulpit he made a big pitch to the children in the congregation to come forward to the "praying rail" and show their love of Christ. My mother sat in her chair. The preacher then looked directly at her and said, "You, child, do you not love Christ?" Defiantly, she continued to sit, not answering. "Do you not want the love of Christ?" Do you not want to be one of His flock?" Still no answer. Finally he gave up, but later that night her mother drew her aside and asked, "Daughter, do you not love Christ?"

"Yes, I do," my mother replied.

"Then have you some sin to hide?"

"No."

31

"Calvinist suspiciousness," my mother used to say at the end of the story. But she gave my grandmother credit for being fair, for the latter did not pursue the question further.

As a matter of fact, my mother showed me her impishness as well as her love. I remember only two of the songs she sang to me when I was a child. One, a lullaby, was "Mighty Lak a Rose":

> Sweetest little fella,
> Anybody knows,
> Don' know what to call him,
> But he's mighty lak a rose.

The other, sung when she wanted me to go to sleep and I was crying was "The Bells of Hell":

> Oh, the bells of Hell go ting aling aling,
> For you but not for me.
> For me the Angels sing alinga aling,
> Throughout eternity.
>
> Oh Death where is thy sting aling aling,
> Oh Grave thy victory,
> Oh the bells of Hell go ting aling aling
> For you but not for me!

The day she arrived to visit me at West Point in 1941 was a Sunday, a pleasant one for December, so we walked from the barracks a mile along the Hudson to the Thayer Hotel, where we were going to have a midday dinner. She was worried about the possibility of war and what would happen to my father. I spent the whole walk assuring her there would be no war, that the Germans were bogged down in Russia, and that the Japanese were too fearful of American sea power.

We got to the Thayer a bit early, so we stopped off at the gift shop to buy my father a Christmas present. The radio was playing some classical music when the announcer broke in to say that the Japanese had attacked Pearl Harbor. It was 7 December 1941.

3 ★★★★★★★★★★★★★★★★★★★★★★★

The Fall of the Philippines

When my father was first ordered to the Philippines, my mother and I might have persuaded ourselves that he was safer there than in Europe. The attack on Pearl Harbor and the simultaneous bombing raid on Clark Field in the Philippines denied us that comfort. And within a week, it became clear that the Philippines would be the most dangerous place of all.

Before Pearl Harbor, when my father first received his orders to the Philippines, my mother had decided to wait for him in San Antonio, where her sister lived. But first she wanted to spend as much time with me as she could during the Christmas holidays of 1941. In those days, a West Point class got its first holiday off the reservation eighteen months after they had entered the academy, their second Christmas. Any cadets whose homes were close enough wanted to go and see family and friends, especially girlfriends. All cadets, wherever they went, wanted to have a good time. The idea was to paint the town red—the home town if possible, if not, any town that was convenient. Air travel was rather primitive in 1941, and taking a train all the way to San Antonio and back would burn up the whole holiday. My roommate, Bill Naylor, was in the same boat, since his home was Oregon. So my mother took a small apartment near Times Square for the holidays. Bill and I could spend the nights painting the biggest town of all, and my mother and I could be together during the days—or at least from about noon, when Bill and I dragged ourselves out of bed.

Bill was dating a girl from New York at the time, and they liked to go dancing. I was not so lucky. A number of times I went alone to the German-American, a beer hall near the Bowery

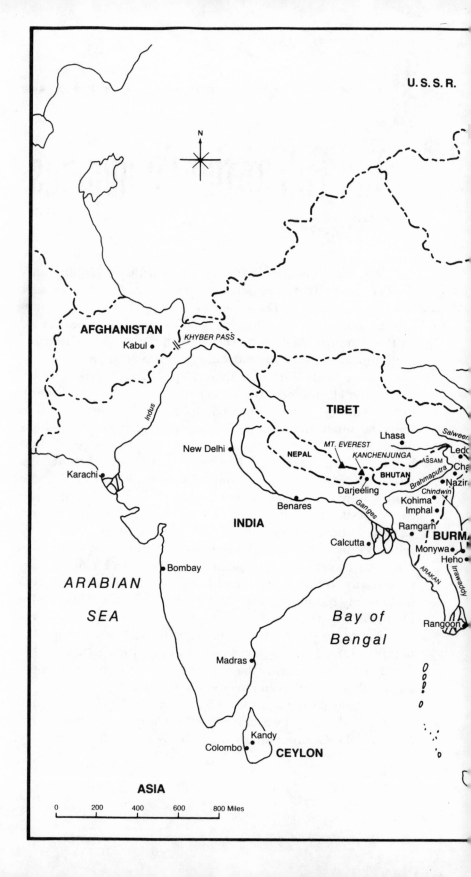

where college students went to drink beer and sing. The GA, as we called it, had three floors, each with a couple dozen tables for six to eight people and a piano with a player to bang out old, familiar songs. There I could take up with a group of students from one college or another. And one weekend Posy Callahan came up from Maryland. But she and I had drifted apart in the fifteen months I had been back at the Point, so we simply joined the others at the GA.

This forced attempt at gaiety during our ten short days of freedom kept gloom at arm's length, at least in the evening. But news from the Philippines brought it back during the day.

★ ★
The Attack on the Philippines

When my father arrived in the Philippines in early November 1941, General MacArthur immediately sent him to the southernmost island of Mindanao to take command of a cadre for what would become a division defending the port of Davao. Davao, the only major port in the southern Philippines, turned out to be the key to Japanese plans for invading Borneo and the Dutch East Indies.

The Japanese planned to attack American air bases in the Philippines at the same time they attacked Pearl Harbor, but on 7 December they were delayed by fog at their base in Formosa. They feared that the news of Pearl Harbor would alert American forces, but when their bombers reached Clark Field the American planes were still lined up in neat rows. The U.S. Air Force in the Far East was virtually wiped out.

Over the next few days, the Japanese made several small landings to cut communications lines. The main landings did not begin until a fortnight later.

The main landing on Luzon came on 22 December at Lingayen Gulf, about 125 miles north of Manila. A smaller landing was made two days later at Lamon Bay to the south. The idea was to form a giant pincer around Manila and Corregidor, the island fortress at the mouth of Manila Bay. Rather than fighting against such odds on an exposed plain, MacArthur declared Manila an open city and put into effect the longstanding Plan Orange, shifting the American and Filipino forces to Corregidor and the Bataan Peninsula, which together dominated the entrance to Manila Bay. So long as the Americans and Filipinos held Corregidor and Bataan, the Japanese could not use Manila as a port.

In the southern islands, specifically Mindanao, the main attack came on 20 December—two days earlier than the attacks on Luzon—and it came at Davao. So it turned out that my father was in command of some of the very first American ground troops in World War II.

It was a poignant time. The papers were full of the attack on the Philippines, including reports about my father and the fighting at Davao. America was hungry for heroes, and the press seized on my father's little force to help fill her stomach.

★ ★
The Battle of Davao

Actually, Davao was not really much of a battle. The Japanese attacked with five thousand regular army troops, including an armored unit and a battalion of divisional artillery, all carried in fourteen transport ships. The transports were escorted by a naval force consisting of a destroyer squadron, a cruiser squadron, the aircraft carrier *Ryujo*, and a seaplane carrier. The cadre my father commanded numbered eight hundred regular Philippine army soldiers equipped with rifles and six machine guns, plus about a thousand reservists. Considering the odds, they gave a fairly good account of themselves. They mounted the machine guns on trucks and protected them with sandbags, keeping the vehicles safe behind the beaches. When the Japanese landing force was launched they moved the trucks up to the point of landing. One machine-gun squad was able to inflict heavy casualties on Japanese infantry in their landing craft before it was knocked out by a direct hit from a Japanese shell. Once the Japanese were on shore the defenders were quickly overrun, but losses were great enough to force the Japanese to commit an additional detachment that they had intended to save for the invasion of Jolo Island, a steppingstone on the route to Borneo.

By nightfall, only about a hundred of my father's force were still together, with their backs against the jungle outside the city. They broke off contact with the enemy and marched all night to get well into the mountains and jungle.

From there the little band made their way straight over the central mountains of Mindanao, one of the larger islands of the Philippine Archipelago. At the center it was uninhabited and unexplored, although many years later, in the 1970s, a tiny tribe of primitive people was discovered there.

In the first two or three days of the march, before they entered the uninhabited areas, my father and his men were able to get some rice from villagers, but not enough to last for more than a few days. The journey to the other side of the island took a month, and most of that time they lived on monkeys, snakes, and grubs.

They reached the other side of Mindanao toward the end of January. The Japanese, using Davao as their port, had already attacked the Netherlands East Indies. Manila had fallen, but American and Filipino forces fighting on Bataan and Corregidor maintained radio contact with the outside. The Japanese had not yet attacked any of the other southern islands, and my father was ordered to take command of the island of Negros.

I learned about Davao and the march across Mindanao later that spring from Father Manuel Ortiz, a young Jesuit priest who was chaplain to Manuel Quezon, president of the Philippines. President Quezon and his party were evacuated from Corregidor on 19 February 1942 by the submarine *Swordfish*, and the party spent a few days at my father's headquarters in Negros on their way to the Del Monte airfield in Mindanao, which had not yet been attacked. From Del Monte they flew by B-17 to Australia. When Ortiz, who had been a cadet at the Ateneo de Manila when my father was commandant, finally got to the United States, he came to see me at West Point. My father had told him the story of the trek across Mindanao and given him some letters and snapshots taken on the journey. These included pictures of the monkeys they had had to eat.

38

★ ★
General Douglas A. MacArthur

On 12 March 1942, shortly after dark, General MacArthur, his wife, his child, the child's amah, and seventeen officers escaped Corregidor in four PT boats for Mindanao and the Del Monte airfield, where they were picked up a few days later by B-17 bombers flown in from Australia.

The news came to West Point of the escape of MacArthur and his family at dusk one day when the cadets were forming up to march to dinner. A lot of us were shocked. At first I didn't believe it. "No American general," I argued, "would leave his troops at such a time. It's just a vicious rumor." We hadn't known that MacArthur was keeping his own family with him when the families of all the other officers had been evacuated. It seemed to the cadets more like what a Roman proconsul would do than an American general. It was only later that we learned that President Roosevelt and General Marshall felt that MacArthur was too valuable to waste in a prison camp; Roosevelt had personally ordered him out to take command of Allied forces in the southwest Pacific. Even so, MacArthur insisted on delaying his departure until he was sure it would not be such a blow to the morale of the men on Bataan and Corregidor that the defense would collapse.

MacArthur, of course, was a supreme egoist, a driving, ambitious personality. His statement on leaving the Philippines, "I shall return!"—"I," MacArthur, rather than "we," the Americans, and the very proper "shall" rather than the colloquial "will"—is itself revealing. Most of his public statements were delivered in pompous purple prose. He was not above a little petty plagiarism; he would adopt a turn of phrase he liked, perhaps without knowing it was someone else's but certainly without embarrassment or apology. One of these, obviously borrowed from the Duke of Wellington's line about the playing fields of Eton, is inscribed on the walls of the gym at West Point:

Upon the fields of friendly strife
Are sown the seeds
That upon other fields, on other days,
Will bear the fruits of victory.

In later years I got to know an officer who had been one of two aides-de-camp to MacArthur for a period between the wars, and I asked him if MacArthur spoke this way naturally or only on state occasions. The aide said it was entirely natural, and he told me a story to make the point. One night, when General MacArthur was visiting Paris, he went off to have dinner with the American ambassador. The two aides stayed at the hotel, in the room next to MacArthur's. Those were the days when the *maisons de haute couture* would send a collection of their gowns with models to your hotel room. Officers would have dinner in their rooms and view the gowns with an eye to buying one or two as gifts for their wives. The champagne flowed, and the two aides had what they thought was a brilliant idea. They bribed one of the models to climb naked into the general's bed—he was divorced from his first wife at the time. Chuckling, they waited for his return.

About midnight, clump, clump, clump, the general came down the hall. The key turned in his lock, his door closed. A few moments later the door opened, clump, clump, clump, and there was a pounding at their door. All innocence, the aides opened it. "Get that strumpet from my bed forthwith!" he yelled. Did I think MacArthur's pompous prose was not natural?

The aide swears the story is true. Of course, the number of fanciful tales circulated in the army about MacArthur is fantastic. My father often told one about the general's relationship with his mother. When MacArthur entered West Point, his mother took a room at the hotel on the reservation where she could see his window in the barracks and check to see if he was studying. She stayed the entire four years. This part is documented. According to my father, however, her watchful oversight continued until after he had retired from the army. In 1936 the elder Mrs. MacArthur came to visit the Philippines, after a voyage of about a month on one of the ships of the old President Line. MacArthur turned out the troops to greet her. The army band and any officers not on urgent duty were assembled at the foot of the gangplank at old pier 7. When Mrs. MacArthur was halfway down the gangplank she spotted Douglas, stopped, and held up her hand for silence. Then she put her hand on the shoulder of a woman standing beside her and turning back to her son, who was at least fifty feet away, said sonorously, "Douglas, I've found the perfect wife for you."

This story was widely repeated, and I believed it without question. But when well-researched biographies of MacArthur were published, I learned that the story was a wild fabrication. The reason it had been given such credence in the army was that it fit the image that much of the army had of the the relationship between MacArthur and his mother. In fact, while the elder Mrs. MacArthur had indeed accompanied the general to the Philippines in 1935, she was ill and confined to her cabin during the voyage. She died a month after they arrived. The woman MacArthur took as his second wife had been a passenger on board the same ship, bound for a tour of Asia. She and the general were taken with each other, she canceled the rest of her trip to stay in Manila, and they were married in 1937.

What is interesting in this case, however, is that truth exceeded fiction. MacArthur's mother was constantly conniving and politicking to further her son's career. During World War I, when he was a colonel and chief of staff of the Rainbow Division, she regularly wrote the secretary of war urging that her son be promoted. Even when he was chief of staff of the army in Washington, she lived with him and supervised his supervision of the army.

★ ★

The Surrender of the Philippines

Bataan fell on 9 April 1942, Corregidor on 6 May. From the southern islands came nothing but silence. Later that year Japanese forces published a picture taken on Negros and somehow *Life* magazine got hold of it. (*Life* labeled it incorrectly as the surrender on Corregidor.) Anyone who knew them could easily have recognized my father and his adjutant, Edward Mason. With them were a Filipino aide carrying a white flag, a Japanese colonel, and another officer. Clearly, my father had surrendered. At least we knew that he had survived up to that point.

It was only after the war that we learned what had happened. On 8 April the forces on Bataan had surrendered. The

41

Japanese then landed on Corregidor itself, and on the morning of 6 May General Wainwright decided that he must surrender, too. Several days earlier, in a desperate effort to stave off surrendering the whole of the Philippines, Wainwright had turned over command of the forces in the southern islands to General William F. Sharp, whose headquarters were in Mindanao, and told him to report directly to MacArthur in Australia. Sharp, in turn, put the Visayan islands, those between Luzon and Mindanao, where he had his headquarters, under a separate command with headquarters in Cebu.

In the meantime the Japanese received reinforcements from Borneo and Malaya, and on 10 April, one day after the Bataan campaign ended, they landed on Cebu and Panay. On both islands, American and Filipino forces quickly withdrew to the mountains. Shortly after the attacks began, my father was ordered to report to headquarters in Cebu City and take over as chief of staff of the new Visayan Command, now separate from General Sharp's force on Mindanao. He landed on Cebu and set off on foot. Just before dark, he met some Filipino forces in full retreat and almost immediately caught a glimpse of advancing Japanese patrols. He spent that night in a chicken coop, and the next day made his way back to Negros by dugout canoe.

When Wainwright surrendered, the Japanese commander, General Masaharu Homma, refused to accept the subterfuge that the American was not in command of all the forces in the Philippines. Homma insisted that if the fighting was to stop, Wainwright must surrender all his forces in the Philippine islands, American and Filipino. If the fighting on Corregidor continued, it would mean at the very least that as many as several thousand more American and Filipino soldiers would be killed. In addition, although no such threat had been made, Wainwright believed that if he didn't surrender the whole of the Philippines, the Japanese would execute the Americans they already held. In any case, he radioed General Sharp, rescinding the earlier order and putting Sharp and his forces back under his, Wainwright's, command.

After seizing Davao, Japanese forces were fully engaged on Bataan and Corregidor and so left the rest of the southern islands alone. American and Filipino forces were preparing to defend only the larger islands—Cebu, Panay, Negros, Leyte, Samar, and Bohol. However, the commanders of these islands soon realized that it would be impossible for them to repel a landing, so they concentrated on getting ready to continue the struggle in the mountains as guerrillas.

When General Sharp received the order to surrender, he decided to wait for the arrival of Wainwright's emissary before obeying. This man, Colonel Jesse T. Traywick, Jr., arrived with several Japanese officers on 9 April. Sharp found himself in the same position Wainwright had been in. Traywick told Sharp that if the forces in the southern islands did not surrender, the Japanese would probably reject the terms agreed upon and resume the fighting. According to the historical record, he added that the Japanese would probably open fire on the prisoners they already held. Again, no such threat had been made, but rumors were circulating that Japanese guards had told their American prisoners that for each day that the surrender was delayed, ten American officers would be executed. Seventy-eight thousand Americans and Filipinos who had been fighting in Bataan were now in Japanese hands, and even though the facts of the Bataan death march were not yet known, many of Sharp's officers were inclined to believe the rumors.

What actually happened was as follows. About sixty-six thousand Filipino soldiers and twelve thousand Americans surrendered to the Japanese on Bataan. They had been fighting for three months in a difficult climate and terrain and with inadequate food and medical supplies. On the eve of the surrender at least one-third were sick with malaria, dysentery, and other diseases. Japanese military custom forbade surrender, and the Japanese had simply not considered that they might be responsible for feeding a substantial number of prisoners. In fact, the Japanese themselves were short on food and medical supplies, so it isn't surprising that the prisoners got even less. The march out of Bataan was uncoordinated and chaotic. Some groups proceeded without harassment, but most traveled in a series of forced marches, needlessly exposed to the tropical sun and crowded at night into unsanitary assembly areas.

Japanese soldiers were accustomed to being treated callously and even brutally by their superiors, and to treating anyone under them the same way. Since Japanese military tradition, training, and indoctrination taught them they should never surrender, they tended to hold in contempt anyone, friend or foe, who did. Some of the Japanese guards on the march out of Bataan were humane and occasionally kind. But many were sadistic, bayoneting men who fell down and sometimes torturing them. Neither General Homma nor any of his officers showed concern about what was happening to the prisoners.

Brutality, fatigue, disease, and a lack of food, water, and medicine—all of this resulted in an extremely high death rate on the march and in the weeks after the prisoners reached Camp O'Donnell, their destination. In fact, twice as many died in the two months following the surrender as died on the march itself. Only about four thousand of the twelve thousand Americans who surrendered on Bataan survived until the end of the war. Casualties among the Filipinos were probably about the same.

The officer couriers that Sharp sent to commanders in the Visayan islands repeated the threat that if they continued fighting as guerrillas, the prisoners on Corregidor would be executed. Even if the threat to execute was unfounded, the Japanese had every right under international law to resume the fighting on Corregidor if American-Filipino forces elsewhere in the Philippines did not surrender; this would put eleven thousand American and Filipino soldiers, wounded, and nurses at extreme risk. Sharp decided he had no choice but to capitulate.

Most of the island commanders had established mountain bases and were prepared for operations as guerrillas. Their bases were capable of prolonged resistance, and none of them wanted to surrender. Some also felt since Wainwright was already hostage to the Japanese, his orders had been issued under duress and should not be obeyed. And in response to Sharp's order, one commented that he didn't see any reason to surrender just because the people on Corregidor had agreed to "shell-shocked terms." "I must have MacArthur's okay," he radioed, "otherwise it may be treason." But the only word from MacArthur was that he no longer had communications with the Philippines. In fact, he didn't reply to any of the messages subsequently sent to him.

My father, for his part, decided that although the battalions under his command had the capacity to resist for a time, the cost they could inflict on the Japanese was not worth the risk to the lives of the people on Corregidor. Today, when I read my father's cables in official military histories, I can almost hear his voice. The workings of his mind—at best and worst—are familiar, especially the competition between his romanticism and his self-image. As a young officer he had collected photographs and letters of the officers who died with Custer at the Battle of the Little Big Horn. The temptation to take to the hills as the leader of a guerrilla force around whom myths might grow must have been strong. But his image of himself as a soldier—brave and loyal and totally committed to doing his duty—was equally strong.

His cables indicate how he reconciled the conflict between the two, or at least how he rationalized it. This time my father's enthusiasm didn't lead to self-delusion but to a sort of MacArthur-like rhetoric. In a cable to his fellow island commanders, he said that no matter what personal risk might be incurred, they had to do their duty and surrender "or be classed as deserters by our own country and as outlaws by international law."

Under a flag of truce he met with the Japanese commander, Colonel Kumataro Ota, who offered the same terms as those given to General Wainwright—my father would have to surrender the whole of his force or the fighting would continue. My father agreed and issued the orders.

But he quickly discovered that merely issuing an order was not enough. As part of the preparation for guerrilla warfare, Negros had been divided into five sectors, and the battalion commanders in each sector had been released from central control. When my father got written orders to surrender, he called these commanders to a conference to arrange the details. Not all the battalions under his command obeyed. He was faced with what amounted to a mutiny.

Several commanders were convinced the prisoners from Bataan and Corregidor would be killed anyway and their only chance of staying alive themselves was to hide in the hills. In the meantime, a number of Filipinos simply threw away their weapons and uniforms and faded into the population. Troops and civilians began to loot Japanese and Chinese commercial

45

establishments. One of the groups in the hills was holding 196 Japanese internees as hostages.

General Wainwright wrote about what happened next in his memoirs:

> At the risk of his life he [Colonel Hilsman] went into the mountains in search of the mutinous leaders, who had threatened to kill any American who attempted to communicate with them. When these expeditions failed he twice talked the ranking Japanese officer on the island into extending the time by which the surrender must be effected.
>
> These extensions were all the more remarkable because three Filipino envoys—a Colonel Valariana and his two aides—were murdered by a demented Filipino soldier as they advanced under a flag of truce.[1]

By the expiration of the second extension, my father had succeeded in persuading about 95 percent of one battalion and 30 percent of two others to come down out of the hills. Two other battalions, in spite of the risk their actions held for their fellows and for the prisoners on Bataan and Corregidor, disbanded and faded away. Finally convinced my father had done his best and no organized forces remained in the hills, Colonel Ota agreed to accept his surrender with the troops he still controlled.

After the war we learned that Colonel Ota had treated my father with dignity and respect. The temporary prison camp that had been set up lacked the most rudimentary facilities and, for a time, even a reliable system for supplying the prisoners with food and other necessities. Ota visited the camp several times and tried to correct the deficiencies. On one occasion he sent a Japanese army cook to prepare a meal for the Americans because they didn't know how to handle the unfamiliar rations.

Many years later, this incident aroused some interest in Japan. In 1963 President Kennedy promoted me from the post of director of the Bureau of Intelligence and Research at the State Department to assistant secretary of state for Far Eastern affairs, replacing W. Averell Harriman. When the Japanese press learned of my wartime background, they were afraid I would be prejudiced against their country. The State Department arranged for

---

[1]General Jonathan M. Wainwright, *General Wainwright's Story* (Garden City, New York: Doubleday, 1946).

me to meet with Japanese correspondents in a special conference to allay their fears. Their press contingent in Washington was—and still is—the largest of any country's, a total in those days of about twenty-five. The senior correspondent, Yoneo Sakai, who had remained in Washington throughout World War II, put the question bluntly. "Mr. Secretary," he said to me, "you fought against the Japanese during the war. You were severely wounded by Japanese troops. Your father spent three and a half years in Japanese prison camps. How do you feel about the Japanese?"

To the question of fighting against and being wounded by them, I replied that soldiers must do their duty. I did mine, and the Japanese soldiers did theirs. And I harbored no personal resentment. The only thing I added, somewhat wryly, was that my experiences had taught me that the Japanese were very good soldiers indeed. As for my father, I told them of his surrender to Colonel Ota and of Ota's personal visits to the camp to see that conditions were improved. Colonel Ota, I said, was a regular officer who had behaved in the samurai tradition.

Some of the reporters giggled at that comment. Part of the reason, I was told by Japanese friends later, may have been nervous relief. I had allayed the reporters' fears. But part of it was my use of the word *samurai*. The reporters knew that, being an American, I was equating the samurai tradition with chivalry. The samurai code did include courage and heroism, but the samurai also had a reputation among Japanese for uncivilized cruelty.

★ ★
On Leave

That ten days in New York over Christmas in 1941 was the only let-up my class had for six months. Classes and training time were stepped up, and free time cut. But at the end of the second year, the summer of 1942, my class was finally given a whole month's leave. So I traveled to San Antonio by train to spend it with my mother. Or at least I spent the mornings and early afternoons with her. Johnny Mattfeldt had grown up in San Antonio and his parents still lived there, so he was also in town and we formed a team. Late afternoons, we would loll around the swimming pool of the Officers' Club at Fort Sam Houston with the other army brats, mainly female. Nights, Johnny and I usually double-dated, making the rounds of San Antonio's cheaper nightclubs. Normally we would have a different date each night. Texas had a bottle law; we would buy a fifth of rum, the only liquor available in those wartime days, and make the rounds.

Matty had a huge repertoire of college football songs, ballads, West Point ditties, and the usual high-school chestnuts, and we would end the night with our dates in the old square in the Mexican part of town singing with one of the regular guitar players. A typical ditty, and one of our favorites, was "The Persian Kitty":

The Persian kitty, perfumed and fair,
Went out to the kitchen, to get some air.
A tomcat, lithe and lean and long,
Dirty and yellow, came along.

He sniffed at the perfumed Persian cat,
As she walked around with much éclat,
And thinking a bit of time to pass,
He whispered, "Kiddo, you sure got class."

"It's fittin' and proper" was her reply,
As she arched her whiskers over her eye.
"I'm ribboned and I sleep on pillows of silk,
And daily I'm fed on certified milk."

"Oh, I should be happy with all that I've got,
Oh, I should be happy, but happy I'm not.
I should be happy, I should indeed,
Because I'm highly pedigreed!"

"Cheer up," said the tomcat with a smile,
"And trust your new-found friend for a while.
You need an escape from your backyard fence.
My dear, what you need is experience!"

New joys of life he then unfurled,
As he told her his tales of the outside world,

Suggesting at last with a lurid laugh,
A trip for the two down the primrose path.

The morning after the night before,
When the kitty got home 'bout the hour of four,
The innocent look in her eyes had went,
But the smile on her face was a smile of content!

In after years when the people came,
To see the Persian kittens of pedigreed fame,
They weren't Persian, they were black and tan.
She told them that their Daddy was a travelin' man
—a snatchin', scratchin', travlin' ma-a-an!

The third Christmas, in 1942, my class also had ten days' leave, and I spent them with Eleanor Hoyt and her family at Sparrows Point, just outside Baltimore on the Chesapeake Bay. My roommate, John Myrtetus, was in Baltimore with his grandmother, so three or four evenings during those ten days we double-dated, I with Eleanor and Myrt with any one of several different girls. We made the rounds of Baltimore's beer cellars, which were a lot like the German-American in New York.

But Eleanor's family was so much fun that she and I spent most evenings with them. Her mother Nell played the piano with the virtuosity of a bawdy-house professional. She could read music at a glance, and if you hummed a tune for her, she would wiggle her hands up and down for a minute or two and then belt it out. Eleanor's father, Eb, who had a deep bass voice, had sung in the church choir as a boy and in the glee club at Hamilton College. With Nell at the piano, Eleanor, Eb, Eleanor's older sister Mary Katherine, and I would gather around and sing all the songs we could remember. We drank bourbon when we could get it, and rum when we couldn't. And when we got tired of singing, we would play twenty questions, charades, or who am I?

★ ★
Graduation at West Point

Shortly after the attack on Pearl Harbor, a decision was made to graduate the West Point class of 1943 in January rather

49

than June, and to graduate my class, the class of 1944, a whole year early, in June of 1943. The traditional three-month vacation at the end of the third-class year was cut to one month, and the pace of academic and military instruction was stepped up.

We cadets were not long in recognizing the urgency of preparing ourselves. Most of us quickly came to understand that we were going to have to fight a rough war. But even the most hardheaded and realistic of us probably didn't realize just how rough it would be for our particular class. We would be the lieutenants. Members of our class would see action on all the D-days except for North Africa. Some, in the ground forces, would lead the troops ashore at Normandy and in the Pacific at all the landings from Guam to Okinawa. Others, in the air forces, made the raid on the Ploesti oil fields in Rumania in which 10 percent of the attacking American planes were lost. And they were on every raid that followed in both Europe and the Pacific. Our casualty rate was horrendous. Some of West Point's Civil War classes, with only a dozen members, had a higher percentage rate, but for total number of killed and wounded the class of June 1943 holds the all-time record, with the Korean War class of 1951 coming in second.

Both of my two roommates were in the air corps. One of them, John Myrtetus, was the pilot of a B-24 on a raid to France. The plane was badly shot up, and he ordered the crew to bail out. But one man was too severely wounded to jump, so Myrt single-handedly tried to take the plane back across the channel. He never made it.

My other roommate, Bill Naylor, lucked out, but the very improbability of his surviving illustrates the danger the class ran. Bill not only made the Ploesti raid with its 10 percent casualties but was co-pilot of one of the pathfinder aircraft whose job it was to lead the way and mark the targets with smoke. He developed food poisoning halfway to the target but urged the pilot to keep going. His vomiting was torture enough, but what was excruciating at the high altitude was the bloating gas accompanying his diarrhea. He fainted several times from the pain. Once as he began to regain consciousness he was entranced by a line of sparkling lights approaching on the horizon.

Then he realized the lights were the tracers from the guns of the attacking Messerschmitts coming at them head on.

In the infantry it was even worse. One of my classmates, Bill Debrocke, led a platoon of about fifty men ashore at Guam and took a bullet straight through his St. Christopher medal. His wound was what the British called a blighty—serious enough to serve as a ticket back home. Exactly one year later a planeload of wounded arrived from the Pacific, and the fellow they put in the bed next to Debrocke was the fiftieth leader of his own platoon.

The company of regular infantry I was with when I first saw combat in Asia went into battle with six officers and 232 enlisted men. The battle lasted fifty-five days, and at the end all six officers had been killed or wounded. So had another six sent in as replacements, and so had a third group sent in to replace them. In 55 days, 18 officers had been killed or wounded, and of the original 232 men, only 23 were left. I myself lasted just under two weeks.

My particular group of friends was hit hard. Tommy Farrell and John Myrtetus have already been mentioned. In addition, Fred Kramer and Jim Browning were killed in France, and Johnny Mattfeldt in Czechoslovakia. Argonne Dixon, my fellow "intellectual," was also killed. His death I had expected. During World War I Argonne's father had "found himself" in the Battle of the Argonne, for which he had named his son. Not surprisingly with a name like that, Argonne felt he had a destiny, "a rendezvous with Death at some disputed barricade," in the words of Alan Seeger, where he, too, would find himself. I got a letter from him when I was in Burma. "The mountains of Italy," he wrote, "are tall." My reply was returned, marked KIA.

As I said, it was not long before it dawned on the men of my class what was in store for them. By 1943 I was thinking of Eleanor as something more than just a buddy. She was now at Barnard College in New York, and she began coming up to West Point for weekend dates. For June Week, at graduation, cadets are supposed to invite their OAO's, one and only's. Eleanor was the girl I invited, and she came. I kissed her for the first time at the graduation dance, on the balcony of Cullum Hall overlooking Flirtation Walk and the Hudson River.

51

Many of us at West Point had begun to realize that any more permanent relationship than a date might be cruel to inflict on our girlfriends. What would a young woman do who was widowed in her early twenties and perhaps with a child?

It was the custom among West Point classes to put a brass plaque on the walls of Cullum Hall in commemoration of any classmate killed in action. Years after the war I was invited to the academy to give a lecture, and Eleanor, now my wife, and I paid a visit to Cullum Hall to see if we could find the plaques for my classmates. We rounded a corner and came upon a single huge one with all the 1943 names on it. I wasn't prepared to see all those names at once, and the memories of so many overwhelmed me.

On graduating, cadets choose their branch—engineering, artillery, infantry, and so on—according to academic ranking, with engineers being the most prestigious. Though I ranked 45th in the class of 514 and had a choice, I still selected infantry. I liked to think of this as idealistic—infantry was the "queen of battle." But when the war was over I began to wonder if my motive hadn't been more deep-rooted, connected somehow with my father and the fact that he had been a prisoner of war.

4

★ ★

Overseas at Last

As I said, in June 1943 my class graduated. We got another month's leave, and I spent it in San Antonio with my mother. This leave differed in only one respect from the one a year before—I dated one girl more frequently. Her name was Pat, and she was very pretty, very sexy, and lots of fun. Her interest in me was about the same as mine in her; she wanted to have fun. She was actually one of the more calculating young women I have known. She had decided that it was as easy to fall in love with a rich man as with anyone else, and that was what she was going to do. In the meantime, however, why not enjoy? Things went along swimmingly for a time, but then her mother called mine one day to ask when the "kids would be getting married, since they are so much together." Both Pat and I began having other dates.

However, later, for a short time, I had more romantic notions about Pat. After our month's leave we were sent to branch schools for officers' basic training in the summer of 1943. For the infantry this was Fort Benning, Georgia, and Pat's father had been transferred to Maxwell Field in Alabama. Benning had lots of men but few women. The hard training, the constant talk of war, and the fighting that lay ahead depressed us. There seemed to be so little time left.

When I heard that Pat was at Maxwell Field, only 125 miles away, I began to romanticize. She came to Fort Benning for a weekend, which was fun, sexy, and sentimental. For at least the next two weeks I thought I might be in love. Then I got a weekend pass and went to Maxwell Field. On the way, rushing to get there in time for the dance, I missed a turn, ran over some railroad tracks, and got two flat tires. I was late, and Pat was irritated, petulant, and thoroughly disagreeable. I saw her only once again, on a weekend in New York, when our relationship resumed its natural course of fun and partying.

★ ★
Infantry Training

Fort Benning was combat training for real, even though it lasted only three months. It was minimal training, designed mainly as an overview of what the junior officer needed to know. Detailed training would come in the next stage, when officer trainees joined a division.

Perhaps there was some benefit in associating with other trainees and instructors, which gave us a sense of identification with those who had gone before. The army was full of stories of heroism, and these helped when things got rough. One was a story from World War I that I remember being repeated at Benning. A group of young officers, the story goes, speculated about what to do if a machine gun opened fire on you when you were in the middle of a perfectly flat field. If you tried to run back to your own lines, you would not last two seconds. If you fell flat and tried to dig in, you might last as long as three or four minutes. The only possible hope, the young officers decided, would be to run straight for the machine gun. This might just rattle the gunners, since they would have to elevate their barrels, which required more coordination than other adjustments. Later in the war one of the officers was caught on—of all things—some tennis courts. He ran straight for the gun. He was wounded, but not before he got near enough to throw a grenade. The gun and gunners were destroyed, and the officer lived to get a medal.

★ ★
General John J. Pershing

The stories that I remember most vividly from the three months at Fort Benning, however, were of an entirely different order. At the end of each company's row of barracks was a small shack that served as a branch post exchange (PX). You could buy toilet articles and other sundries there, and at night, beer. The concession was given to a retired noncom, and late one night I found myself alone there, drinking beer and talking to the grizzled old sergeant. As we chatted, he mentioned that he had been General John J. Pershing's first sergeant when the latter had been a captain commanding a company in an isolated part of Mindanao following the Philippine insurrection. He had also been with Pershing on the punitive expedition to Mexico in 1916. My ears perked up. I had heard a lot of stories about Pershing when I was growing up in the army, and here was a sergeant who might be able to confirm them.

In one story, it was said that Pershing, while commanding a company in the Philippines, had fathered an illegitimate family by a local girl. The story first circulated when he was made brigadier general over the heads of 862 officers senior to him, along with the charge that his former father-in-law Senator Warren had threatened to cut off the army's appropriations if Pershing wasn't promoted. I had always assumed it was a vicious fabrication. Everyone concerned denied the story about the illegitimate family, including the Filipino woman who was supposed to have been Pershing's common-law wife, but the story persisted. So when the old sergeant said he had served with Pershing, I jumped at the chance to check on it. When I asked the sergeant, he looked at me for a moment and said, "Well, son, let's just say this—any man who won't fuck won't fight, and the general was a fighter."

As for the several stories about how Pershing got his nickname Black Jack, the sergeant didn't really have anything new to add. In the mildest version, he was called this because of the color of his hair. According to another, the nickname came from his having commanded some black troops. Third, Black Jack described his personality. It was said that he had been the most diligent of all his classmates in hazing plebes at West Point, and that he continued to be cruel and unfeeling throughout his career. He reputedly came up to inspect troops in the early days of World War I when the colonel commanding, a classmate, heartily greeted him with a loud "Hello, Jack!" Pershing replied with ice in his voice, "The days of West Point are long gone. You are hereby relieved of command."

That particular story is usually told in conjunction with the one about the debate in the American Expeditionary Force over where to send officers who had been relieved of command for incompetency. Some members of Pershing's headquarters wanted to send them to Blois—Americans usually pronounced it "blooey." As it turned out, they were sent to Cannes, which was just as well, since it could be said that they had been canned.

My father's slight experience with Pershing was enough to convince me of the man's cruelty. For a few months in 1928, my father had served on the staff of the army chief of staff in what was then the equivalent of the Pentagon, the old state-war-navy Victorian wedding cake of a building next to the White House, which now houses agencies of the Executive Office of the President. Staff officers sat at desks in a huge room, and on the other side, away from the door, were the offices of the chief of staff and several other senior officers, including Pershing, who was by then writing his memoirs. Pershing would arrive mid-morning, someone would shout, " 'Ten-shun!" and everyone would stop work and stand at attention. Most mornings Pershing would say "At ease," and everyone would go back to work. However, one morning, according to my father, the general looked over the assembled group and said, "Gentlemen, today is a red-letter day for me. I have succeeded in getting even with the last son-of-a-bitch in the army who ever did anything to me!"

Nor did I need the sergeant's help to confirm the story of the young French mistress Pershing had had when he was commander in chief of the U.S. Expeditionary Force in World War I. Pershing's wife, the daughter of the powerful Senator Francis E. Warren, and three of his four children had died in a fire at the Presidio in San Francisco in 1915 while Pershing was with his troops on the Mexican border. During World War I he was a widower, and he remained unmarried the rest of his life. So the story seemed credible, and I heard a confirmation of it when I was still at West Point. In the years following the war, Pershing spent a lot of time in France in his capacity as head of the Battle Monuments Commission. The cadet across the barracks hall at

West Point was an army brat whose father had been military attaché during this period, and his family were friends of Pershing. The cadet had actually become a favorite of the French mistress. His story was that Pershing wanted to marry her but was dissuaded by his first wife's family.

When we were at West Point, the French mistress was living at the Mayflower Hotel in Washington and visited the general at Walter Reed Hospital daily. Every so often she wrote my fellow cadet the latest news on the general's health.

The sergeant confirmed another story about General Pershing that I had heard before in the army but never quite believed. Pershing had recruited prostitutes for his troops on the punitive expedition to Mexico against Pancho Villa in 1916. When I asked the sergeant in a skeptical tone whether this was true, he was disgusted with me. "Of course it's true." All through history, he said, armies have suffered more from disease than from battle, and most diseases were venereal. Pershing recruited a bevy of prostitutes and had them screened by the medics. When the expedition made camp in Mexico, he had an outer fence built around the main camp and in the center of the main camp a fenced compound for the women. Their compound had only one entrance and one exit. To get in, you had to show your dogtags and your money to an MP and your genitalia to a doctor. The way out was through a prophylactic station. Pershing's expedition, the sergeant said proudly, had the lowest VD rate in history!

★ ★

Maneuvers

At the end of our time at Fort Benning, in early fall 1943, Johnny Mattfeldt and I requested assignment to the Ninety-seventh Infantry Division because it was stationed only a few hours from San Antonio. We both got our wish, but within a week of reporting for duty the division was sent to the Louisiana maneuver area for a month of simulated combat.

The maneuvers were reasonably realistic. We marched long distances, dug innumerable foxholes, had mock battles

57

with the "enemy," and, frequently out of touch with field kitch-ens, ended up eating K-rations or nothing at all. And we learned something. Combat entails long periods of tedium and occasion-ally of cold and wetness and hunger, interspersed with short pe-riods of utter terror. On maneuvers the simulation is speeded up so the tedium is less than in actual combat and the terror is absent. But on maneuvers I was actually colder and wetter and hungrier for longer periods than I ever was in combat. We learned how to scrounge and squirrel away food and how to keep as warm and dry as possible while camping out—some-thing my children tried several times to get me to do as they were growing up but never succeeded. Maneuvers even gave me my fill of picnics.

We also learned a little something about terrain, about what makes a good defensive position, and about how to use terrain to move troops into a position for an attack with a mini-mum of casualties.

One unexpected consequence of maneuvers was that the physical deprivation did something peculiar to a young man's priorities. As it happened, at the end of maneuvers Johnny Matt-feldt and I were in the advance party that went ahead of the division to its new station at Fort Leonard Wood in Missouri. Johnny had gotten leave to drive his car to our new post, and the evening after we arrived we drove on the highway until we found a diner with a lot of trucks parked outside—a certain sign of hearty food, Johnny claimed. Sure enough, the plate of the day was a sirloin steak dinner with french fries. Johnny and I finished one plate each, looked at one another, and ordered a second.

Two days later, on Sunday, we took the car and headed for Jefferson City, the nearest town of any size. Johnny was a small-town boy from Texas. "This is what we're going to do," he said. "If Missouri is anything like Texas, there's a little village near Jefferson City with a small boarding house or hotel where we can get real home-cooked food. We'll pick up a couple of girls and offer to take them to Sunday dinner if they'll tell us where to find one." The very first girls we asked took us to a little fam-ily place in Westphalia, Missouri, where we had a meal I'll never forget. It took a little time to prepare, and so we danced to a jukebox. Then the cook put a huge plate of country ham on the table, another huge plate of fried chicken, still another of hot biscuits, and kept refilling them. The two girls were young and pretty, but we had been on maneuvers for a month and eating was better than kissing.[1]

★ ★
En Route Overseas

Shortly after the troops arrived at Fort Leonard Wood from maneuvers early in 1944, the division was "cadred"—all the enlisted men were sent to replacement depots in England where they stayed until the time came for them to replace casualties. The officers and noncoms of the Ninety-seventh were to remain with the division and begin the year-long training of a whole new set of recruits. It was disheartening.

At that time a call came for officers and noncoms with "jungle experience" to volunteer for a special force. Jungle experience suggested the Pacific theater. If my father was still alive, he was there. So I volunteered. As for jungle experience, I pointed to my three years as a child in the Philippines, and no one questioned it.

The assembly point for the volunteers was Fort Meade, Maryland, thirty miles from Eleanor Hoyt's home on the Chesapeake Bay. For the four weeks we were at Meade, I went there every weekend. Not long before, Argonne Dixon, who had also gone through Fort Meade, had been spending weekends with the Hoyts. Rather than resenting so many young soldiers camping with them on the way to war, Eleanor's family seemed delighted.

Somehow, in spite of wartime shortages, there was always

---

[1]Forty-two years later, a woman telephoned me in my office at Columbia University. It was one of the two girls. I asked her how on earth she had remembered our names. "Oh," was her improbable answer, "you were such handsome young officers." All I can say is, if that's why she remembered us, she must have been very disappointed over our obsession with food. She told me she had learned the words to "The Persian Kitty" that day and had sung it at parties ever since.

alcohol to drink at the Hoyts. Just as we had during Christmas of 1942, we spent a lot of time singing around the piano and playing parlor games. Any time left was spent in heavy, tipsy philosophical and political argument. Eb, with his sly sense of humor, discovered that the word *splutter* meant "confused noise," and he thought the word so apt that it became the name of their home—The Splutter.

The chance to be part of this fun-loving family before shipping out was too good a thing to miss for either Argonne or me. But I had another interest—Eleanor. What with the singing and the parlor games and the arguments, we did not have much time together. But by the time I shipped out I had made a promise to myself that if I did come back, the first thing I would do would be to look Eleanor up.

The volunteers for the special "jungle force" sailed from Newport News in one of the big, fast passenger ships of the United States Lines that had been converted to a troop ship. It was packed to the gunnels with over five thousand men and fifty nurses for the Twentieth General Hospital. The enlisted men were in five holds, a thousand men to a hold in hammocks stacked four high. The officers slept twelve to a cabin in bunks three high. Meals were staggered from 0600 to about 2100. The ship proceeded without convoy at top speed from Newport News to Capetown, South Africa, zigzagging every two or three minutes.

There was nothing at all to do, except watch old movies that were replayed several times so everyone would have a chance to see them. When the men weren't milling around the deck, the chief amusement was playing craps. Each officer was nominally responsible for a platoon of fifty men, and one young lad in my platoon had more luck at craps than any man I have ever known. He started the trip with fifteen cents and borrowed a dime to get into a game. Just before we got to Capetown, he came to me with part of his winnings in small bills, about fifty thousand dollars. He asked if I could arrange to have it taken care of. It was much too bulky to carry around, and he was afraid to go to sleep at night. He got rid of some of the money by buying a diamond in Capetown, but he still had more than he could carry. I had the purser put the money in his safe. By the time we reached Bombay, he and the big winners in each of the other four holds had begun a super game. If the voyage had lasted another two weeks, one soldier would have had most of the cash in the ship.

The officers played bridge, or at least some of us did. We raced for the lounge immediately after breakfast to get a table and played straight through until bedtime, breaking for meals. A captain named McKnight and I formed a team. He was a brilliant bridge player, daring and imaginative. Our agreement was that I would play strictly by the book; he would supply the pyrotechnics. The system worked like a charm, and we triumphed over all comers. My only regret was that we weren't playing for money.

McKnight had been married two days before we sailed. Shortly after we were committed to combat, he somehow got cut off from the company he commanded and was captured. In a counterattack we found his body bound with ropes to a tree. He had been bayoneted to death.

The fifty nurses, surrounded by about five hundred officers, didn't lack for attention. But I doubt if anything more than friendship developed; no niche of the ship was occupied by any fewer than five people. The only opportunity for anything resembling a date was during the one night the ship stopped over in Capetown.

The South Africans—the English-speaking South Africans, that is—gave us a tremendous welcome. Dances were held all over Capetown for the enlisted men, and there wasn't a bar in the city where an American could pay for a drink. At least two country clubs put on dances for the officers, who found they couldn't pay for a drink either. The drink itself turned out to be a problem. British beer was available, a South African champagne, and a very young brandy. Few of us had any reservations about drinking. I got terribly sick in the suburban train station returning to the ship and made it back in time for curfew only because one of the nurses took pity on me and helped.

As the sergeant at Fort Benning said, throughout history armies have suffered more from disease than from bullets. Knowing this, our commanders reminded everyone to take precautions. For three days before the ship docked in Capetown, the men had been lectured over and over about the importance of "taking a prophylactic," which since the Mexican War has meant having a stinging germicide shot up the penis. "If one of your buddies brags about his success," we were told, "make sure he has a pro!" One poor lad in my platoon came staggering back just before curfew and did just that, bragged. He swore he had had the pro but that he had lost the paper certifying it. His buddies marched him down to the medics and saw that he had another. Drunk as he was, he lost that paper too and bragged again to another group, which marched him down for a third! It took him the rest of the voyage to recover.

My most poignant memory of that voyage was the optimism and lightheartedness of the men who were bound for combat—or more accurately, their innocence of what was to come. One night the officers in our cabin began to speculate about the ribbons they would sport on their uniforms when they came back. At the minimum, they would get one ribbon for having served in World War II, one for service in the United States, one for serving in the China-Burma-India theater, and one for each campaign in which they fought. "If you make it back," one of the older officers said, "most likely you'll get a Purple Heart as well." Purple Hearts are awarded to anyone who is wounded (or killed). The rest of the officers hooted in derision. None of them planned to be wounded!

Their optimism reminded me of a story my father used to tell about World War I. A newsman watched a commander tell his assembled company that they had been picked for an extremely dangerous mission—so dangerous, in fact, that only one of the company could survive. The newsman, astonished at how calmly the men took the news, collared one of them afterwards. "I don't understand this. The captain says that only one of you guys'll survive and you just stand there, not saying a word. What the hell was going through your mind?" "Oh," said the soldier, "I felt really sad. I'm going to miss the fellows."

Of that group of twelve officers who hooted at the thought of a Purple Heart, only two didn't receive one. And six of the twelve never came back at all. After some time in combat, these men became battle-hardened. When they heard of another death their only question was, "Did he die hard or easy?" It wasn't death they came to dread so much as dying hard, or being helplessly maimed.

From Capetown on we had destroyer escorts, up the coast of Africa and across to Bombay. The part of Bombay where we docked was strange looking. I had never seen a harbor city before with buildings no closer than fifty feet from the water. The explanation was chilling. Some months before, an ammunition ship had blown up in the harbor. Thousands were killed and most of the buildings at the water's edge had been flattened.

★ ★

Across India by Troop Train

The troops were required to change all their money into rupees or send it home by money order. The big winners in the crap game sent the bulk of their money home; the rest of us converted to rupees. To save time, two lieutenants from each of the five holds collected the men's money, delivered it to Indian money changers, and then gave the rupees out on the troop train. Another officer and I were designated to do the job for our hold. In spite of the big winners at craps, we collected several thousand dollars, about seven or eight dollars a man. The rate was something like four rupees to the dollar, so we ended up with about thirty-two thousand rupees to dispense. But when we got toward the end of the money, we discovered that the money changers had been using a rate taken to the hundredths, about 3.95. So we were four hundred or so rupees short, or $100. Since a lieutenant's pay was $135, this was a disaster. The big winner at craps heard about our plight, laughed, and tossed out the difference.

The troop train consisted of third-class cars of India Railways. They had wooden seats with an upper bunk that folded down. Four days and four nights we chugged across the hot dry plains of the subcontinent. Stops were frequent, and at each one we cleaned the vendors out of their mangoes and melons and boiling hot tea.

A British officer and two soldiers, serving aboard the train as liaison, took it upon themselves to teach us about the country and how to behave. They even endeavored to teach us some

Urdu, the Indic language developed after the Mogul conquest for use in "the court and camp." *Cha* was tea. *Pani* was water and drinking water—water that had been boiled—was *pinaka pani. Chota* meant small, as in a *chota* peg of whiskey; *thora,* little; *thanda,* cold. *Thora thanda pani* was a little cold water. To get your laundry washed, the expression was *saf karow.* And the man who did the laundry was the *dhobi,* in soldiers' Urdu, the *saf karow wallah. Wallah,* in fact, was pervasive. The *pani wallah* was the water bearer, as in Kipling's Gunga Din. A *base wallah,* spoken with derision by combat soldiers, was someone with a noncombatant job. Our British guides even taught us a little ditty to remember some of our Urdu:

> I love a lassie,
> A bloody, black *Madrassi*
> She's dirty and she's stinking,
> And she smells.

> She rubs her teeth with charcoal,
> And *saf karow*s her arse hole,
> With a *thora thanda pani*
> From the well.

But the GIs were also inventive, putting individual Urdu words together into phrases that were really American slang. Their favorite was the combination of *hai,* a form of the verb "to be"; *upra,* literally "up"; *kuh,* literally "what"; and *jig jig,* "to fornicate." Thus, *Upra kuh jig jig hai?* in the American use of Urdu becomes, "What the fuck's up?"

The train ride was slow, leisurely, and hot. We killed the time singing and talking and playing cards and craps. We also speculated about where the hell we were going and where we would be fighting. The little news we received concerned Japanese attacks on India, at Imphal and Kohima. Maybe we were going to be fighting on Indian soil, to repel a Japanese invasion. Or perhaps we were going to be part of a counterattack, an attempt by the Allies to invade Burma. Still another theory was that we were on our way to China to serve as a ground-force equivalent to the American Flying Tigers.

Late one afternoon we arrived at Ramgarh, an Indian army post somewhere east of Calcutta. The plan was told to us the day before we arrived. After several weeks of organization and training, we were to become the second regiment of Merrill's Marauders. The Marauders were a long-range penetration unit modeled after the British Chindits, the brainchild of General Orde Wingate. The idea was to have a light infantry unit trained for long rapid marches and that could also be transported by parachute and glider deep into enemy territory. Once there, it could disrupt communications, blow up supply dumps, ambush, and generally make trouble. In the mountainous terrain and jungles along the borders of India and Burma, and in northern and eastern Burma, such an outfit had a reasonable chance of going in, raising hell, and making it back out, as the Chindits had in 1943. In any case, when the time came to reconquer Burma and the rest of Southeast Asia, units of this kind would be extraordinarily useful for penetrating enemy territory and seizing airfields in advance of the main attack.

But the officers who met us at Ramgarh were grim-faced. The first regiment had indeed made a long-range penetration march into Burma and successfully seized an airfield. As a result, the Japanese had gathered their forces and were preparing to counterattack. But even worse was news that the first regiment of Marauders had camped in an area infested with mite typhus and over 50 percent had already collapsed. Doctors believed that in a matter of days the first regiment would cease to exist as a fighting force. Our group was to be flown in to replace them immediately, without either reorganizing or training.

We spent that first night issuing arms and ammunition, and the next morning we boarded C-47 aircraft, one platoon to a plane. We flew to an airfield in northeast India, in a town called Ledo on the Brahmaputra River, which flows west to join the Ganges and then to Calcutta and the sea. Ledo was one of the air bases used by the Americans to fly the "hump" over the Himalayas to China. From it you could see the snow-covered, brooding escarpment of mountains. At Ledo we would refuel and fly on to the airfield the Marauders had seized in Burma, a place called Myitkyina.

65

5

★ ★

Burma !

So Burma was where we would fight! That night in Ramgarh we were briefed on the terrain, health hazards, military
events since the Japanese invasion in 1942, and Allied plans for
the immediate future. Some British liaison officers and men
from Merrill's Marauders who had been evacuated for wounds
or disease filled us in on the gory details.

When we looked at the map we saw a country that seemed
to originate in the Himalaya range, with its peaks up to twenty-
five thousand feet. Parallel ridges of shorter mountains curved
southward through Burma. One range defined the border between India and Burma. Alongside it ran the narrow Hukwang
Valley, carved out by the headwaters of the Chindwin River.

For several hundred miles, the Chindwin is a torrent raging between mountain walls. Gradually the mountains turn to
hills, and finally the river enters a broad central plain, where
five hundred miles to the south, just below Mandalay, it merges
with an even bigger river, the Irrawaddy. Then another ridge of
mountains separates the headwaters of the Chindwin from
those of the Mogaung River, which is smaller and shorter, joining the Irrawaddy further north among the foothills. Then
comes another range, and then the narrow valley at the headwaters of the Irrawaddy. At a huge bend in the Irrawaddy, still in
the foothills, lies the town of Myitkyina (pronounced *mich-chi-
naw*). Beyond Myitkyina are more ridges, and beyond them the
mighty Salween River flows. More ridges and headwaters lie
further on.

It is three hundred air miles from Ledo to Myitkyina—
three hundred miles of some of the most rugged terrain Ameri-

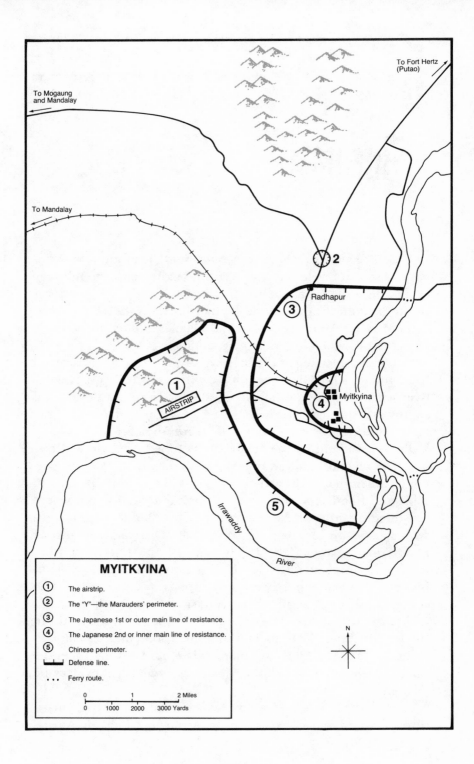

To Fort Hertz (Putao)

To Mogaung and Mandalay

To Mandalay

②

Radhapur

③

①

AIRSTRIP

④ Myitkyina

⑤

Irrawaddy

River

MYITKYINA

①   The airstrip.

②   The "Y"—the Marauders' perimeter.

③   The Japanese 1st or outer main line of resistance.

④   The Japanese 2nd or inner main line of resistance.

⑤   Chinese perimeter.

━━   Defense line.

...   Ferry route.

N

0	1	2 Miles
0	1000 2000	3000 Yards

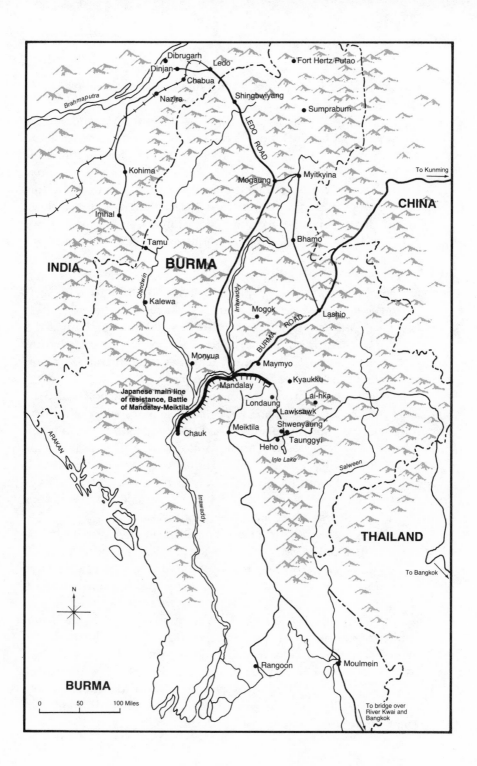

Dibrugarh
Ledo
Dinjan
Chabua
Fort Hertz/Putao
Nazira
Brahmaputra
Shingbwiyang
Sumprabum
LEDO ROAD
Kohima
Mogaung
Myitkyina
To Kunming
CHINA
Imhal
Bhamo
Tamu
BURMA
INDIA
Chindwin
Kalewa
Irrawaddy
Mogok
Lashio
BURMA ROAD
Monyua
Maymyo
Japanese main line
of resistance, Battle
of Mandalay-Meiktila
Mandalay
Kyaukku
Londaung
Lai-hka
Lawksawk
Chauk
Meiktila
Shwenyaung
Heho
Taunggyi
Inle Lake
Salween
ARAKAN
Irrawaddy
THAILAND
To Bangkok
Rangoon
Moulmein
N
BURMA
To bridge over
River Kwai and
Bangkok
0   50   100 Miles

cans have ever fought in and with one of the most inhospitable climates.

Covering this incoherent jumble of mountains and valleys are several different kinds of jungle. In the rain forests of the western mountain slopes, the trees are twenty feet in diameter at the base and rise straight and clean of branches to a dense roof foliage at eighty to one hundred feet. The gloom of the forest prevents undergrowth, but the forest floor is covered three to four feet deep with rotting vegetation, and walking is difficult. In the valleys between mountain ridges, the trees are smaller and more scattered and the undergrowth is rank, full of briars and entangling vines. Bamboo patches are common, often so thick that when a path is chopped through the forest floor, the matted vegetation overhead makes a tunnel. Clearings are rare, and usually covered with razor-sharp elephant grass four to six feet high. Some of the Marauders, recruited from troops serving on Guadalcanal, testified that Burmese jungles were worse than those in the Solomons.

Burma has a tropical monsoon climate. The colonial British used to say that there were three seasons there—hot-dry, hot-wet, and "simply lovely." The hot-dry season begins in January, and it gets steadily hotter and dryer until the rice fields crack. Unhappily, however, even in the driest weeks, the humidity is high. Marauders found that their clothes were always damp, giving rise to fungus infections, "jungle rot." Weapons had to be disassembled and oiled every day.

In June the monsoon rains come. In the morning it may be clear, but then the clouds gather and by late morning the rain comes down in pelting sheets. It can pause for a while in early afternoon; soon the clouds thicken again and the downpour resumes. The average rainfall in the mountains of northern Burma varies from 150 to 250 inches a year. In Shingbwiyang, where the Seventy-ninth Evacuation Hospital was located, it is over 400 inches. If you ride in a jeep from India on the Ledo road, when you come through the pass and first see the valley it will be raining. By the time you're about a third of the way down the valley the skies will clear and the sun will break out. Then what looks like steam will start rising from the valley floor, clouds will form, and before you reach the bottom it will be raining again.

In September the rains lighten up, and by late October the simply lovely weather begins and continues through December. This period resembles the best of English springs. The days are warm and sunny, the nights cool enough for a sweater and a fire. Unfortunately for the Marauders, their fighting began in February and continued until August, when those who were left were disbanded.

In such a climate, the insects are unbelievable. The mosquitoes rival those of the Maine woods, and there is a monstrous variety of ticks, spiders, and other pests. But what no one who fought in Burma will ever forget are the leeches. As you complete a bend in the trail an ordinary bush will suddenly come alive, its twigs wriggling all over. They are covered with leeches, which, alerted by your scent, rear up to catch hold of you as you brush by.

I still have dreams about those animated bushes. A hungry Burmese leech is about an inch long and no thicker than a kitchen match. The Marauders wore nylon jungle shirts with flaps that could be buttoned down at the collar and sleeves, nylon pants that had flaps at the flies and legs that tucked into their boots. They had leather parachute boots, or jungle boots with nylon tops and sneaker bottoms. But the leeches would still find a way to crawl in at the wrists or under the belt. They would even go through the eyelets of your boots and fasten onto your ankle or foot. Frequently, you would take off your boots at night to find you had been walking in blood. When a leech attached itself to your skin and began to suck blood, it would swell up to the size of a garden slug. If you tried to pull the leech off it would break in two, leaving the head still dug into your skin. The only way to get a leech off was to burn it with a lighted cigarette.

With the climate and the insects, every conceivable disease thrives. I once saw a world map shaded to show different tropical diseases; all the ovals and circles overlapped on Burma. Malaria was unavoidable. After the six-week course of pills to cure it, you were immediately reinfected. All you could do was take a suppressant and wait until you were shipped home for the six-week cure.

Bacillary dysentery was also unavoidable. Periodically, it just happened. When it did you took handfuls of sulfa pills.

Amoebic dysentery was more serious, requiring a hospital stay. Of the 2,997 Marauders in the first regiment, 503 were evacuated for amoebic dysentery. Dengue, or "break-bone" fever, was common but almost never fatal. It was probably one of the principal causes for the evacuation of the estimated 950 Marauders who suffered from "miscellaneous fevers."

Cholera, plague, typhus, and all the other tropical diseases were also threats. Probably the most serious, mentioned above, was mite typhus, or Japanese river valley fever. One battalion, which apparently camped for a night in a place infested with the mites, was particularly hard hit, sustaining most of the 149 cases of this disease. None of the known drugs worked. The only thing medical personnel could do was give the victims good nursing care. With the heat and humidity it was hard to provide such care in the bamboo *basha*s that served as wards, so bricks were flown in to build wards that could be air-conditioned. Everyone in the hospital, from the general down, laid bricks.

But these were not the diseases we feared most. The dreaded ones included elephantiasis. Like malaria, it is mosquito-borne, and we found it impossible to avoid being bitten. The symptoms were horrible, as you could see among the native Kachins. Elephantiasis blocks the lymph system, which can cause an arm or a leg to swell to grotesque dimensions. I once saw a man with a testicle the size of a watermelon; he had to carry it in a special bag over his shoulder when he walked.

The other disease we feared so much was liver fluke, also called snail fever or *shistosomiasis*. The liver fluke is a parasite rather than a germ, and it has a complex life cycle. It inhabits livers of humans and other mammals. Its eggs are discharged into the host's bowels and so deposited in streams, rice paddies, and other bodies of water, where they are ingested by snails. The liver fluke leaves the snail in the form of a tiny worm and swims free. When a mammal wades through a stream, the parasite penetrates its skin, travels to the liver, and starts the cycle all over again. It doesn't kill quickly, but debilitates the host over the course of many years. And the disease is not easily cured. Until recently the only effective measure was to cycle all the blood in the victim's body through some sort of filter. What made us so fearful was the fact that in the middle of a war, it was impossible to avoid wading through streams.

Sometimes it was hard to follow even the most simple precautions, like not drinking contaminated water. One group, for example, was crossing a paddy field in the late morning when it met Japanese machine-gun fire. Part of the rear force still under cover in the trees kept the Japanese from attacking, but every time the men in the paddy moved, the gun would open up again, spitting bullets just a few inches above their heads. They tried crawling, but halfway back they saw that from the gunner's vantage point he could see anyone crawling that last 100 feet or so. So the men had to wait until dark to move. The sun was fierce; by midday their canteens were empty. Under that blazing, hot sun they got parched, but just up on the hill, draining into the paddy field, was a row of privies used by the nearby village. The water in the paddy field was the color and consistency of pea soup. The soldiers pinned in the paddy field had halazon tablets, and after a couple of hours, they filled their canteens with green soup, added the halazon, and drank. Later, they also ran out of halazon, and their thirst became unbearable. Finally the men drank the green soup without halazon, and inevitably they came down with dysentery.

★ ★

The Military Situation in Burma

In 1937, four years before Pearl Harbor, the Japanese had invaded China. By 1939 they occupied all of China's ports and all of the major cities except those deep in the interior. From that time on, any supplies the United States sent to the Chinese had to go over the "Burma road." They traveled by sea to the port of Rangoon, by rail alongside the Irrawaddy River to Mandalay, then by rail over the mountains past the ancient ruby and jade mines of Mogok to Lashio. From there they went by truck to Kunming, China, on cart tracks and trails, widened for truck traffic in 1937 through 1939.

Marco Polo took this same route on his way back to Venice from Cathay, and it was already ancient in his day. In fact, it is one of the oldest trade routes in human history. Jade has been traded over it since paleolithic times, just as amber has been traded down the equally ancient route from the Baltic to the shores of the Mediterranean and up the valley of the Nile.

★ ★
The Japanese Attack on Burma, 1942

The Japanese invaded Burma in January 1942. They quickly overwhelmed the defenders—a combined British, Indian, and Burmese force totaling just over one division, very little artillery, and sixteen obsolete fighter planes. Rangoon fell on 8 March 1942. A Chinese force under the command of General Joseph "Vinegar Joe" Stilwell was sent in from China to keep the Japanese from closing the Burma road, but it, too, was overwhelmed south of Mandalay. One Japanese column turned west and occupied Akyab, on the Arakan coast near the border of India, driving part of the British force before it. Another Japanese column occupied Kalewa in central Burma, also near the Indian border, and a third struck north and east to Lashio. This third column then split into two. One half pushed toward China along the Burma road until it reached a good defensive position; the other made its way due north to Myitkyina. Using Myitkyina as their base, the Japanese established a screen of troops along the Indian border and thence east, between China to the north and Burma, Thailand, and Indochina to the south.

Although Burma and India were under the same British colonial administration, communications between the two had been solely by sea. Neither roads nor railroads connected them. So the Allied forces had to retreat on foot. Those British and Indians who were not driven into India along the Arakan coast retreated across the Chin Hills to Imphal and Kohima. Stilwell and the Chinese retreated north until they reached Myitkyina, then cut west toward India through Shingbwiyang at the headwaters of the Chindwin. From there they crossed another ridge of mountains to get to Ledo in the northeast corner of India.

74

With the Japanese occupying Burma, the Chinese forces under Chiang Kai-shek, whose nationalist government was in the mountains of Chungking, were now cut off by land and sea. The only way to get supplies to them was by air. Supplies went by sea to Calcutta, then by rail or river steamer to Ledo on the Brahmaputra River in upper Assam. A complex of American airstrips was built in the area from which a fleet of C-47s and C-46s flew the supplies five hundred miles over the Himalayas to Kunming. This last route was called the Hump.

But the planes couldn't carry enough to provide the Chinese army with anything but high-priority items such as radios, medical supplies, and the gasoline and bombs to maintain minimum operations by the forty planes of the Flying Tigers, an American air force unit under General Claire L. Chennault. And just to get four tons of precious gasoline to Chennault, the cargo planes had to burn up three and a half tons themselves.

In October 1942, the Japanese attacked from Akyab along the coast, actually occupying a portion of Bengal. The British and Indians succeeded in holding them there. In the spring of 1943 the Chindits, a long-range penetration force of British and Indian troops under the command of Orde C. Wingate, marched three hundred miles along back trails in the mountains and jungles into Burma. For four months the Chindits, supplied solely by airdrops, blew up bridges along Japanese rail and road-communications lines, ambushed, and gathered intelligence. Then they broke up into small units and made their way back to India.

★ ★
Allied Plans

What the Allies intended was for the British to defend India along the borders of southern and central Burma and to reconquer Burma whenever their strength grew large enough to permit it. But the European and Pacific theaters had first priority. The China-Burma-India theater got only what the others could easily spare. So it was not until January 1944 that the Allies could hope to take the offensive.

The plan was for the British to drive toward Rangoon along the Arakan coast. In the north, the Americans and Chinese were to attack across northern Burma to reestablish a land link with China. On the heels of the retreating Japanese, engineer troops would build an all-weather road to hook up with the old Burma road at Lashio, south of Myitkyina. This came to be called the Ledo road, from the base in India where it started.

Myitkyina was the strategic key to the entire plan in the north, since it had the only hard-surface, all-weather airstrip in Burma north of Mandalay. As Chinese divisions attacking from Ledo maintained pressure on the Japanese Eighteenth Division, which was responsible for defending northern Burma, Merrill's Marauders would slip around the Japanese over mountain and jungle trails in a series of end-runs designed to seize both the airstrip and the town of Myitkyina itself.

Once the Marauders got the airstrip at Myitkyina, four brigades of Wingate's Chindits were to enter Burma by parachute and glider and to seize a point on the rail line eighty miles south of town to block Japanese supplies and reinforcements. At the same time, a fifth brigade of Chindits were to fight their way overland, on foot, cutting Japanese supply lines as they went.[1]

In addition, the Office of Strategic Services (OSS), the newly created American intelligence and special-operations organization, had succeeded in parachuting agents with radios into some of northern Burma's villages, which Western, mainly Irish, missionaries identified as friendly. The people were Kachins, a mountain people much like the Sherpas who would help Western mountain climbers on Mount Everest and other Himalayan peaks after the war. The Kachins scouted Japanese locations, and their information was radioed back by OSS agents. Several American lieutenants had also been parachuted in to train Kachins as guerrillas. Kachin harassment along the Japanese line of communications proved enormously valuable.

In January 1944, Chinese forces crossed the border and penetrated one hundred miles into Burma, where they engaged

---

[1]The airplanes and gliders were those of the American First Air Commando Group, commanded by Colonel Philip G. Cochran, made famous as Colonel "Flip" Corkin in the comic strip "Terry and the Pirates."

elements of the Japanese Eighteenth Division. The Marauders were committed in late February. The plan was for Chinese forces to keep the Japanese occupied on their front, while the Marauders made long-range flanking penetrations behind Japanese lines to ambush and to block supply lines. Over the next two and a half months this operation was repeated three times, culminating in the seizure of the airport at Myitkyina.

Myitkyina was the main Japanese base for northern Burma because it was the terminus of the rail line from Rangoon and Mandalay. The Irrawaddy was navigable to Myitkyina, so the town was served by river steamer as well. Beyond Myitkyina, a dirt road continued up the narrow valley of the Irrawaddy's headwaters to Sumprabum, where the Japanese had established their forward outpost. From there they conducted active patrolling north toward the Himalayas, east toward Yunnan, and west to the headwaters of the Chindwin. Fifty miles north of the Japanese outpost, at a place called Fort Hertz, the British had an outpost, supplied solely by air and manned by a tiny force of Gurkhas and Kachin Levies. Over the massif west of Fort Hertz, in the Chindwin Valley, was the British outpost of Shingbwiyang. By the beginning of 1944, the Ledo road had been pushed this far, and the American Seventy-ninth Evacuation Hospital had been installed in native *basha*s, huts of bamboo covered with broad nipa leaves.

★ ★

The End Run to Seize Myitkyina's Airstrip

Aware of Allied intentions to build a link to the Burma road, the Japanese had meanwhile reinforced their troops in Burma by 185,000 men, including two new divisions. In mid-March 1944, they attacked from central Burma across the Chin hills to cut the supply line from Calcutta and overrun the airfields around Ledo. Though the British were preparing for an offensive in the Arakan, they had suspected that a counterattack might be launched at Imphal and detached their IV Corps to defend the area.

Using the tactics of infiltration and envelopment, the Japanese completely surrounded the IV Corps in Imphal. They also surrounded a strong point at Kohima on the only road to Imphal from India, a strong point manned by a single Gurkha battalion. Supplied completely by air for eighty days, the British and Indian forces held. Then an entire division, including mountain artillery and mules, was flown in to reinforce the surrounded garrison at Imphal.

The Japanese were exhausted and overextended. Their supplies had to come over mountains and jungles by trails that their engineers had tried with only modest success to convert into roads suitable for trucks. Rather than launch the planned offensive on the Arakan coast, the British counterattacked from Imphal. As General William Slim, the commander of the British Fourteenth Army said, "The Japanese showed us the route into Burma."

In the north the Marauders' flanking maneuvers and Chinese tactics of pressure on the Japanese front worked well at first. But General Stilwell concluded that a much stronger force would be needed for the third maneuver, to seize the airstrip at Myitkyina. By mid-April, when the time came, the Marauders had lost about 700 of their original 2,997 men to disease and wounds, and no American replacements were available in the entire theater. Therefore a company of American-led OSS Kachin guerrillas was added to one of the Marauder columns and a whole Chinese regiment was attached to each of the two other columns, bringing the entire force to 7,000 men.

Beginning on 11 May, the Marauders made a five-day march guided by a Kachin over supposedly impassable mountain and jungle paths to avoid being seen by the Japanese. En route, they encountered two native Kachins, whom they took into custody. Then, fifteen miles before they reached the airstrip at Myitkyina, the Kachin guide was bitten by a poisonous snake. Two American officers slashed the fang marks and spent the next two hours sucking out the poison. Knowing that the Marauders could never find their way without him, the Kachin rallied and was able to mount a horse. He led the Marauders on, and they continued to elude the enemy. They seized the airport from its handful of surprised Japanese guards on 17 May 1944.

General Merrill flew in immediately and established his headquarters at the strip. Myitkyina was situated at a point on the Irrawaddy where it began to make a great U-shaped bend. The airport was just a mile north of the other end of the U and three miles west of the town. The railroad came up from the south several miles to the west, went north past the town to avoid some hills, and then through a gap approached the town from the northwest, passing about two miles north of the airstrip. A couple of roads headed toward the town from the north, one from the Japanese outpost at Sumprabum, the other from Shingbwiyang and the Mogaung Valley. The two roads met in a Y three miles north of town.

Merrill ordered defensive blocks to be put in on the railroad and the Mogaung road to the north. The bulk of the Japanese Eighteenth Division was still many miles northwest of Myitkyina; the number in the town itself was small. Over the next few days Chinese troops coming in by air succeeded in establishing a perimeter around the airfield and then in pushing south a few hundred yards so that the southern edge of the perimeter reached the river.

Then the Japanese began filtering down from the north. Within a few days they outnumbered the Allies. The blocks on the railroad and Mogaung road were pushed back to the perimeter around the airfield.

From the northern edge of the airfield over to the Irrawaddy River was a three-mile gap. It was through this that the roads came from Mogaung and Sumprabum. And down these roads came streaming the various units of the Japanese Eighteenth Division that had earlier been bypassed.

The reinforced Japanese attacked roadblocks and forced the Americans back to the airstrip perimeter. Japanese artillery succeeded in bringing the strip under intermittent fire, and then Japanese infantry began to probe the perimeter, steadily tightening the noose.

By this time the first regiment of Marauders was no longer an effective fighting force, even with their Kachin and Chinese reinforcements. Of its 2,997 men, 424 had been battle casualties, and 1,970 had been evacuated for sickness. A number of these had returned to duty, but only 1,310 had reached Myitkyina and all of them were exhausted from eleven weeks of marching and fighting. On several occasions Marauders fell asleep in the midst of a Japanese attack.

The fate of the whole campaign depended on holding the airstrip, but few reinforcements were available. One of the battalions building the road had been trained as combat engineers. It was equipped and rushed to Myitkyina.

It was at this time that my group, the second Marauders regiment, arrived at Ramgarh. We spent the night drawing ammunition prior to flying to Myitkyina. The Chinese troops who had been putting pressure on the Japanese were ordered to march to the nearest airstrip. They too would be flown in. Hospitals and the convalescent camp at Dinjan were told to rush "any man fit to carry a rifle" back to Myitkyina. Two hundred convalescing Marauders were duly shipped out. Doctors at Myitkyina sent fifty of them back to the hospital, but the rest had to stay. What was left of morale in the first regiment of the Marauders collapsed. As soon as reinforcements began to arrive, most of the original Marauders were evacuated to India.

★ ★
The Second Regiment Flies In

As we listened to the briefings while being issued rifles and ammunition that night at Ramgarh, I got to thinking about the maneuvers in Louisiana. In World War I, fronts were stabilized by trench warfare and men were fed hot meals from field kitchens. In the hopes that World War II would be a mobile war, the army had developed three different kinds of "mobile" rations. The best was called ten-in-one. Packaged like a case of canned goods, it consisted of meals for ten men for one day or one man for ten days. All the meals were varied—canned scrambled eggs, spam, turkey, beef stew. Next best was the C-ration. C-rations came in three or four different varieties, but all I can remember are canned corned beef and beef stew. The "hardest" ration of all the hard rations was K. It was designed to feed a man for a three-day patrol. But if my experience in maneuvers was any indication, we were going to end up eating K-rations for however long the battle lasted. It was a lot easier to get K-rations to the front lines than any of the other rations, and if the snafus of maneuvers had resulted in nothing but K-rations, then actual combat would produce the same.

The trouble with K-rations was that the taste was so pronounced. After eating them for a week or so the mere sight of any of the cans would bring on nausea. The only good thing was that different people reacted to different foods, and the men would trade off what nauseated them for something that didn't. Some ended up eating nothing but scrambled eggs, others nothing but spam, still others nothing but biscuits.

Remembering this from maneuvers, I persuaded the men in my platoon to pool their assets—money, candy, and whatever else they had that could be traded—and sent our most enterprising sergeant to bargain with the base wallahs. Before the night was over, he had succeeded in getting each of us four cans of C-ration to take into combat. Those cans would make a world of difference.

As the arms and ammunition were issued, it began to dawn on us that we were going to be committed to battle with considerably less equipment than our training manuals described. Each man was given a rifle, some ammunition, and two grenades. But the only machine guns were British light Brens, and each platoon got about half the number it was supposed to have. The tables of organization called for heavy machine guns as well. There were none. The same with mortars. Some 60-millimeter mortars were issued, but fewer than the tables of organization specified, and there were no 81-millimeter or 4.1-centimeter mortars at all. To make matters worse, none of us had been trained with the Bren gun and some had not even had adequate training with American-made rifles.

We asked if the differences would be made up at Myitkyina. Everything that got to Myitkyina, we were told, had to come by air, and as a consequence nothing was available except additional ammunition. Furthermore, the only artillery was a few pack howitzers that the first regiment had brought on mules in their long-range penetration, and these had been fired so much that their barrels were badly worn. Since World War I infantrymen had called artillerymen two-percenters because two percent of artillery shells were normally expected to fall short and land on the friendly side. With these howitzers, the percentage would be closer to twenty.

The next morning we loaded into C-47s in alphabetical groups, the system that had been used aboard the transports, with one lieutenant in charge of fifty or so men. This is the way we flew to Myitkyina and this is the way we were committed to combat—in alphabetical order, piecemeal, with no training as a group, and with officers that barely knew the names of the noncoms, much less the men. As our C-47 neared the airport at Myitkyina, the control tower radioed us to circle and kill some time. A Japanese patrol had a machine gun within range of the runway. When the go-ahead finally came, we were instructed to load and lock our rifles. The plane was to land, disgorge the men, and take off immediately. As each man jumped out of the door he was to run straight to the edge of the runway, hit the dirt, and wait for orders.

★ ★
The Battle for Myitkyina Town

Our plane banked sharply, darted for the ground, landed, and taxied off to one side of the strip. We jumped out and ran for the bushes, and after hitting the dirt waited for orders. A few minutes later a staff officer showed up and directed us to the section of the perimeter defense that we had been assigned.

We trudged behind him and looked around us in wonder. Myitkyina was the strangest airport I had ever seen. It consisted of a single strip, with what must have once been a taxi runway parallel to it but was now the drop zone for supplies being parachuted or falling free. There were no buildings nor any sign that there ever had been any. Strewn along both sides of the strip were wrecked aircraft—some Japanese Zeros that had been destroyed on the ground, but mainly American C-47s that had been damaged on landing. There had been neither the time nor the facilities to repair them, so the planes were simply dragged out of the way and abandoned. The control tower itself was a wrecked C-47 that had been jacked up to give the controller a decent view from the pilot's seat.

While C-47s loaded with incoming troops were landing on the runway, others with their side doors removed were coming in over the drop zone in a steady stream at an altitude of about five hundred feet. As each plane reached the drop zone, a "kicker" would shove out the drop. Ammunition or weapons came down with brightly colored rayon parachutes. Sacks of rice came in a free fall, fifty pounds in a hundred-pound sack to keep the rice from bursting. Drops this day were for the Chinese troops, and as each load hit, Chinese soldiers would run out to gather up the supplies before the next plane made its drop.

Accidents were inevitable. I saw one Chinese soldier who had been arguing with his fellows turn, step into the drop zone, and hold out his arms to catch one of the free-falling bags of rice. It hit him full in his chest. The soldier had made a bet that he could catch one of the bags. He didn't live long enough to argue whether being crushed by a fifty-pound sack falling at seventy-five miles an hour qualified as catching.

Just about the time my plane arrived, another group of the second regiment made a lunge for the Y and succeeded in establishing a perimeter around it. But there were no defenses between the perimeter at the Y and the northern end of the airstrip or between the Y and the river.

My planeload of fifty men spent the first two days and nights in the perimeter around the airstrip. The previous occupants of the sector had dug foxholes and Bren-gun emplacements. Our men needed no encouragement to spend their time improving them. Periodically we took artillery fire, but no attack came on our sector. By the third day we had grown to company strength, four platoons of about fifty men each. So we were ordered to turn our sector of the perimeter over to some later arrivals. Then we marched north to join the force clinging to the Y.

Trying to fill in the gap between the airstrip and the Y on one side and the Y and the river on the other was a frightening task for our green troops. They would attack a Japanese position one day, then the next have to turn around and attack a new position that the enemy infiltrating down from the north had established in their rear.

It took almost two weeks and many casualties to fill that gap. But this was only the beginning. For the road to go through, the Japanese had to be either pushed out of Myitkyina or destroyed. All signs indicated that they were determined to hold, digging in and turning Myitkyina into a fortress.

Myitkyina was originally a town of nipa and bamboo shacks, a few wooden houses built mainly of teak, in the Southeast Asian style with high ceilings and open verandas, some warehouses made of corrugated tin, and a rabbit warren of shops in the "downtown" district. A town like this does not lend itself to the solid defenses of a city of brick and stone, and by the time the Marauders seized the airstrip most of these structures had been leveled by Allied bombs. The jumble of ruins provided good cover for the complicated network of deep dugouts and pillboxes that the Japanese had been busy building. Every ruin concealed a pillbox of logs covered with several feet of earth and rubble, and the Japanese defenders had established telephone communications between them all. The troops that manned the defenses were highly trained soldiers with a lot of experience in combat.

On our side, some of the Chinese troops had combat experience, but many of them were new recruits. Some were so-called overseas Chinese whose ancestors had come to India and Burma generations earlier, and their motivations were mixed. Many were not much more than mercenaries. The second regiment of Marauders, as described above, were raw recruits and had not been organized in any way except by alphabetical order. Their equipment was that of a light-infantry, long-range penetration unit—what men could carry on their backs. As for the specialized weapons used for winkling an enemy out of pillboxes— flamethrowers, tanks, and the like—there were none at all.

The only advantage Chinese and American troops had was air power. In the first two or three weeks the Japanese were able to mount several raids with Zeros, attacking C-47s in the air and on the ground. But American losses were not heavy, and believe it or not, one C-47 brought down a Zero. The terrain around

Myitkyina included parallel ridges. When a Zero locked onto the tail of this particular C-47, the pilot hugged the ground, dodging and turning as best he could. A Zero couldn't make turns as tightly as a C-47, and on one turn, rising over a ridge, the Zero crashed. When the C-47 got back to its base in Assam, the pilot had the crew tie down all the loose equipment and fasten their seatbelts. To the delight of the entire China-Burma-India theater, the plane did a victory roll over the field before landing.

But by the time the Chinese-American force began its assault on the pillboxes at Myitkyina, Zeros were no longer to be seen and Allied control of the air was complete. A squadron of P-38 fighter-bombers would be brought in for two or three days to provide bombing and strafing support. These planes had what must have been the shortest bombing run in history. They took off, banked right, flew straight for a few seconds, banked right again, dropped their bombs and strafed, banked right, flew straight for a few seconds, banked right again, and landed for a new load.

The Strategic Bombing Survey, a study conducted after the war of the effects of the Allied bombing of Germany and Japan concluded that strategic bombing was not decisive and that the enormous outlay for it would have been better spent in air power for close support. The United States had to learn the lesson again in Korea and still once again in Vietnam. The Chinese-American troops at Myitkyina might not have won without close air support; at the very least, winning would have taken not fifty-five days but several hundred.

Air power alone wins neither wars nor battles. Artillery is much more accurate than bombers, and if something heavier than worn-out pack howitzers had been available to attack those pillboxes, casualties might have been much fewer. As it was, the Americans and Chinese at Myitkyina had to attack them by sending individual soldiers straight forward against withering machine-gun fire—hoping that someone would get close enough to throw a grenade. This is why the casualties were so high.

It should also be said that artillerymen were not the only "two-percenters." P-38s hit their own troops often enough to make some of the Marauders dispute the statement that they couldn't have won at Myitkyina without air support. It is true that the percentage of U.S. bombs that fell on our own men was considerably over two, but in defense of the air corps, it should be said that P-38s traveled at a ground speed that made it difficult to be as precise as they would have liked. I myself was content to take my chances with air support.

Many years later, in arguments both before and after the bombing of North Vietnam, I was able to turn the P-38 misses into a little profit. In lectures at the National War College in Washington and at the Air War College at Maxwell Air Force Base, I used to say, much to the amusement of air force officers, that I had been bombed and strafed by the U.S. Army Air Corps too many times to believe that air power alone could win either wars or battles.

The Battle of Myitkyina lasted fifty-five days from the time that the first regiment of Marauders seized the airfield until the last of the Japanese defenders was killed. At the start, the Japanese Eighteenth Division probably numbered about fifteen thousand men. By the end, two hundred had been captured— not because they surrendered but because they were badly wounded—and no more than a few hundred were able to escape by clinging to logs drifting down river. The rest were killed.

But the Japanese extracted a price for their casualties. The first regiment of Marauders racked up more casualties from disease than from battle—67 percent from the former, 13 percent from the latter. With the second regiment the figures were reversed. As mentioned earlier, my company of Marauders suffered about 90 percent enlisted casualties, and all six of the original set of officers were either killed or wounded. So were all of two sets of six replacements—a total of eighteen officers. The casualties for the second regiment as a whole were only slightly less.

6 ★

An Incident on Patrol

Even before the gaps had been closed between the Y and the river on one side, and between the Y and the airstrip on the other, a decision was made to probe in the direction of the town of Myitkyina itself. We needed to know where the Japanese were setting up their MLR (main line of resistance) in order to plan for an assault when the gaps were finally closed.

There's an old saying in the army: "Keep your mouth shut, your bowels open, and never volunteer for anything." Violating that principle, I volunteered to take a patrol near town to try and locate the MLR. We headed toward Myitkyina, skulking along the edges of the dirt road. The first landmark was the remains of a Japanese outpost wiped out in the earlier fighting. The bloated bodies of two Japanese soldiers lay unburied beside the road, and from there on what assailed us was the characteristic stench of the battlefield. It is an odor that is never forgotten.

Shortly afterward we came to a piece of terrain that would make a good MLR, a rise high enough to dominate the ground. I turned command of the patrol over to the sergeant and moved forward with two scouts, keeping well to the edges of the road. We got to the crest and found nothing.

We repeated this procedure two more times. The third time we discovered a cluster of ruined huts, what was left of the hamlet of Radhapur, the rise that commanded the terrain. As we neared the crest, the scout to my left suddenly held up his hand. We all stopped and crouched down. "Lieutenant," he said, "I think I see something under that bamboo clump ahead. Give me your glasses."

87

I pulled out my field glasses and tossed them over. Then all hell broke loose.

There was a Japanese machine gun in a pillbox under the bamboo clump, aiming straight down the road. And there was another machine gun in a pillbox on the rise to our right. The two of them must have been connected by field telephones, for they opened fire simultaneously. The gun straight ahead took the scout on my left with a burst of six bullets full in his chest. He was dead before his body hit the ground.

The gun on the right took me. I was crouched forward with my left hand on my carbine, and my shirt had blossomed out in the breeze. The initial burst went through the shirt without hitting me. The bullets tore the carbine from my hands and sent it whirling through the air. I spun for the ditch with bullets from both machine guns cracking by my ears. Suddenly it felt like someone hit me with a baseball bat, propelling me even faster into the ditch.

After that nothing seemed quite real. It wasn't pain that I felt but a numbing, tingling sensation like hitting your funny bone. Finally it dawned on me. "I've been hit," I reported to myself. "I've been hit bad." I could feel a warm liquid soaking the back of my right leg. Blood. Lots of blood.

I felt the back of my leg tentatively and was swept into sudden euphoria. My canteen had a bullet hole in it. The temperature was well over 100 degrees, and nice warm water was trickling down my leg! "I'm not hurt at all," I said to myself, "that goddamned canteen just bruised me."

I lifted my shirt to examine the bruise, and even before I saw the wound I knew the truth. My nostrils were assailed with the smell of fresh-cut meat. It was like walking into an old-fashioned butcher shop. What I saw was an open gash running from the top of my right hipbone to just above the navel. Again I was relieved. It's just a graze, I thought. I'm not hurt badly at all.

It wasn't just a graze, but I didn't know this. As far as I was concerned, the problem was no longer the wound but getting back to the perimeter. I peeked over the ditch and there, about thirty yards away, advancing under the cover of their machine guns, was a line of Japanese infantrymen, their backs to me as they moved toward the spot where I had left the patrol.

Another dozen more had broken off from the line and were heading straight in my direction, not twenty yards away, poking their bayonets into every bush.

My heart pounded wildly. A reddish tinge clouded my vision. I felt sick to my stomach. Something in my mind kept repeating, "Please, God, I don't want to die. Please, God, I don't want to die." I cowered in the ditch, clutching the dirt with both hands. But then I realized this feeling was familiar—having your heart pound, your vision tinged with red, being dizzy with nausea. This was *panic*. I remembered the feeling from being hazed in those clothing formations as a plebe.

Part of military training and indoctrination is the aphorism, Do something! The idea is that doing something and doing it energetically, even if it's the wrong thing, is better than standing there waiting to be shot. I got up and made a break for the brush. Again, a hail of rifle and machine gun fire. But this time they missed.

What saved my life was the fact that I was familiar with the feeling of panic and therefore able to handle it. The more I have thought about it, the more I have come to believe that this is the true explanation for the forms of boot camp that so many armies throughout history have adopted. Boot camp is a way of simulating the panic a soldier is bound to feel on the battlefield. For the recruit, panic becomes almost as familiar as a friend. He learns to suppress or control it, and he learns to pursue a line of action in spite of it.

The purpose of boot camp isn't to instill discipline or to make the soldier obey the commands of his superiors. In the days of the Greek phalanx, of the Roman legion, and, in the eighteenth century, of closed ranks discharging volleys of fire on command, blind obedience might have been necessary. But that kind of fighting was on its way out by the late eighteenth century, as American colonials knew when they tried to teach General Braddock how to fight like the Indians. In modern war, soldiers in combat are on their own much of the time, and what they need is initiative, coolness under fire—the ability to handle feelings of panic.

Once into the brush, I hit the ground and began to crawl. Then my luck changed. Two of my men had been on flank guard about twenty-five yards parallel to the road. Not having heard the command for the patrol to stop, they continued for almost a hundred yards before they stopped too. So they were just opposite the place where I was hit. With them was the second scout, who had had just enough time to make the underbrush before the two machine guns finished with the other scout and me.

All four of us started back toward our own lines, keeping down as best we could to avoid stray shots passing between our patrol and the Japanese.

I could walk, but I certainly wasn't thinking very clearly. Again, training took over. "Take your sulfa"—this had been repeated endlessly. Justified or not, I had the distinct feeling that if I didn't hold on to my belly, my guts would fall out. So I was pressing it with my left hand, afraid to let go. At some point after my carbine was sent flying, I had pulled out my .45 pistol. Now, still walking, I put that back in its holster and with my right hand fumbled for the first-aid packet on my belt. I got it out and worked loose the sulfa pills.

Then, abruptly, we were being fired on from the road. We had reached a point opposite the Japanese force, which had finished routing our main patrol. I threw the pills away and grabbed my pistol to make at least a show of returning fire. But their bursts were going over our heads. Because of the underbrush they didn't realize that the ground sloped down from the road. Luckily, I realized this before firing back and revealing our position—and just in time to stop the others from firing back as well. As quietly as possible, we continued toward our lines.

What kept me going must have been adrenaline. As we got nearer and the tension lessened it became more and more difficult for me to walk. My right leg was dragging, so I put the pistol back in its holster and used my right hand to pull on the leg. When we got in sight of our lines one of the flank guards began yelling, "American patrol coming in!" and with the realization that we were so close to safety, what strength I had left began to fade rapidly. I had made it on my own for almost a mile, but I had to be helped the last fifty yards.

Our patrol had, of course, found what we had been sent to

were

look for—the Japanese MLR. (Actually, it turned out that the Japanese had constructed two such lines, a first or outer MLR about two miles outside the town of Myitkyina, and a second or inner MLR inside the town itself.) Over the next few days, the combat-engineer battalions that had been working on the Ledo road ~~was~~ brought in to close the gap between the airstrip and the river, and their first assignment was to assault the MLR our patrol had located at the same spot, Radhapur hamlet. Repeated attacks by the engineers failed. It was only when the Japanese line was broken almost a mile to the north and Radhapur was flanked that the Japanese pulled back to the second MLR in Myitkyina itself. The engineer battalion's casualties were horrendous.

Once in the perimeter, the medics were all over me, cutting away my clothes, dumping sulfa in the wound, applying a pressure bandage, shooting me with morphine, administering blood plasma. Shortly afterward the doctor at the battalion aid station made doubly sure that the bleeding was stopped.

Then came a long wait. The gap in the north was not as big as it had been, and most of the Japanese Eighteenth Division had probably already passed through. But small enemy groups still occasionally arrived from the north, and individual snipers and even groups of three or four infiltrators were known to sneak into the gap from Myitkyina. As a result, the area between our perimeter at the Y and the guard perimeter around the airport was often dotted with Japanese. So the wounded had to be littered back under the protection of a combat patrol, one large enough not only to protect the wounded but also to drive away snipers. Only one such large patrol could be spared each day, after enough wounded had accumulated to justify it.

Late in the afternoon, the patrol with its collection of wounded started out. Dopey from morphine, I was only dimly aware of what was happening, but midway through the journey the drug began to wear off. Then the hurt began in earnest, and as it did some Japanese snipers opened fire. The bearers dropped the stretchers and began firing back. No sense of helplessness and vulnerability that I know can match the feeling of lying on a stretcher with snipers popping away while your people are firing back and using your body as a shield. The ludicrous thought came to me that now I knew what it was like to be one of Custer's horses.

Miraculously, no one was hurt. The snipers were silenced—no one bothered to tell the wounded how—and our party resumed its trudge back to the airport. Further along, behind the first outposts, jeep ambulances were waiting. The stretcher cases were strapped across the backs, one to a jeep, and the walking wounded rode in the passenger seat or stood on the running board.

★ ★

Dr. Gordon Seagrave and the Portable Hospital

Waiting just outside the airport perimeter was Dr. Gordon Seagrave, the "Burma surgeon" and chief of the portable hospital at Myitkyina. (At the time of the Korean War, a portable hospital was called a Mobile Army Surgical Hospital—a MASH. Hereafter I use the term *MASH*.) Quickly he went through the triage procedure, dividing the wounded into groups of three: those who would recover and could wait for treatment, those who would die and so could also be put aside, and those whom prompt treatment might save.

The morphine had worn off almost completely by now, and I was quite conscious of what was going on around me. In fact, I was feeling better. I still believed that my injury was only a flesh wound from a single bullet—a grazing blow across the front of my abdomen. But the truth was that I had been hit four times. One of bullets was a superficial graze, but it was across my chest, not the abdomen, and I wasn't aware of it until later. What had happened was this: As I spun for the ditch, a burst of three bullets hit me in the right side and slightly toward the back, each emerging in front. At least one hit the crest of the ilium, the top of the hip bone, and shattered it. From the front, the wound from these three bullets looked like a single deep gash. It was the fourth bullet that grazed me across the chest.

Seagrave walked beside the jeep reading the tag describing

92

my wound. Abdomen, chest, and head wounds rang alarms.[1] He climbed on board, peeled back my lips to look at my gums, peeled back my eyelids, and took my pulse. With wonder in his voice he said, "You know, I think you're going to make it." That was when I knew that my wound wasn't just a graze.

Seagrave stayed on the jeep with me, and in the operating room worked on me himself. The room was a blackout tent about one hundred feet long and twenty feet wide stretched over one end of an earthen revetment that the Japanese had built to shelter their airplanes. The revetment was a U-shaped wall about twelve feet high and twenty feet wide at the base, the open part of the U wide enough for a single airplane. The fact that we were in a revetment was a comfort, for Japanese shells began to thump down every few minutes in the general neighborhood. Two rows of ammunition boxes the size of orange crates were lined up in the middle of the tent with bright gasoline lanterns strung above. The stretcher bearers had plunked my litter down on two of the boxes. That was the operating table.

The anesthesia was local. Seagrave rolled me on to my left side, jabbed needles all around the wound, and began the debridement of damaged tissue. All during the operation, he chainsmoked cigarettes in a long elegant holder. The ashes kept dropping in the wound. Noticing my perturbed expression, he grinned. "After all," he said, "they're sterile."[2]

---

[1] Later when I ended up at the Twentieth General Hospital in Ledo, there were sixty bedridden casualties, of which only one had a head wound, only two an abdomen wound, and only three a chest wound. The abdomen and chest are much larger targets than other parts of the body, but most men wounded there died before they made it back to the hospital.

[2] In his book, *Burma Surgeon Returns* (New York: W. W. Norton, 1946), Seagrave says that the first thing American medical units had to do in the jungle was to shelve "Park Avenue" methods. Sterile gowns were hard to get, so they used the few they had only when working on abdominal cases. The day I was hit, the casualty rate was high, and they had quickly run out of gowns. When Seagrave operated on me, he was bare to the waist—and sweating! Seagrave also says that they never used a mask at all, again except for abdominal surgery. Even then, they never masked the nose, but only the mouth. My wound was abdominal, but he could not have known that the peritoneum had not been punctured until he had cut away the damaged flesh. So the reason he didn't wear a mask was apparently his addiction to tobacco!

Facing me a few feet away was a Chinese soldier whose arm was being amputated. He had been wounded several days earlier, but enemy fire kept him pinned inside a foxhole while his arm putrefied. It stank like the battlefield. It wasn't long before I forgot all about him, in spite of the smell. Either the anesthesia began to wear off or Seagrave was cutting deeper than he had anticipated. An aidman saw my distress and sat down by my head, holding my hand and feeding me drags on a cigarette. At some point I either passed out or Seagrave ordered a general anesthesia.

When I woke up I was in the recovery room, still in the same revetment, but in a pyramid tent with half a dozen other wounded. My belly hurt like hell. What hit me more was that battlefield stench. In a few minutes I also became aware of swarms of flies buzzing over me. I tried to shoo them away and, looking at my stretcher, the same on which I'd been lying during the operation, discovered the problem. Little piles of my raw flesh lay there decomposing in the tropical heat.

Seagrave's MASH unit had been built around his mission-ary hospital staff, so his nurses were all Kachins. One of these appeared with morphine shots and tea, and things began to look slightly better.

Infection sets in quickly in the tropics, and within a few hours I must have become slightly delirious. My mind wavered in and out of consciousness. I woke to find my stretcher and I were no longer in the tent, but lined up alongside other stretch-ers in bright sunshine on the airstrip beside a plane. A sergeant came by collecting shoes, helmets, and other equipment. Sup-plies were only getting into Myitkyina by air, and every item salvaged from the wounded saved cargo space. As he neared, it dawned on me what he was doing. The SOB was going to take my .45 pistol!

A pistol was the most precious possession a man could have in Burma. In rear areas people like MPs carried pistols, but in combat zones pistols were issued only to machine-gunners as a defense of last resort. A pistol was prestigious, something of a macho symbol, and everybody schemed and plotted to get one. Actually, there was a sensible reason for carrying one. The jun-gles of Burma provided an unusual opportunity for snipers, and the Japanese made the most of it. A man in the woods with his pants down and his carbine leaning against a tree is hopelessly vulnerable; with a pistol on his belt, he can at least give himself some covering fire. I had traded a lot for that pistol, and in my semidelirium it seemed vital that I not lose it now. I took hold of it, pointed it in the direction of the sergeant, and said something to the effect that he would have to kill me first. I still have that pistol.

★ ★

The Seventy-ninth Evac

The plane took us to Shingbwiyang, to the Seventh-ninth Evacuation Hospital. An aidman was the first medic that a wounded man saw. His job was to head off shock. The blood of a person in pain tends to collect in the abdomen. This and loss of blood leaves the brain and major organs inadequately supplied with oxygen. The result is quick death. The aidman first tried to stop the bleeding, by compresses or tourniquets, then the pain, with morphine. If the patient had already lost a lot of blood the aidman administered blood plasma with a needle, a tube, and a bottle tied to a rifle whose bayonet was stuck in the ground. He also tried to head off infection by dousing the wound with sulfa. This was exactly the procedure the aidman followed with me.

The next stop was the battalion aid station. Here the doctor made sure the bleeding was stopped, using emergency surgery if necessary. He administered more plasma if indicated and did anything else he could to stabilize the patient for the journey to the MASH unit.

The MASH was where major surgery was done. It was emergency surgery, not corrective or therapeutic. A MASH could not provide nursing care. As soon as the patient stabilized, he was moved on—in a matter of hours or at the most a very few days.

Evac hospitals were intermediate between the MASH surgery and a general hospital. Patients with minor wounds never got any further. They stayed at the evac hospital for as long as thirty days and, if ready for duty at the end of that time, went back to their units. Patients who required corrective surgery or a longer convalescence were transferred to a general hospital—for the Burma campaign the Twentieth General at Ledo, at the foot of the Hump.

The stay at a general hospital could be as long as three months. If cured, patients returned to their units. If disabled or requiring longer treatment, they were transferred to the "zone of the interior," home to the United States. As mentioned earlier, in World War I British soldiers called a wound serious enough to take you home a blighty. In the India-Burma part of the China-Burma-India theater, Americans adopted the same word.

I was now at the point of being transferred to an evac hospital. The plane from Myitkyina loaded with our stretchers landed in a drizzle at Shingbwiyang, the place that got four hundred inches of rainfall a year. It was met by military ambulances, the litters were loaded, and we started out down one of the bumpiest dirt roads I can remember, which might have been because the driver seemed to think he was going to a fire. Gasps and moans from the wounded quickly turned to screams, until one of the less seriously wounded succeeded in intimidating the driver enough to make him go slower.

The first thing I remember after the litters were unloaded was a nurse kneeling over me and yelling, "Doctor, this patient is bleeding badly." They carried me into the ward, transferred me to a bunk, stripped off my clothes and bandages, and went to work on the spot.

Newly bandaged, pumped with plasma, and comfortable with a shot of morphine in me, I was finally able to look at the Seventy-ninth Evac. What I saw from the bunk where I would spend thirty days was a collection of dirt-floored bamboo *bashas* built in the shape of hospital wards. The beds, with frames for mosquito nets that were pulled down at night, were lined up on each side of the long room as in a traditional ward. At one end of the ward were two rooms, one the nurse's office and the other a little kitchen and storeroom for medicine and bandages. A simple but marvelous place!

The staff of the Seventy-ninth Evacuation Hospital had

been recruited from Los Angeles, doctors, nurses, and all. They were all of them bright, physically attractive outdoor types, solicitous of the patients, and cheerful.

Presently a nurse came in with my clothes, the nylon jungle-green shirt and trousers. She held them up with a bemused look and said, "Lieutenant, there are four bullet holes in you. But I've counted sixteen in your uniform." Somehow the canteen had stayed with me, and she held that up too, with its hole. "This is seventeen." Then she held up the cigarette case that my father had given me. One of its corners was crumpled. "And this is eighteen. You're a very lucky guy."

One of the doctors pointed out that the bullet that had grazed my chest was the one that hit the cigarette case. The corner of the case deflected the bullet just a few degrees, enough to make it graze my chest rather than perforate the heart.

That wasn't all my luck. A couple of weeks later when a doctor was changing my bandages, he hoisted my head up for a look at the wound. The surgeon's removal of damaged tissue had left a gaping hole the size of a football. Pointing to the peritoneum shining at the bottom of the wound, the doctor said, "Every man in the Marauders had dysentery, including you. If a bullet had gone through that it would have perforated your gut, and the infection would have been impossible to control."

Actually, I had two infections. One was a simple cold, along with a cough. Nothing to worry about, but with a gut wound a cough could be harrowing. The more serious infection was in the wound, probably caused by bits of dirt and clothing carried into me by the bullets. The doctors tried sulfa for a week or so without success. Then one day a doctor appeared with a small vial of brown liquid. "Okay," he said, "we'll try the miracle drug." It was penicillin, part of the first shipment to arrive in our theater. Little was then known about the proper dosage or how it was to be administered, so the doctor simply poured it into the wound. It didn't work.

Months later, on liaison duty with the British Fourteenth Army, I contracted a strange tropical infection and received another dose of penicillin. By this time they had learned that the antibiotic must be introduced into the body slowly and steadily if it is to work. This time the doctors rigged a stand with a bottle of penicillin and ran a tube down to a needle implanted in my leg so the penicillin could enter me drop by drop all day long. It was agony. Penicillin is as painful as iodine. Every minute or so the drop hit, and it was like having a hot iron twisted in your leg. After twenty-four hours, deciding I was only getting worse, the doctors abandoned that technique as well. Eventually, researchers found a way to mix penicillin with novocain to kill the pain and with beeswax to permit it to seep into the system slowly; that seemed to work.

I was back on sulfa. The problem with it was to ingest enough liquids to prevent the formation of sulfa crystals in the bladder and urinary tract. The nurses tried every trick they could think of to get us to drink the quantities of liquid required. They held contests to see which patient would produce the most urine each twenty-four-hour period, rewarding us with gifts of food they had received from home. And they tried to concoct appetizing drinks. But the supplies were meager and the mainstay other than water was pineapple juice. To this day, almost fifty years later, the mere smell of pineapple juice nauseates me.

Apart from sulfa, the most important medicine was morphine. Even men who were bothered by needles welcomed that one! It should be mentioned that constant practice made the nurses skilled in administering needles. The fellow in the next bed, Stan Barker, had to have daily intramuscular injections of some kind, requiring deep penetration of the buttocks with an exceptionally long needle. The nurse who administered it was a specialist, and she had a sense of humor. After rolling Stan onto his belly and pulling down his pants, she would cast the needle and syringe into him like a dart. I can still see that syringe rocking back and forth in Stan's behind.

It's hard to exaggerate how important morphine was to the wounded. Pain was constant, and at night it was especially hard to bear. Morphine let us sleep, and sleep had healing power. I remember with particular warmth the last shot of the day, just before lights out. The pain would gradually increase in sharpness as the earlier shot wore off. Then the nurse would appear, needle in one hand, cotton swab in the other. A quick jab in the thigh and the morphine would gradually begin to take hold. First the pain would recede. Then a feeling of well-being and security would follow. Here we were, warm, dry, and safe in our beds. A sort of sleepy euphoria would follow. I distinctly remember that before dropping off to sleep my whole body would seem to rise a few inches above the bed and float lazily in the air.

I have no doubt that all of us became addicts, though we never knew it. At first the shots were given every hour or so, then they were cut one by one until we got only the final shot of the day at bedtime. Long before we were ambulatory, and able to go hunting for drugs, that final shot was also eliminated. As a result, we associated morphine not with pleasure so much as the alleviation of pain. Because morphine prevented shock in the wounded, I carried a package of morphine syrettes when I went back into combat. I had to use them several times on wounded men; it never once occurred to me to use one on myself.

Most of us were confined to our beds, so we got to know only those in nearby beds and the few who were ambulatory. Stan Barker, from the state of Washington, was in the bed on my right. A burst of machine-gun fire had broken his right leg above the knee and completely shattered almost three inches of bone above the ankle. He had a cast that went from his foot right up to his crotch. Of Scandinavian descent, Stan was a handsome blonde with a wry, self-deprecating sense of humor. He had been a delivery man for a bakery back in Washington, and he delighted in stories about how delivery men would use their pencils to poke holes in the wrappings on their competitors' products to make them go stale. He was also bright and had a philosophical bent. In the middle of the night, when sleep was elusive, Stan and I would carry on whispered conversations about life, and God, and what we wanted to do if we ever got through this war. Stan was an aggressive atheist, following in his father's tracks. He showed me a line in a letter from his father that he particularly relished: "Your mother's prayers are with you, Son, and my fervent hopes."

Stan's thirty-day stay in the evac hospital ended two days before mine. When he got to the Twentieth General he conned the staff into saving the bed next to his for me, so that we had another sixty days together. Then we parted. I recovered and went back into combat. His wound was a blighty, and he was shipped back home for another two years in the hospital. I did see him once again. A couple of years after the war, when I visited my parents in San Francisco, he flew down to spend two days with us. His wound still bothered him. Clots had formed in the damaged veins in his leg, and every so often one would break loose and cause trouble when it traveled to his lungs. I didn't understand why the doctors hadn't just amputated the leg. Five years after I last saw Stan—seven years after the war— he was sitting at a bar when suddenly he fell off his stool, dead. A large clot was responsible.

I've forgotten the name of the man who lay to my left in the Seventy-ninth Evac. This was undoubtedly a psychological slip. He was thoroughly unlikeable. His talk was largely of women, not in itself unusual, but his stories all told of how he had bested and humiliated them. An example was the wife he had divorced. After the separation, having schemed to seduce her and succeeding, he brought her to the verge of climax and left her there. And this fellow openly schemed about how he might fool the doctors into sending him home.

I met a few selfless, fearless heroes in World War II of the kind *Reader's Digest* extols, but very few. Most of us dreaded the prospect of going back into combat, speculating privately about how we might escape it. But usually we felt guilty about those speculations.

What men in combat long for is a wound that will get them out of battle but not be maiming—an honorable way out. I had imagined an ideal wound would be one on my left side that didn't perforate the intestines. The only difference between the wound I had prayed for and the one I got was that mine was on the right.

I began to think about my father in a prison camp and wondered if he was still alive. How could I even imagine going into a noncombatant job while he sweated in a prison camp? What would he think of me if I sat out the rest of the war in some cushy situation? I began to have trouble sleeping.

In the bed beyond the cynical misogynist was a lad from Texas. A mortar shell had gone off just behind him, and his buttocks were riddled with shell fragments. It took the doctors hours to pick the pieces out of him. One they had to leave in. It was a thumb-sized hunk of steel lodged next to his spine, too close, the surgeons said, to be removed. He spent all his days face down. It was as awkward as it was humiliating. "What am I going to tell girls who ask where I was wounded?" he lamented. But he cheered himself with the prospect of applying for a pension on the grounds that his wounds had made it impossible for him to continue his civilian career. In Texas he had worked on an oil-exploration crew operating a magnetometer, a device used to measure the earth's magnetic field and so sensitive the operator couldn't even wear shoes with metal eyelets.

Directly across the dirt aisle was a lieutenant who had commanded one of the few tanks that participated in the first few days of the penetration. When the Marauders started out, a squadron of tanks accompanied them until the road petered into jungle trails. They had seen only one major engagement, and in that they had suffered terrible losses. Roadbound by jungle and mountain, they were sitting ducks for any antitank gun, including a bazooka-type hand-held rocket launcher. A direct hit set this lieutenant's tank on fire. As he climbed out of the red-hot turret, his hands had been so horribly burned that bone showed through the flesh, and his legs, dangling in the flames, received even worse damage. The treatment for burns at the time was the pressure bandage, which had to be changed every day in a procedure that a medieval torturer would have envied.

The lieutenant was a brave man, and he took the daily torture stoically at first. But gradually days stretched into weeks and the daily agony broke him down, as it would anyone. By the time I arrived at the Seventy-ninth, the mere appearance of the doctor at the door of the ward would reduce the lieutenant to blubbering. The chief nurse was a dragon lady, a bitter regular army woman in her forties. Much of the lieutenant's time awake was spent pleading with her to give him something, anything, to ease the pain. She would lash out at him, saying he was getting everything they could give him and that he was past the stage where anything would help. The rest of us cringed in our beds, hating her. It was only later that I began to realize that her ramrod treatment of him was a defense—against helplessness in the face of so much pain and so many deaths.

101

Next to the burned tank man was a doctor, Fred Zombro. Fred had actually come overseas with the Seventy-ninth, then volunteered for duty with the Marauders on the march into Burma. There he had contracted a debilitating tropical disease. By this time, however, he was ambulatory and went around the ward using his medical skills to do things the overworked staff doctors didn't have time to do. He was kind and gentle and big-hearted, at the same time the foulest-mouthed man I have ever met. He couldn't utter a sentence that wasn't rife with curses. Sometimes he even split words to provide space for one—"irre-goddamn-gardless."

Zombro made it his business to see that the tank man did not lose the use of his hands. Patiently and sweetly, dispensing profanities, he inveigled the lieutenant into gripping his hand, into playing cards, and into anything else that would exercise his fingers and keep them from atrophying. Because of Zombro, the tank man recovered to lead a normal life.

Both Zombro and I ended up on convalescent leave in Darjeeling in the Himalayas, where we spent a lot of time together. I never did figure out what was behind that odd combination of gentleness and foul language. I asked him once, and he gave a tongue-in-cheek answer. He had been born with a natural love of humanity, but the nature of his medical practice in Hollywood and Los Angeles probably made him cynical. He was a urogenital specialist. In Hollywood and Los Angeles, that meant you dealt mainly with three problems—venereal disease, premature ejaculation, or inability to achieve an erection. After years of listening to the details of such troubles, profanity he said, was the only recourse.

Bedridden as I was, the only patients I got to know in the Seventy-ninth Evac beyond those in the nearby beds were two ambulatory men. One was a fellow from Boston with a thick Irish brogue who liked to be called Xavier, his middle name. Prancing up and down the aisle, he regaled us with wildly funny tales of the Irish and of Boston politics. And he poked fun at both the hospital and its patients. He had been in the company next to mine at Myitkyina. "This West Pointer comes along to Myitkyina," he said pointing at me, "full of duty, honor, and country. 'Why are we sittin' here in our foxholes?' he says. 'The

inimy is over there and that's where we should be.' Sure, he
volunteers to take out a patrol. And the next thing I see is he's
being carried by on a stretcher!"

The other ambulatory patient was a British officer from
the Black Watch regiment who had been liaison officer to the
Marauders from the Chindits. He was making the most of what
he regarded as the only opportunity he would ever have to be
so close to a bevy of American nurses, and he came in every
night late and tipsy. It was something of a mystery where he
was able to get the drink, even more of a mystery how he had
managed to have sent to the hospital his full-dress Black Watch
uniform, including kilts and bagpipes. It was a highlight of the
war when he appeared one night in full dress, tipsier than usual,
and gave us a bagpipe recital as he paraded up and down the
aisle.

★ ★
The Twentieth General Hospital

At the end of thirty days, I was transferred to the Twentieth
General Hospital at Ledo. Compared to the Seventy-ninth Evac,
it was plush. The floors were concrete and the wards were Quon-
set huts. A lot of the nurses had been on the ship with us, so it
was a little like coming home. The hospital was designed to care
for fifteen hundred patients, but the battle at Myitkyina had
provided it with three thousand. Our particular ward had only
bed patients, about sixty of them, far more than the one nurse
and one medical corpsman on duty could handle. Their shifts
were twelve hours, six days a week, and they were always on
the verge of exhaustion.

Caring for these sixty patients was more than routine. They
were not just injured, they had also been under severe mental
stress. Some would probably have been evacuated fairly soon
for combat fatigue, the circumlocution for neurotic problems,
had they not been wounded. At night, when they were asleep,
they filled the air with the sound of grinding teeth, moans, and
screams.

I saw an extreme example my first night in the ward. At

the end of the row across the aisle was a six-foot 280-pound lieutenant whose thighbone had been shattered by a bullet below the hip joint. He was in traction, and the doctors had some hope of saving his leg. He was having nightmares about being back in combat and he thrashed around so violently that he fell out of bed, with his leg still tangled in the trapeze above. The medical corpsman was in the mess hall, and the nurse was only five foot two and weighed about 105 pounds. She struggled frantically. By this time, Stan had begun to experiment with going to the bathroom on crutches; he hobbled down to help, and only succeeded in falling himself. The nurse ran for help. It was fifteen minutes or more before they got the lieutenant untangled and onto a stretcher. The doctors operated immediately, saving the man's life, but not his leg.

The casualty rate that the Marauders had suffered appalled the hospital personnel. I think the nurses who had been on the ship with us were especially affected. They had made friends among us, and all had lost at least one of those friends. Whether by accident or design, each nurse seemed to become guardian angel for at least one of us. My self-appointed guardian was sweet and plump, about five foot two, and named Millie. She came by at least once a day, bearing whatever gift of food or drink she had from home or could scrounge.

Then the time came for the secondary closure, the operation to close my wound after the cavity had filled with scar tissue. The choice was between skin grafting and a procedure that involved cutting under the skin above and below the scar tissue, pulling the two pieces together, and sewing them up. The doctors chose the latter. They gave me spinal anesthesia, but in the middle of the operation they discovered they had to cut higher than they had expected. Local anesthesia helped, but not much. Finally they just gave me a surgical lamp to hold on to and went ahead.

The problem with a spinal is that if the patient raises his head, or if there is too much agitation and the fluid gets to the brain, the result is a monster headache and twenty-four hours of nausea. That happened to me. Knowing what retching would do to a man with a belly wound, and knowing that the night nurse and corpsman wouldn't be able to devote much time to me, Millie came around six in the evening when her own shift was finished and spent the next twelve hours tending me. The only sleep she got was dozing in the chair between my episodes of retching.

When a patient recovers enough to dictate a letter home, the hospital chaplain dragoons everyone on the hospital staff to help. While bedridden in the Seventy-ninth Evac, I had dictated several letters to my mother and others, but I hadn't received any mail since. My mother was getting my letters, and the fact that I hadn't gotten any from her was driving her crazy. She was writing every day, sometimes twice, sending copies to the Seventy-ninth Evac, the Twentieth General, and the Marauders' APO (army post office). A Red Cross worker had made inquiries, but still no mail. After I recovered enough from the secondary closure to manage crutches, I hobbled down to the APO and filled out all the forms I could find. Within a few days I was inundated with mail. When I was first registered at the APO, they had mistaken my name for Kilsman, and that record went forward with me to the Twentieth. My mail had been circulating endlessly between the Twentieth and the APO and the Seventy-ninth. I read every letter, happily wallowing in all my mail.

As I made my way back from the APO, I rounded a corner and came face to face with the sergeant who had been second in command of the patrol on which I was wounded. He turned pale. "Is that you, Lieutenant Hilsman?" he said in a cracking voice.

"Sure," I said. "Great to see you."

"It's great to see *you*. The doctor at the aid station said that with that gut wound you didn't have a chance in hell of making it past the portable hospital. Seeing you alive was a shock. You must have been damned lucky."

I agreed.

7

★ ★

Rest, Recuperation, and the OSS

Men who were seriously wounded got thirty days' leave for rest and recuperation. When "base wallahs"—headquarters, line-of-supply, and other noncombat personnel—got R & R, they were sent to one of the old British hill stations in the Himalayas, usually Darjeeling. But combat soldiers, who wanted bright lights and a town to paint red, were sent to Calcutta—as sinful a city in the midst of World War II as anyone could wish for.

The blighties were already on their way home. Those of us given R&R expected to go back into combat, so the incentive to live it up was strong. It took a strong incentive indeed to do any high living in late August in Calcutta. The monsoon was in full swing. The days were hot, very hot. And the humidity was unbelievable. Before you could put your shoes on in the morning, you had to scrape the fungus from inside them. Sleeping under mosquito netting cut off what little breeze there was. Two, sometimes three times a night, we would get up to take a cold shower. After a few days I had prickly heat from the roots of my hair down to my toes. It was miserable.

My mood was as bad as the climate. Between the fear of having to go back into combat and the guilt of wanting to avoid it, sleep was difficult. When sleep did come, it was disturbed by nightmares. You would wake up screaming that the Japanese were right behind you, or someone else would wake you screaming. Even when the fellow in the next bed didn't scream, he

107

would wake you up with his moans, grinding teeth, and thrashing.

Even the recreation was depressing. Calcutta, in either war or peace, is one of the poorest cities in the world. Vendors and hawkers milled around in streets lined with market stalls selling spicy foods and cheap sundries. Barbers cut hair, trimmed beards, and shaved their customers by seating them on portable stools on the sidewalks. In the midst of all the crowds, all the shouting, gesticulating, and frenetic hurry, were the dull-eyed, listless poor. The estimate was that something like half a million people in Calcutta had no home except the streets. The homeless weren't just derelicts and bag ladies, but entire families.

The derelicts were more dramatic than any I had ever seen. One, a man six feet four with the hair and beard of a prophet, strode stark naked up and down the narrow alleyways of the market waving his arms and hands elaborately and shouting long litanies in what I supposed was Bengali. One of the Marauders recuperating from wounds was a battalion medical officer, and his curbside diagnosis was that the man had central-nervous-system syphilis. Another naked man was the GIs' favorite. He was most often seen reclining in a traffic island, sporting a gigantic erection.

After a humid, sleepless night, dawn brought more heat and wetness. I would get up at first light and go for long walks on the streets of Calcutta. It was 1944. The great famine that had struck in the midst of the war had peaked in 1943, but it was far from over. Down the middle of each street an Indian army truck slowly made its way. *Sepoys*—private soldiers—walked beside the truck picking up the bodies of street people who hadn't survived the night and hoisting them into the truck. Each block would net two or three bodies—men, women, and children.

Big city though it was, Calcutta offered little to distract us from our misery. After you had seen what sights there were, gorged on badly cooked curries at restaurants, and drunk as much of the cheap booze as you could, the pickings were meager. The United Service Organizations made a noble attempt with table tennis and the like. They even tried to put on a dance with phonograph records. But there were very few Western women, and Indian women were only to be found in the brothels. No major hospital was situated in Calcutta, so nurses were rare. The few British females who were not themselves off to war were in Darjeeling or one of the other hill stations. The handful of American USO women in Calcutta tried to dance with as many GIs as possible, but with as many as two or three thousand in town, even their most heroic efforts were senseless. The nightclubs were not much help. It was so hot and humid that dancing wasn't any fun. Most of us were terrified of venereal disease, and when we did dance, with taxi dancers, it was very gingerly. The general opinion was that the only thing to do was get drunk.

★ ★
AWOL at Darjeeling

After less than a week, my prickly heat began to get infected. No number of cold showers helped. Another officer and I went to the commandant of the rest camp and told him that if anyone wanted us, we could be found at the Everest Hotel in Darjeeling. "You'll be AWOL," he said looking at me. "How will that look on the record of a career officer?" At that point, I couldn't bring myself to care.

Going absent without leave in the European theater might have been difficult, but it wasn't in India, at least not in Calcutta. The train station was a madhouse. There were no American MPs, and the British and Indian army police had their hands so full handling fights and drunks they couldn't begin to think of checking papers. The only problem would be getting from Darjeeling back to the combat zones. As you neared the front, security became tight indeed. But that was a bridge that could be crossed later. We bought tickets and boarded the train. It took a day and a night to get to the foothills of the Himalayas.

The train journey itself was worth going AWOL. Each station was a kaleidoscope of multiracial India. Eating, sleeping, arguing, people of every kind thronged the station platforms. Sikhs with turbans, Bengalis in their *dhotis*, all milled around shouting and gesticulating. Seat reservations were required for first-class carriages, and they were available, so we were all set. The other cars were first come, first served, and every car on the train was jampacked. When the train got to an intermediate station, the only way people in the middle of a car could get out was to throw their luggage through a window and climb out after it. More people fought their way aboard at each stop. By the time we had made half a dozen stops, people began climbing on the roofs of the cars, clinging to any handhold they could find.

The toilet facilities were ingenious. Just before nightfall and again at dawn, the train stopped in the middle of nowhere. As if by signal, the men piled out one side of the train to relieve themselves and the women out the other. That was strange enough to an American. What was even stranger was that the women stood up straddle legged to urinate, while the men squatted down, carefully arranging their *dhotis* to maintain privacy.

Darjeeling is about five-thousand feet up in the Himalayas. The first sight was disappointing. Since it was the tag end of the monsoon, clouds obscured the mountains and continued to do so day after day. But after about a week, they suddenly broke and there hanging over heads was Kanchenjunga, the third highest mountain in the world. It seemed so close and so high it made you cringe. A mile or two out of town on the trail to Nepal, you could see the whole magnificent range of the Himalayas and even Mount Everest off in the distance.

Cloud cover or not, Darjeeling was cool, and the humidity was low. The best climate in the world can be found at hill stations at an altitude of several thousand feet and within 30 degrees of the equator. The days are warm, 70 to 90 degrees, and the nights are cool. You can wear shorts in the daytime, but you need a sweater at night and a fire in the fireplace. And much of the year, except for the monsoon, the sun shines brilliantly. It's like a perpetual English spring. Within twenty-four hours, my prickly heat had almost disappeared.

This alone made going AWOL worth the risk. We checked in and were assigned to a suite of four rooms that had been turned into a dormitory for Americans, four men to a room. There we had an even more pleasant surprise. A contingent from the Seventy-ninth Evac had arrived for their R & R a few days

110

earlier. Three of the doctors were there, including my fellow patient Fred Zombro. They reported that four of the nurses from
the Seventy-ninth were in a similar suite in the hotel annex.

The Everest Hotel was a huge, spacious Victorian example
of the British Raj at its most luxurious. Wartime or not, the place
swarmed with servants. Tea was brought to your room as part of
the wake-up call. The dining room was resplendent with its silver
service and white, white linen. Only the food left something to be
desired, partly because of wartime shortages, partly because the
cuisine was basically British. The only decent dish was a British
interpretation of Indian curry. I remembered Voltaire's witti-
cism, that the British are a nation of a thousand religious and one
sauce. But rid of the prickly heat and surrounded by friends from
the Seventy-ninth, including nurses, I thought Darjeeling and the
Everest Hotel were the closest thing to paradise.

The British tea planters who lived in Darjeeling and the
British authorities were generous in their hospitality. Since
only headquarters *wallah*s and hospital personnel were sent to
Darjeeling, just a few Americans went there, and that must have
made generosity less onerous that it was in Calcutta. The two
or three British clubs in Darjeeling opened their doors to both
American and British military.

Even so, there wasn't much to do. Shopping in the bazaar
could kill no more than one morning. You could borrow rac-
quets and play tennis at one of the British clubs. You could play
pool or billiards at any of them. You could get a picnic lunch
from the hotel and go hiking on one of the mountain trails—not
something that appealed to Marauders. You could play bridge.
The clubs even managed to put on a dance once a week.

The problem with the dances, of course, was the shortage
of females. It was made clear that native women were not allowed, and in any case the only native women anyone ever saw
were servants who spoke very little English. The middle-aged
planters' wives did their best at the dancing, but it was like
dancing with your aunt, at best. Of the dozen or so younger British women in Darjeeling, half were the wives of British officers
at the front, leaving only half a dozen who were unattached to
be added to the three or four American nurses on leave. So the
dances were not as popular as they might have been.

111

What most of the American soldiers did in the evenings was drink and compare their war experiences. The drink that was available seemed not only ample in terms of quantity but also, for wartime, at what was nearly the end of the Allied supply line, amazingly varied. British-type beer made in India was plentiful. There was also gin, vodka, scotch, and even bourbon. How in the world could anyone get that wonderful assortment in India in the middle of World War II? When asked, the bartender and the hotel manager merely shrugged their shoulders. The taste gave a clue. The scotch was awful, the bourbon even worse. We found the answer by reading Indian English-language newspapers. "Distilling firm wants scotch and bourbon experts," the ads read. "Must bring own formulas and secret ingredients." All the strong spirits were grain alcohol. The difference between gin, vodka, scotch, and bourbon was the flavoring and secret ingredients. Still, it was better than what the Marauders had manufactured at the base camp in Ledo. They had discovered that coconuts have three soft spots at the top, the umbilical cords to the tree. They would bore one of these out, drop in a handful of raisins, and cork it up with a twig. Several days later, the twig would pop out, and the brew was ready. The taste was sickly, the hangover atrocious, but the effect was exactly what was sought. The ersatz scotch and bourbon were better than fermented coconut. Nonetheless, most of us switched to beer or vodka, a few of the bolder souls to gin.

★ ★
Liars' Dice

The context for the drinking and talking was provided by a marvelous game borrowed from the officers' messes of the Indian army, liars' dice. It was played by as few as four people and as many as ten grouped around a bar, a table, or, in the messes in the field, a packing crate. Five poker dice were used. Each had one face with an ace, a king, a queen, a jack, a ten, and a nine. The first player would shake the dice in a cup, turn the cup down, and without letting the others see what was under it, examine his throw. Then he would announce what, according to him, was under the cup. The player on his left then had to accept or reject what he was being passed.

However, the package could be negotiated. If the player on the left was offered two pair with aces high, he might negotiate for two pair with kings high, or even a pair of aces with a king high. In any case, he had to pass to the player on his left something higher than he had accepted. For example, if a player accepted two pair with aces high, he might assume the second pair was nines and pass on two aces and two tens. When the pass reached two aces, two kings, and a queen, the next pass had to be three of a kind. By the time the dice reached the third or fourth player, the negotiations could become a little tense.

If the player on the left refused to accept what he was passed, the dice were exposed. If what had been asserted to be there or something higher was actually there, the challenger lost. He put a rupee in the pot and was eliminated from that particular round of the game. If what had been asserted was not there, the player who tried to pass it forfeited the rupee and dropped out.

A variety of strategies were available. It paid in the long run to build up the notion in the mind of the player on your left that you usually undercalled—that is, you usually passed less than there really was. If he came to believe that you almost always undercalled, he would believe you when you actually had to lie about what was under the cup. You built up the notion that you felt the fellow on your left was a good guy, but that the fellow two or three players on *his* left was a villain you were out to get.

Suppose you are lucky and roll four aces and a king. The strategy is to pass to the fellow on your left four aces and a jack. He looks under the cup and, without rolling, passes four aces and a queen. The next fellow passes four aces and a king—what is really there. The fellow that accepts the four aces and a king is the one with the problem. His best chance is to expose the four aces and roll the king—and then, without looking under the cup, offer the next fellow five jacks. If that next fellow accepts, he can either try to pass five queens without rolling, or roll the die hidden under the cup and then try to pass five queens.

In any case, it is a grand game for people with nothing to do but drink and talk. The game moves around the table. Talk

113

proceeds until the game reaches your part of the table. Then everyone in your area pauses to watch the action and play. When the dice move on, the talk resumes. It is an unusual mixture of luck and psychology, similar to poker but requiring negotiating skills as well as the art of bluffing.

Drink and talk were enough as far as I was concerned, and that is what I did except for the last five days. A new contingent from the Seventy-ninth arrived then, and among the nurses was one who had been on my ward for a time. For those five days, I was one of the lucky ones with a date.

Those who were neither so lucky nor so content with drink and talk groused constantly—belly-ached, to use the GI phrase. One of the unattached British women tried to remedy the situation almost single-handedly. She was very attractive and she accommodated almost every discontented officer. She favored the Americans, so much so, in fact, that she was known as Miss Reverse Lend-Lease. For accounting purposes, supplies furnished to the Americans by the British were totted up against those furnished to the British by lend-lease—reverse lend-lease. So far as the Americans at Darjeeling were concerned, she, unaided, had evened the score.

There was considerable debate as to whether she was an eager patriot grateful to the Americans for their contribution to the war or a bona fide nymphomaniac. One incident made me lean toward the latter school of thought. This particular night, the people in my dormitory room were awakened by her excited moans and the curses of her companion. For want of a better place, one of the Americans she had favored had brought her into the dorm. In the midst of her passion, oblivious to everything, she had bitten his ear until the blood ran and raked her long fingernails up and down his back until it looked like the whole British fleet had whipped him with the cat-o'-nine-tails!

★ ★
Back to the Base Camp

As leave came to an end, I had to face the problem of getting through MP checkpoints and back to the base camp at Ledo. Fred

Zombro and the group from the Seventy-ninth had to go back at the same time. I arranged to go with them. Just about that time I caught a terrible cold. "That's it!" said Fred. He bundled me up, fortified me with medicine, and got the nurses to go to work on me with their makeup. When they were through, I looked worse than I felt. At each checkpoint Fred would put on a surgical mask and his gravest doctor's demeanor. He identified himself to the MPs as a doctor, explained that he was taking me back to the Twentieth General, and said that he wasn't sure what was wrong with me but that he suspected a rare form of highly contagious Asian plague. Zombro didn't have to be persuasive; none of the MPs showed any interest in seeing my papers.

The Marauders' base camp was as depressing as Calcutta. The death rate had been high. So had the number of blighties. When you added those who had escaped disease and wounds to those who had recovered from wounds and were fit for further combat, the total could not have amounted to more than 25 percent.

We lived in pyramid tents in a sea of monsoon mud. We ate three reasonable meals a day. We played cards. We took showers to cool off. The camp was miles from the Twentieth General and the nurses, and there had to be some official reason to borrow a jeep. Our rations included one case of beer once a month; most of us drank it up in two days.

Normally, half a case a beer would have dulled the boredom for at least a day, but in the circumstances you didn't get as much beer as that. There was no ice and no refrigeration. The beer was so hot that when you opened a can, you had to clap it to your mouth instantly and gulp away until you had almost drained it. Any slip and the beer would explode in foam. The only substitute was one of those coconuts primed with raisins.

So the days were mainly spent in boredom. In that, and in venom. The Marauders in the second regiment, mine, had never seen General Merrill, much less General Stilwell. But the first regiment knew both or had heard their officers complain about them. Because Merrill had suffered a heart attack early in the campaign, Colonel Charles N. Hunter, officially the second in command, had done most of the commanding in combat. The first regiment admired and liked Hunter. They thought he should be the general, and be rewarded for doing a heroic job in impossible circumstances. For Merrill they had no affection or even sympathy, for they saw Merrill as a protégé of Stilwell, and they hated Stilwell with a passion.

Stilwell had never paid a visit to their training camp. Moreover, when they had had to march several days from the railhead to the jumping-off place for the long-range penetration to Myitkyina, they passed within a half a mile of Stilwell's headquarters and he hadn't bothered to come out and wave to them.

For the officers of the Marauders, Stilwell's nickname, Vinegar Joe, was mild. In their view he was self-centered and egotistical. They felt he was a second-rate general who surrounded himself with incompetent sycophants. His claim to command in our theater, they believed, was that he was the only high-ranking officer who spoke Chinese.

The historical record seems to support the Marauders' view of Stilwell. He certainly showed little regard for the welfare of the troops. He spent most of his time in petty quarrels with Mountbatten, the Allied supreme commander, and with the generalissimo, Chiang Kai-Shek (whom Stilwell, in letters to his wife, called Peanut, referring to his bald head). It was Stilwell who had ordered Marauders time after time into impossible situations without the supplies or reinforcements that were needed. It was Stilwell who had sent wounded Marauders back to Myitkyina so long as they could still carry a gun.

Things were bad enough in the base camp. This venomous hatred made it worse.

And so we waited. What we were waiting for was a decision about our fate. Here at the end of the world, information about the war didn't exist. All we heard were rumors. One rumor turned out to be true. After the Battle of Myitkyina, Colonel Hunter had said something to General Stilwell about the lack of supplies and reinforcements. The newspapers back home had printed stories of men being sent back into combat with their bandages still on, and of their resentment of General Stilwell. Stilwell took his revenge. He relieved Hunter of his command and sent him home by ship rather than air.

The decision about what to do with the remnants of the Marauders had become a political problem. Publicity had been extensive—the physical hardship of their long march through mountain and jungle, the extraordinary disease rate, the heavy casualties. The stories carried an undercurrent of doubt about the high command, implying that supplies and medical evacuation had been mismanaged. The order that had sent convalescents in bandages back to Myitkyina seemed to be the crowning proof.

Finally, a decision was made to give every Marauder a complete physical exam. Apparently, instructions were issued that anyone who had been wounded would automatically be treated as a medical problem.

My case seems to have presented the doctors with a dilemma. Although severe, my wounds had not damaged me in any permanent way. With much of the muscle tissue on my right side replaced with scar tissue, I would never be a star athlete. But it was just a matter of weeks before I would be fit for the duties of an infantry lieutenant again. Those Marauders of the second regiment who had not been wounded were encamped at Myitkyina. Several weeks later this group became the cadre for a new outfit, the Mars Task Force. The doctors were reluctant to send anyone who had been wounded back to join them. The suggestion was that I be assigned to a rear-area MP unit.

This put me in a dilemma. I had volunteered for the Marauders because my father, if still alive, was in a Japanese POW camp. I was a regular officer, and there wouldn't be much of a postwar career for someone who had spent all but a few weeks of the war as an MP. As a result, I asked for permission to see if I could find another assignment on my own. No one objected, and I started on my quest for another "combat outfit." It must have seemed quixotic to others, and thinking of it now makes me cringe in embarrassment.

The Marauders were the only American ground forces that had had a combat role in the India-Burma part of our theater. The Third Air Force had fighter-bombers engaged in close support of British divisions fighting their way into Burma on the Arakan coast and into central Burma from Imphal and Kohima. Individual Americans were assigned as advisers and liaison officers to the Chinese divisions, but those jobs required some training in the Chinese language. So I hitched a ride on one of the

C-47s flying supplies over the Hump to Kunming in China. Everyone I met was courteous, if not a little puzzled by my quest. As it turned out, the only "combat" opportunities in China outside the air force were those adviser and liaison jobs.

The sole profit of that excursion was flying the Hump. From Ledo, where the Twentieth General Hospital, the Marauder convalescent camp, and the network of airfields were all located, you could see the snow-covered escarpment of the Himalayas not too far away. Now that the Myitkyina airfield was secure, the route to Kunming didn't pass over the highest of the Himalayas, but still they were breathtaking.

The trip back was equally stimulating, but in a different way. The C-47, the military version of the DC-3, was a marvelous airplane, the kind, pilots would say, that forgives you any pilot error. The pilots of the Hump put it to tests beyond reason. When we started back to Ledo from Kunming the weather was bad. Not an hour out we got caught in a thunderstorm. Lightning was striking all around us, and the C-47 bounced around like a cork in a raging sea. Later the pilot told me that at one point the plane was diving straight down but his altimeter showed it was actually rising. The up-draft currents were that strong.

The end of our trip was worse. India was covered in cloud. The pilot said he was "virtually certain" we were past the Himalayas. India itself had plenty of hills, trees, and other obstructions. The plane started circling slowly, creeping lower as it went, while the pilot searched for a glimpse of the ground. This went on for an hour. Those of us in the back of the plane were sweating. Then, all of a sudden, the plane banked sharp left and dove almost straight down. A break in the clouds had revealed the green of a paddy field and the pilot wasn't about to wait for another. If we couldn't find the airfield, he reasoned, we could land in a paddy field. We started circling again, looking for a landmark. We quickly found one, and in another hour we were home.

The Marauder convalescent camp was more depressing than ever. Each night I relived Myitkyina in nightmares. The terror I tried to avoid facing was going back into combat. The MP job offered safety and physical comfort. But every time I let myself think of it, guilt descended on me like a shroud. Without actually spelling it out to myself, I dreaded the prospect of seeing my father after the war and telling him that while he was in a POW camp, I was patrolling the rear areas as a policeman. At night, the hours free of combat nightmares were filled with dreams of my childhood, especially of confrontations with my domineering father. Looking back at that time, I think I must have been headed for a breakdown.

Then I heard more details about the group that had trained the Kachins, Detachment 101 of the super-secret Office of Strategic Services.

★ ★
The OSS and Detachment 101

The United States did not have a permanent intelligence organization until the CIA was formed after World War II. The army's G-2, the air force's A-2, and the Office of Naval Intelligence did have their corps of military attachés. These gathered overt information from their diplomatic posts and occasionally—sporadically and amateurishly—ran espionage agents. But the service intelligence organizations were mainly engaged in research and analysis.

In war, most military information came from the interrogation of prisoners, patrolling, and air reconnaissance. During the Civil War the United States government hired the Pinkerton Detective Agency to seek out such information. In World War I, it relied on information supplied by French and British secret intelligence services. But at the beginning of World War II President Roosevelt called in William J. "Wild Bill" Donovan, gave him the title coordinator of information, and told him to set up a professional U.S. intelligence service. Donovan was an Irish-Catholic Republican who had won the Congressional Medal of Honor for heroism with the "Fighting Sixty-ninth" in World War I, and who had spent the intervening years as a successful Wall Street lawyer. For President Roosevelt, the combination of Irish Catholic, Republican, war hero, and successful lawyer was politically very useful.

Donovan had earned his nickname the same way he earned the Medal of Honor, by reckless disregard for his own safety. To his detractors, this impulsiveness was his greatest fault. But it had a positive side. He was enormously inquisitive and unbelievably energetic. After the war, for example, when I was at Yale working on a Ph.D. dissertation about the role that the research and analysis branch of intelligence might play in the making of foreign policy, someone told Donovan about my work. He turned to his secretary and said, "I want to talk to that fellow. Get him here—today!" They tracked me down in the stacks of the library at Yale, and he insisted over the phone that I come to New York immediately. I got to his office about two that afternoon and spent the rest of the day and part of the night trailing him around as he worked. Every free moment he had, he interrogated me about the study I was doing.

That same omnivorous curiosity was the hallmark of the organization he built. Donovan was willing to try anything at least once, even the most harebrained scheme. The first thing he did was hire a bunch of historians, regional specialists, and other experts and put them to work in the Library of Congress. At the time, the Allies were planning their landings in North Africa, and the information the OSS people dug up on roads, railroads, bridges, tunnels, and so forth turned out to be enormously useful. The next thing Donovan did was fly to Great Britain to pick brains in the British intelligence services. From then on, he sought ideas wherever he could find them. He set up divisions of OSS for espionage, for forging documents, for inventing new gadgets, and so on down a long, long list that included "black propaganda"—"news" hurtful to the enemy that was forged to appear to have come from his own government.

In the China-Burma-India theater, OSS had an office at Stilwell's headquarters in New Delhi, one at his headquarters in China, and one at Mountbatten's headquarters in Kandy, Ceylon. One of the operating arms of OSS ran agents into Burma on the Arakan front by torpedo boat. An operating arm in China had liaison officers both with the Communists and with the nationalist forces and ran some agent nets itself. But by far the most active was the arm that operated in Burma, Detachment 101.

Detachment 101 was the brainchild of Stilwell and Donovan. Stilwell believed that one of the reasons the Japanese had "given us a hell of a beating" in Burma in 1942 was their "fifth-column" operations. These supplied them with excellent intelligence and permitted them to set up ambushes behind Allied lines. Stilwell wanted an American-led intelligence outfit of this unconventional type, and Donovan was sure that the OSS was it. A reserve officer Stilwell had known while stationed in Hawaii seemed just the kind of unorthodox fellow to command the organization. His name was Carl Eifler. Eifler was six feet two and weighed 250 pounds. He had lived among the Chinese and Japanese in Hawaii, and he had served for a time with the border patrol on the Mexican border. Donovan arranged for Eifler to be assigned to the OSS, and he in turn recruited half a dozen other officers, including Captain William R. "Ray" Peers, who became its commanding officer when Eifler's health failed at the end of 1943.

Stilwell told Detachment 101 of his plan to try and open a new Burma road to Kunming from Ledo through northern Burma. He gave them the task of infiltrating intelligence agents and guerrilla units into the area around Myitkyina, which was the linchpin of his plan. They set up a training camp in the midst of a huge British-run tea plantation at Nazira in Assam, about fifty miles from the Ledo-Chabua-Dinjan triangle. No amount of skin dye could disguise the tall Americans as native Burmese, so 101 concentrated on recruiting and training sympathetic natives, usually from one of the mountain tribes, such as the Kachins.

As mentioned earlier, the British still held one lone outpost with an airfield in northern Burma, Fort Hertz or Putao, near the China border. The Japanese hadn't bothered to attack it because their attention was focused west, toward India. The first attempt to form a network of agents and guerrillas involved flying an eight-man 101 team into Fort Hertz, and from there infiltrating it through the Japanese lines.

Probing patrols looked for a soft spot, with the result that every promising one quickly filled with Japanese soldiers of the Eighteenth Division. The answer seemed to be "vertical infiltration," by parachute. The group was parachuted deep into Burma, about 250 miles from the airfield in Assam, 250 miles south of Fort Hertz, and 100 miles south of Myitkyina.

Their mission was to blow up bridges and other parts of the rail line from Myitkyina south. They succeeded in planting about half a dozen charges, but the Japanese were hot on their trail. Some of the group were lost; the rest finally made their way back to Fort Hertz. What made escape possible was that they put themselves in the hands of Kachin villagers, who guided them on little-known trails, backtracking and circling the Japanese posts until they reached Fort Hertz. It took the group three months, and they covered over a thousand miles, yet the minor damage they had inflicted on the rail line took the Japanese no more than a day or two to repair.

In a second attempt, a similar team was parachuted even deeper into enemy territory. They had a pure intelligence mission, locating Japanese installations. The group was immediately captured by the enemy.

★ ★
The Kachins

Detachment 101's first real success came when it established itself with the Kachins. The Kachins were animists and, like many primitive mountain peoples, more responsive to the appeals of Christian missionaries than valley peoples with their more highly developed religions. It was with the Kachins that Gordon Seagrave, the Burma surgeon, had worked, and his reputation helped Detachment 101. But the real groundwork had been laid by two Irish-Catholic missionaries, Fathers Denis MacAllindon and James Stuart. They had escaped from Myitkyina shortly after the Japanese arrived and made their way to Fort Hertz, where they joined 101.

Kachins are of Mongolian stock, their ancestors having come down from the Himalayas in the border area between Tibet and China several hundred years ago. Rarely over five feet six inches, they are of stocky build. They worship *nats*, the spirits of the wood, stream, and mountain. Shrines to the *nats*, little bundles of leaves and bright cloth on a stick, dotted every Kachin village and sometimes trails and the areas near springs.

Kachin men wear a *longyi*, a rectangular or tubular skirt tied at the waist, which they hike up high and tie up like a G-string when they have to do heavy work or move fast. The women wear brightly colored, usually red, hand-woven woolen skirts with yellow and black designs. Both men and women go bare-chested, or wear something similar to a bolero jacket when it is cold. The men always carry a *dah*—a sort of long machete—and a bamboo tube as a canteen. Sometimes the tube is used to carry other things as well. And both men and women carry enormous burdens in baskets on their backs.

Many Kachin villages sit atop mountains, for defense against animals, mainly tigers, and against the Shans to the south and Chinese tribes to the north. They grow vegetables around their villages, upland rice by the slash-and-burn method, and at the more civilized southern edges of Kachin country, wet rice in paddies.

Kachin is a Burmese word. The Kachins call themselves Jingpaw, "the people." Their myths explain their condition. After the *nats* created the world, they sent a written message to all its different peoples inviting them to come and receive a portion of the good things it had. The Jingpaw could not read, and only heard that the *nats* had summoned the peoples. All the other peoples came with baskets and carried away wealth of all kinds. The Jingpaw took away only what they could carry in their bare hands. Later, the *nats* summoned the peoples again, this time for a distribution of the afflictions of humankind. Thinking it was another distribution of goods, the Jingpaw brought baskets while the other peoples came empty-handed.

The Kachins are a simple people, and Westerners immediately come to love them. Straightforward and unaffected, they are friendly and cheerful in the face of unimaginable hardship. Extraordinarily loyal and brave, they are at the same time fierce to their enemies. The practice of displaying the heads of fallen enemies on poles at the village entrance had died out in all but the most remote villages by the time World War II started, but meanwhile the Kachins had developed other ways of tolling victory. Impressed by the successes of the OSS-led Kachins, General Stilwell asked to meet one of their headmen, a *duwa*. In his usual brusque way, Stilwell questioned the *duwa* closely, finally challenging his report of Japanese casualties in an ambush the man had himself conducted. "How do I know you're telling the truth when you say that you killed that many Japanese?" Wordlessly, the *duwa* took a bamboo tube off his shoulder and dumped its contents on the table. "Count them," he said, "and divide by two." It was a pile of ears that had been cut from the corpses of Japanese soldiers.

The Americans who commanded Kachin groups could not help but be awed by their knowledge of the jungle. Kachins could track a tiger or a man through what seemed to be impenetrable jungle as easily as following a highway. Sometimes their knowledge seemed supernatural, as a story told by an American lieutenant, Jim Tilly, suggests. The Kachins wore rattan anklets as decorations, some stained, some natural, and the Americans adopted the custom. Tilly, who commanded a small group operating behind Japanese lines facing the Marauders, developed yaws, and the Kachins explained that he had put on the wrong-color anklets. To cure the yaws all he had to do was to change the anklets to a different color. Tilly pooh-poohed the idea, but the Kachins insisted. Finally he radioed base to parachute him the best and latest medicines for yaws that they could get. His reputation and that of Americans in general was at stake, he said. Nothing worked. Finally he gave up and changed the anklets, and gradually the yaws went away.

Once contact was made with the Kachins, Detachment 101 developed a successful mode of operations. A Kachin would be trained as a radio operator and then parachuted into an area where he knew the people. A few weeks later, after the agent had contacted his friends, an American lieutenant would also parachute in. The two of them would recruit, equip, and train a band of guerrillas. The Kachins, of course, needed no training in jungle lore—the lieutenant's job was to train them in weapons and tactics.

After training, the group would be put to work scouting out

the enemy and his installations. A very high percentage of the intelligence for air strikes normally came from reconnaissance photography, but in this rough terrain air photos were not as revealing as usual. The 101 guerrillas made up the difference.

Detachment 101 also set up an air-rescue network for pilots and flight crews who were forced to parachute when their planes were shot down or experienced engine failure while flying the Hump. Word was passed to Kachin villages all along the route to look out for crews and pass them on to the nearest 101 guerrilla group. Crews were told to try and find native villages rather than avoid them. Of those shot down or forced to parachute because of engine failure, some were killed, some were never located and died of starvation. But somewhere between 25 and 35 percent of the downed crew members were rescued by 101—a total of 425 allied airmen. The operation did wonders for air force morale.

Early in the war, Detachment 101 units tried to avoid combat engagements with the Japanese. Guerrilla groups would lay ambushes on trails leading to their camps as a defense and concentrate on intelligence. But when the Marauders and the two Chinese divisions launched the offensive to open a new Burma road, ambushes and harassing became the first priority. The Kachin guerrillas killed several hundred Japanese in the campaign for Myitkyina.

The more I heard about Detachment 101, the more it seemed to be the answer to my dilemma. I borrowed a jeep and drove to the base at the tea plantation in Nazira. British planters had turned over to the OSS most of their "cottages" and dozens of their warehouses and set their tea workers to building whatever else was needed. The men of the OSS lived well!

I decided they deserved all this and more. A brighter, more imaginative, unorthodox, and dedicated bunch of men and women you could never find. By this time, they numbered several hundred Americans and two or three dozen British and other Westerners. They had an air force of a dozen light planes. These played the same role as helicopters in the Vietnam war, dropping supplies in places inaccessible to bigger planes and landing at tiny fields carved out of a mountainside to pick up wounded or a Japanese prisoner for interrogation. Detachment

101 also included photo specialists, linguistic experts, black-propaganda specialists, forgers of enemy documents, all busily dreaming up new schemes for winning the war.

I should add that 101ers were also irreverent and raunchy, scorning the spit and polish side of military life. A stunt of theirs that became famous was concocted by the photography group. They had started with a well-known picture of Shirley Temple in a fur coat, her hands in the pockets, the coat open. When they got through doctoring the photo Shirley Temple still had on the fur coat, but nothing else.

Most of the other 101ers were just infantry lieutenants. Since they had already been trained in the basics—using rifles, machine guns, and mortars and leading platoons and patrols— it took only a few more weeks of special instruction to turn them into guerrilla leaders. They were people exactly like me.

It became clear when I had an interview with Colonel Peers, by this time the commanding officer of Detachment 101, that being exactly like so many others was my biggest disadvantage. He didn't need any more infantry lieutenants. What was worse, I was still limping, and it would be several more weeks before I was fit for a combat assignment. But it turned out that Peers had one job for which I was slightly better equipped than the others. As a West Pointer, having taken a course in military history, I was a bit more knowledgeable about the way armies operate. As I mentioned earlier, Chinese and American forces were in the north, pushing the last few miles beyond Myitkyina to open the route to China; and the British were fighting their way back into Burma from Imphal and Kohima. This left a gap of several hundred miles between the two forces. One British-Indian division, the Thirty-sixth, flown to Myitkyina to drive straight down the rail line to Mandalay, had narrowed the gap to about 150 miles; this was to be filled with OSS-led guerrilla groups. What Colonel Peers needed was a liaison officer to the headquarters of the Fourteenth Army to coordinate these groups and the British. If I wanted the job, he would approve my request for transfer.

I was enormously relieved. I don't remember whether I gushed when I thanked him, although I do remember asking what it was, exactly, that Detachment 101 did. "Anything the theater commander wants us to do," Peers said.

It was only later that I more fully understood my motives in this quixotic search for a "combat outfit." The guilt of sitting out the war in a safe job which, in any case, wouldn't do much for my future career, was just part of it. If this were the only thing bothering me, the logical thing would have been to waive the not-fully-combat-ready status the doctors had given me and request reassignment to what was left of the Marauders in Myitkyina. They would eventually be reorganized and sent back to combat, in China if not in Burma. In fact, I had been looking for a combat slot that would be less dangerous than the job of infantry platoon leader attacking pillboxes in Myitkyina.

At least since World War I, infantryman has been synonymous with cannon fodder. Infantrymen cower in their trenches or foxholes, battered by the artillery shells of an enemy they often never see before they die or are wounded. In the Marauders, the only Japanese I had seen were those sticking their bayonets in the bushes looking for me. The rest of the time the enemy consisted of shells exploding around me or bullets flying past me. What is so unnerving about the role of an infantryman in modern war is his utter helplessness, his inability to do anything about his situation. Being OSS liaison officer to the British Fourteenth Army was a marvelous solution to my dilemma. Technically, it was combat; once in a great while a liaison officer might get shot at.

Once I admitted this to myself, I began to wonder if I was less brave than the others. My consolation was in knowing that I had a new and interesting job.

8

★ ★

The British Fourteenth Army

To recall, after their march out of Burma in 1942 the British remained in contact with Japanese forces in the Arakan. One side and then the other would launch an offensive, then grind to a halt. The Japanese occupied the rest of Burma, but the mountain ridges that formed the border areas between that country and India were formidable barriers and for a long period they did no more than patrol. In February 1944, Chinese-American forces under Stilwell attacked from Ledo to reconquer northern Burma, capture Myitkyina, and open a new Burma road. Almost at the same time, in March of 1944, the Japanese Fifteenth Army attacked India with a three-division force from their position in central Burma. Their immediate goal was to cut the railroad line from Calcutta and to capture the complex of airfields in the Ledo-Dinjan-Chabua triangle. British and Indian troops stopped the Japanese advance in a heroic stand around Imphal, the capital of a small princely state in a fertile valley completely surrounded by mountains. A single battalion of Gurkhas made an even more heroic stand at Kohima, at the pass through the mountains on the road from Imphal to India. They were surrounded, but held off an entire Japanese division.

After a new British general, William Slim, took command of the Fourteenth Army, he moved forces from the Arakan and elsewhere in India to mount a counteroffensive in Burma. The Japanese had not expected British and Indian troops to put up such a stubborn defense. Their supply lines were badly overextended, they were short of food and ammunition, they were exhausted, and they were hit hard by Burma's panoply of tropical diseases. By the time Myitkyina fell, the British had driven back the Japanese from Imphal to the west bank of the Chindwin River.

The British XXXIII Corps then turned and drove the Japanese still further south along the Chindwin, in the direction of Kalemyo and Kalewa. Here the Fourteenth Army halted to gather itself for the assault across the Chindwin toward Mandalay. The British IV Corps, responsible for the northern sector, stopped on reaching the Chindwin and prepared for an attack across the river to the railroad line that went from Mandalay to Myitkyina. Meanwhile, the British Thirty-sixth Division that had been flown into Myitkyina began its advance south down the railroad line toward Mandalay.

The remnants of the Marauders formed a cadre to create the Mars Task Force. They and the reinforced Chinese divisions were given the mission to take Bhamo, due south of Myitkyina and the linchpin of the old Burma road.

The guerrillas of Detachment 101 had three tasks. Several groups were to work behind Japanese lines facing the Chinese divisions and the Mars Task Force, as they had during the Marauders' campaign from Ledo to Myitkyina. Two more groups were to screen the flanks of the Thirty-sixth Division as it advanced down the railroad line; the guerrillas would ambush, harass, and warn of any Japanese attempt at a flank attack. Four more OSS groups were to fill the 150-mile gap between the British Thirty-sixth Division and the British IV Corps with a screen of patrols.

My job was to coordinate the activities of these four groups with the British attack. I was given a code book, a key-operated, dit-dah-dit radio with a hand-operated generator, and a jeep. I was also given a code name. Code names had to be short, and they were also supposed to be appropriate. Frequently, they became the holder's nickname as well. Since I had been born in Texas, mine was Tex. It was short, yes, and although I had never really lived in Texas and it was hardly appropriate, it became my nickname.

I was also assigned an extremely competent radio operator, Sergeant Joseph Ziino. Ziino was a musician with quick fingers and because of this had been chosen for training as a radio operator. The last week of training school some recruiters came around looking for people with special language skills. Ziino was the son of immigrants from Sicily, and his Sicilian brand of Italian was of great interest to them. Before Joe knew what it was all about, he had volunteered to go to Sicily with the OSS.

Ziino was transferred to an OSS processing center outside Washington, D.C., where he had enough time to make friends in the group to which he was assigned but not enough to get a clear idea of what OSS was. His group was then sent to another camp for specialized OSS training. Ziino was sick the day the authorities briefed the group about the new camp. The briefing included instructions that once the recruits reached the special camp, they were to pretend that they had never seen one another before. No one told Ziino, and over the next several days he became increasingly convinced that he was losing his mind. Desperate, he turned in for sick call. When the doctors diagnosed the trouble, the joke was too good to keep. For that group, the basic premise of the training—pretending not to know one another—had to be abandoned.

Joe never got to Sicily. Instead, he ended up in Burma. His background, however, was not wasted. Every few weeks his parents would send him a food package with *capocola* in it, a peppery sausage made of the whole of a pork tenderloin. For years after the war I wouldn't pass an Italian delicatessen without stopping to look for its equal. Finally I decided that the Ziino family must have made their own.

Joe was bright, friendly, hard-working, and cheerful. His only complaint was the war itself. His heart was back in Milwaukee, with his high-school sweetheart, Dorothy. At times he felt the whole war was a conspiracy to delay their marriage. But he was as good a companion as he was a radio operator.

★ ★
To Imphal and Kohima

We were to report first to the rear-area headquarters of XXXIII Corps at Imphal. The trip took two days by jeep. We spent the first night at Kohima, guests of the commanding officer of the battalion of Gurkhas that had held against the full Japanese division. Most of the evening we spent listening to his tales of the battle—the simple, loyal heroism of the Gurkhas and the unbelievable stoicism of the Japanese as they launched one banzai attack after another and died in the thousands.

At Imphal our first task was to establish radio contact with Detachment 101 headquarters. Then came a short round of briefings on British plans for operations across the Chindwin. In the meantime we tried to adjust to life in the British army.

It was difficult. Everyone was as helpful and friendly as possible, and we all spoke what was supposed to be the same language. But the cultural differences still ran fairly deep. The fact that a British high headquarters in those days was staffed mainly by public-school types from the upper crust accentuated these differences. For instance, our American inclination was to make a good story better by exaggerating things; the British inclination was to improve a story by understatement. Joe and I, referring to an encounter our troop-ship convoy and its escort destroyers had had with a submarine on the way to India, were likely to describe it as "dodging submarine wolf packs." Other Americans would understand that it was not really a serious encounter. A Britisher describing an encounter with a true wolf pack in which his convoy lost half its ships would say that they had had "a bit of a show," and other Britishers would understand that it had been very bad indeed. To the British, Joe and I often sounded like Texas blowhards. To us, they often sounded like Colonel Blimps.

All this was minor, of course. The only concrete consequence was that in awkward moments an Englishman might take to quoting Greek as a way to put down an American. Greek was not a subject taught at West Point, and I would try to shift the conversation to the workings of the internal combustion engine, which was apparently not on the curriculum at Oxford and Cambridge. But we learned to get along.

The first few days Joe and I spent more time setting up housekeeping than anything else. Getting a tent, tables, chairs, and all the rest would have been difficult for a liaison officer who was British; for an American the task was formidable. Things got even more complicated when our jeep was stolen. Ziino took it to see a movie at the British equivalent of the USO in Imphal, and when he came out it was gone. The rule was to take the distributor cap with you when you left your jeep unguarded, but scroungers had taken to carrying spare caps themselves.

Being without transport was a catastrophe. We borrowed a vehicle and searched for days with no luck. Finally, I located a British army repair shop with a clever commanding officer who was a gun collector. We traded him a U.S. army carbine and .45 caliber pistol, and he made us a jeep out of spare parts so that it wouldn't be carried on anyone's records.

Later, Colonel Peers sent us a new jeep and threw in a Harley-Davidson motorcycle. I took the motorcycle out on the only asphalt road in the area and had great fun dodging bomb craters. But it tried to climb a tree as I rounded a turn, and Ziino and I decided to send it back. War was dangerous enough without one of those things.

One part of our work was the routine task of receiving a rather large volume of intelligence messages relayed from 101 guerrilla groups to 101 headquarters and then to us, decoding them, and passing the information to the British. They in turn would give me the information picked up by their patrols and the interrogation of prisoners, and we would send it on to 101 headquarters, which would pass it to the guerrilla groups or the air force. The other part of our work was coordinating guerrilla activities with the British advance.

Things went smoothly enough until Ziino came down with a tropical fever and was hospitalized. My skill with a telegraph key was rudimentary. I was able to contact headquarters and tell them not to worry, we had not been bombed, but nothing else. Shortly thereafter, 101 headquarters sent us a young cryptographer, Pierce Ellis, who could operate the telegraph key in a pinch.

By this time the front had moved sufficiently south that XXXIII Corps headquarters had to shift to the other side of the mountainous India-Burma border, to the village of Tamu, overlooking the Chindwin valley. The trip was fantastic. The road climbed out of the Imphal valley and snaked along the high mountains and on the crests of ridges for about seventy-five miles before dropping down into the valley. It was metaled—

133

that is, made of gravel—but so narrow for most of the stretch that one of two vehicles coming in opposite directions had to find a wide spot and pull over while the other passed. The tanks of an armored unit were being moved to the front at the same time. They were carried on large trailers, and the horseshoe bends in the road were so tight that the tanks had to be unloaded so the trailers could be unhitched and pushed around the bend by hand.

With a narrow road so heavily trafficked and so vital to keeping the troops at the front supplied, there was no hope of repairing vehicles that broke down or towing them back to where they could be repaired without tying up traffic. Disabled vehicles were simply pushed over the precipice. There was hardly a spot on the road from which you couldn't see at least one abandoned truck.

It took us two days to make the seventy-five miles to the new headquarters at Tamu.

★ ★
The Arab

With preparations for the coming offensive going forward rapidly, the time had come for me to do more of the coordinating part of my job. The British briefed me on their plans for the offensive. Colonel Peers then decided that I should pay a visit to the guerrilla group on whose work the British most relied. I was to make sure they understood exactly what was wanted from them, and I was to get as clear a picture as possible of their intelligence and guerrilla capabilities. The American in command of the group was of Middle Eastern extraction, so his code name was The Arab. His reputation was colorful.

It was October, and lovely. The paddy fields were dry and The Arab's OSS guerrillas had leveled the dikes of some nearby fields to make a tiny airstrip. An L-5 light plane, a military version of a two-seater Piper Cub, was arranged for me, and the pilot and I started off. The lower we flew the safer, so the pilot flew at an altitude of fifteen feet, following the course of the

Chindwin River, narrow and winding in these upper reaches. We would appear around a bend and be gone before anyone on the bank really knew what was happening. We drew fire from Japanese sentries only once, and by the time they got their rifles up to fire we were almost out of range.

The landing strip was a paddy field right where it was supposed to be, a few hundred yards south of a village up a small tributary of the Chindwin. There was no sign of life at the strip—not a good omen—and yet we had no choice but to land. We got out of the plane and started for the village.

As we did, a shot rang out. The pilot and I hit the dirt. Silence. The bullet hadn't come in our direction, so cautiously, we started toward the village again. Then another shot. We hit the dirt again, and then again proceeded until finally we came to the group's outpost. Two Kachins were posted there. They were completely at ease, smoking, cradling their Tommy guns, leaning against a tree. They waved us on toward the village.

The Arab's headquarters, and living and eating quarters, was the most luxurious house in the village. It was made of teak, two stories high, and had porches all around. The ground floor consisted of a large hall, with balconies around it leading to bedrooms on three sides. Seated in an easy chair on the front porch was a heavy-set, dark-complexioned man. His head was shaved, he had a full, very black beard, and a livid scar slanted down from his forehead across one cheek to his chin. Both feet were bandaged and supported on stools, and he had a carbine resting on his lap. This, obviously, was The Arab himself.

Behind The Arab were half a dozen guerrillas, and kneeling in front of him was what appeared to be, from his dress, a member of the Kampti Shan tribe that lived south of Kachin territory. He was "hog tied," his hands bound behind him and attached by a short line to his feet, which were also bound, making it impossible for him to straighten up.

As we got closer, the explanation of the shots became clear. The prisoner was being interrogated. One of the guerrillas would put a cigarette in the man's hair, The Arab would ask the prisoner a series of questions, and then he would shoot the cigarette out of the prisoner's hair. The prisoner was a village headman who had turned a downed American airman over to

135

the Japanese. The Arab's guerrilla group had gone to considerable effort to kidnap him in an effort to discourage others who might find downed airmen.

The pilot and I were not prepared for this bizarre scene, but we should have been, for The Arab's reputation had spread throughout Burma. The stories about him described an adventurer who combined the qualities of a character from the comic strip "Terry and the Pirates" and Mr. Kurtz from *Heart of Darkness*.

The Arab had, in the colonial British phrase, "gone native." He wore a *longyi*, carried a *dah*, the short Burmese sword, chewed betel nut, and had taken a beautiful native girl for his common-law wife. Rumor was that he had fathered a child by her.

The bandaged feet were a result of his latest adventure. He had heard rumors that there was a large Japanese ammunition dump some fifty miles to the south guarded by only a skeleton crew. The Arab and a handful of his guerrillas had loaded themselves with explosives, marched the fifty miles, sneaked into the camp, quietly dispatching two guards as they did, set charges with timers, and sneaked out again. They rested for two hours on a hill enjoying what The Arab described as the "best damn Fourth-of-July I've ever seen," then marched the fifty miles back again. One hundred miles of walking through jungle and rice paddies in tennis-shoe jungle boots had so swollen their feet that they had to cut the boots off and do the last dozen miles or so barefoot. Hence the bandages.

There were many stories about The Arab's daring raids and ambushes, and most were at least partly true, but it was the exaggerations and fables that had apparently been cultivated. The Arab's group had rescued a lot of downed aircrews, and some of his success could be attributed to the fact villagers in his area of operations were too frightened of his retaliation to succumb to the temptation of the large rewards the Japanese were giving for fliers. The Arab himself told me one story of a headman who had turned over an American pilot to the Japanese to be executed. The Arab's guerrillas tried several times to kidnap the man, but his village was in the middle of several Japanese installations, and they could never get near enough. So The Arab persuaded headquarters to send him a high-powered sniper's rifle with a telescopic sight. A Kachin sharpshooter on a nearby hill drilled the headman from a range of a thousand yards while he was sitting on his front porch.

Naturally, the army air corps loved The Arab, and they avidly repeated all the stories. Their favorite was the time The Arab had succeeded in kidnapping another quisling headman and then personally pushed him out of the open door of a C-47 into the square of his own village. The Arab believed that his reputation was serving a purpose, so he made no attempt to scotch the stories, true or false. And he had shaved his head and grown a beard to enhance it. The scar, however, was real, the result of an automobile accident before the war.

The Arab was a unique personality. Most of the fifty or so Americans who served behind enemy lines as guerrilla leaders had considerable emotional difficulty adapting themselves to the alien culture of their men and the village society in which they had to live. To the Kachins, torture was the normal way to treat a captured enemy, quite apart from the need to acquire intelligence. They understood the necessity of getting a Japanese prisoner back to headquarters where proper Japanese-speaking interpreters could question him, but there was no need to send a native quisling on, and they behaved accordingly. When they got their hands on one of their own tribe who had worked for the Japanese, the retribution was of a terrible kind. Americans who tried to stop their men from torturing quislings quickly came to understand that they ran a risk of losing their authority and having the men turn on them as well. The result was that Americans either turned their backs on the torture or themselves participated. The result was a sense of guilt, sometimes severe.

Added to the tensions was the constant danger. Two or three Americans serving with OSS guerrillas suffered breakdowns, and most others had emotional problems of some sort. But The Arab seemed to have none at all. He snuggled into the village as if it were Main Street America.

But with all its danger and hardship, life as a guerrilla leader was not nearly so dangerous as being a platoon leader in an outfit like the Marauders, and it was exciting. What is more, Americans who commanded guerrilla battalions wielded enormous power. They were little kings. They were responsible for their men, for ensuring that they were supplied with food and ammunition and ultimately for their safety. They had to lead their men into and out of firefights. If guerrilla commanders did their job well—and anyone who survived by definition did it reasonably well—they were the objects of adulation. They also had power over the villages in the territory where their guerrilla groups operated, commanding the services of coolies to carry supplies of food when airdrops failed. The Arab was one such a king.

I didn't understand a more important aspect of The Arab's personality until after the war. A number of 101ers stayed on with the OSS in Washington, and several more lived on the Eastern seaboard within striking distance. On the first anniversary of the war's end, we decided to have a mini-reunion and rented a suite of rooms at the Shoreham Hotel for the occasion. Almost all of us were having as difficult a time readjusting to life in the States as we had had adjusting to life in the mountains and jungles of Burma. Shortly after the party started, a telegram arrived from The Arab saying that he would be a little late. This prompted the retelling of all the stories about him and his exploits, true and exaggerated. An hour later, The Arab telephoned from the airport saying he had landed and would be at the hotel in half an hour. More stories.

When he finally arrived, everyone in the room stopped talking. He was dressed in a snazzy outfit, very close to the 1946 version of a zoot suit. He was happy to see us, but he wasn't at all interested in exchanging war stories. What he wanted to talk about was his present "deal." He was the manager of a suburban movie theater. He had discovered that certain local wives coming to the matinees were interested in more than the movie, and he had fixed his office up with a couch and other amenities. It was not past glories that were in the forefront of his thoughts, but present conquests. He was the dullest, least interesting person at the party.

Unlike the rest of us, he had made the readjustment to life in America with as little emotional cost as he had made the adjustment to life as a guerrilla. The Arab was not a ruthless ogre, the image he had cultivated. Nor was he the immoral hedonist

138

that most people in Burma had thought him to be. The truth was that he had no morals, good or bad. The Arab was simply unknowing, amoral rather than immoral.

When the pilot and I came into view, The Arab broke off interrogating his prisoner to greet us, and we spent the afternoon at business, going over the maps and exchanging plans and information. By nightfall the business was done. With The Arab were two other 101ers, one a demolitions specialist and the other a radio operator. In addition—and to my astonishment, since we were in a no man's land between Allied armies within easy striking distance of at least two Japanese divisions—The Arab had two guests.

One of the guests was a British lieutenant colonel, a member of the SOE, Special Operations Executive, which was the British equivalent of the American OSS. He apparently had been running an intelligence network in the area near Kohima and, along with the second guest, a young British official who was an assistant district officer in the Burmese colonial service, he had been making his way east in the hopes of finding a new area of operations. The rapid advance of British troops after the fighting at Imphal and Kohima had outpaced him. When the two heard about The Arab, they had come to investigate.

The colonel, not in anything but radio contact with the British forces for several months, was starved for news. The Arab had just received an airdrop that had included several editions of *The Stars and Stripes,* and the colonel read them avidly. One item outraged him, a squib relating that the birthrate in the United Kingdom had gone up. He couldn't understand that, since most of Britain's male population had been off fighting the war. He finally blamed it on the "bloody Yanks," and figured out a way to get even. When the bloody war was over, he said, he would go back to Britain via San Francisco and fuck his way right across the USA!

The Arab had laid on a party. For food there was a variety of curries, with wild boar as the meat. To drink we had a choice between native rice wine or something special from home. The airdrop had included the standard medical chest, and among the sulfa and tourniquets was a quart of medical grain alcohol, 190 proof. The Arab mixed it with canned pineapple juice,

139

which I still found disgusting even with alcohol in it, or canned orange juice, which was more than acceptable. We proceeded to have a party.

At the end of the evening The Arab clapped his hands twice, like one of the Middle Eastern potentates from whom he was descended, and out paraded half a dozen village maidens. Regally, The Arab invited the guests to take their pick. It was the custom, he said: village headmen always offered him young maidens. The village beauties were not too beautiful, and chances were they had one or the other of the array of venereal diseases prevalent in Burma. This was my first experience with guerrillas and villagers behind enemy lines, and I was in a state of mild shock. If I had been one of The Arab's lieutenants I probably would have adjusted to what he insisted were the mores of the villagers, but it would have taken time. To an officer who was still wet behind the ears, the whole thing looked more like what our propaganda accused the Nazis and Japanese of doing. The assistant district officer felt the same. He spent the evening talking to the oldest and most self-possessed of the women, who, he reported, argued that there really wasn't any difference between the Japanese and the Allies—that if anything, the Western colonialists were worse than the Japanese militarists.

This raised doubts in my mind about The Arab's confident claims about villagers' mores. Only a few days later a Kachin guerrilla in another group I visited seemed to confirm them. "Kachin man," he said, "Kachin woman. Shan man, Shan woman. White man, white woman." There were obviously cultural differences between Westerners and Asian villagers, but when headmen offered young girls to the leaders of heavily armed bands in their villages, it probably had as much to do with the politics of might as with sexual mores.

★ ★
IV Corps and Operation Magic

Back at XXXIII Corps headquarters, I found a message from the commander of IV Corps waiting for me. His corps had been named to launch the offensive across the Chindwin and link up with the Thirty-sixth Division coming down the rail corridor. He wanted Ziino and me assigned to IV Corps for the next few weeks, so we packed up and moved. Corps headquarters was set up in the midst of an impressive teak forest, which made things a little difficult to locate. A young Canadian was detailed to show me around the first couple of days. What I remember most clearly about him was his sincere, fervent comment after the first five minutes: "My God, you have no idea how good it is to hear a decent accent again!"

After the war I learned that our short stay at IV Corps almost got me into deep trouble. The United States had broken the main Japanese codes in an operation called Magic. Magic was so precious to the war that security concerning it was extremely tight. Being cleared for Magic required more than a "need to know." No one who ran any risk of being captured was permitted to know of its existence. Any intelligence derived from it could not be used until it had been obtained by other means as well. For example, the Japanese military attaché to Berlin was told of German plans to send a convoy to reinforce Rommel in the North African campaign, and he sent the information to Tokyo via the most secure Japanese code. Magic broke the message, but the Allies couldn't use the information unless they got it some other way. They sent a reconnaissance airplane on a patrol to "accidentally" sight the convoy. The airplane saw the convoy, the convoy saw the airplane, and the Allies were free to attack.

The British IV Corps commander had been told of Magic and of a message intercepted from Rangoon to Tokyo mentioning that the headquarters of a Japanese division on his front was near a certain village. Air reconnaissance showed nothing at the spot and the commander was skeptical. Hoping to confirm the information without revealing the secret of Magic, he told me that a message in simple code had been found on a dead Japanese, that the code had been broken, and that according to the text a Japanese division headquarters was located at that particular village. The corps commander asked me if our guerrillas could send agents to the area to find out if the message was correct.

141

I duly reported what he had told me and the request. Our agents tried to reach the spot, but were turned back by Japanese guards who had put an unusually tight security net around the area. This was enough for the corps commander. He used the information to good effect. After the war I saw a classmate, who was horrified to discover that I had gone from the liaison job to being a guerrilla commander behind enemy lines. His job had been to monitor possible security leaks of Magic, partly by screening message files. They had turned up the incident. I hadn't realized that my information was anything of significance, but had I fallen into Japanese hands, their intelligence people would have quickly figured out that I couldn't have known about the headquarters unless the United States was breaking their codes. "If you want to go on with a military career," he said, "don't ever let General Marshall find out that you left that liaison job to go behind the enemy lines!"

★
Fourteenth Army Headquarters

From IV Corps we moved to the forward headquarters of the Fourteenth Army itself, then at Kalewa. The work was the same, passing intelligence information back and forth and coordinating Detachment 101 guerrilla activities with the advance of the Fourteenth Army.

At Fourteenth Army headquarters we had some visitors. One was Morris Swadesh, a Ph.D. in linguistics. By this time, 101 had all the Kachin, Karen, and Shan agents they needed, but operations were moving south into areas where Burmese predominated, and OSS had few agents who spoke Burmese. Swadesh was to live with us for a while. Eventually he would spend his days going around to ethnic Burmese villages to recruit potential agents.

His skills were finely honed. He had spent the early years of the war on an army project writing language handbooks for GIs for every country the U.S. Army was likely to go to and was one of the authors of a simple system for acquiring the basics of a foreign language. The idea was to memorize a dozen key sentences and a few other rules, on which a larger vocabulary could quickly be built.

What impressed me most about Swadesh's talent was an incident back at the 101 base in Nazira. The standard training session at Nazira culminated in a three-day hike into the Naga hills, where the headman of one of the Naga villages took the 101ers on a jungle-lore tour and then gave them dinner and a party. This way they would get to know what at least one tribe of mountain people was like. Swadesh had never heard of the Naga language, but he fastened himself to one of the guides in the morning and stuck with him all day asking the names of this and that. At the after-dinner campfire, Swadesh stood up and made a ten-minute thank-you speech in Naga. For the trip to Kalewa he had spent a total of three weeks acquiring Burmese.

After the war, during Senator McCarthy's Communist witch hunts, Swadesh lost his job at the City University of New York for refusing to sign the anti-Communist pledge then required by state law. He spent years unemployed, finally ending up teaching somewhere in Mexico. All I knew of his politics came from long talks about the position of blacks in America. I learned a lot from him about their exploitation that was new and shocking. In any case, the loss was academia's. In the years when Swadesh could find no place in an American university, he developed a formula for estimating how long ago a particular people had separated from a parent group by the changes their language had undergone. Anthropologists have told me that it was an extraordinarily useful tool.

Another memorable visitor to Fourteenth Army headquarters was an Englishman named Grant-Taylor. He came to demonstrate how to fight with a pistol or a submachine gun, at which he was expert. Grant-Taylor's method was "instinctive firing." He scorned the idea of front and rear sights for guns such as pistols and submachine guns that were effective only at close range. "Do you use sights to put a pencil on the spot where you wish to write?" he would ask rhetorically.

Instinctive firing was the way the gunmen of the American West had shot, Grant-Taylor argued, and he was fond of telling stories about them to illustrate his methods. His two favorites involved Wild Bill Hickok, and both were probably true. Hickok

bullshit

once walked into a saloon where five gunmen were lying in wait for him, one at each end of the bar, and the other three in the balcony that ran around three sides of the room. They all started firing at once. Hickok shot the two at each end of the bar, and then, badly wounded himself, fell to the ground, spinning. He shot two of the men in the balcony before he hit the ground, then rolled over on his back and shot the third. All five were hit in either the forehead or the heart. "How in hell's name," Grant-Taylor would say, "could Hickok have had time to line up the front and rear sights of his pistols in that short space of time?"

Grant-Taylor's second Hickok story was about the speed of his reaction time. Hickok was eventually killed by a bartender, who shot him with a rifle in the back of the head while he was playing cards—the only time on record that Hickok had ever played cards with his back to the room rather than to the wall. He slumped forward onto the table. The cards—a pair of aces and a pair of eights, known ever since in the West as a dead man's hand—were in his left hand, and in his right was one of his pistols. Hickok had died instantly, but his reaction was so fast, Grant-Taylor insisted, that he had been able to draw in the fraction of a second between the bullet's hitting and his actual death.

All his life, Grant-Taylor had gravitated to where the fighting was. One of his last civilian jobs had been as the number-two man on the Shanghai police force, a period when criminal gangs were fighting each other at the same time Communist and Nationalist forces were. He had been with the Cairo police during one of their worst periods. He had also had some sort of assignment with the FBI at the height of the gangland troubles. In fact, he had been one of those who gunned down John Dillinger outside a movie house in Chicago in the 1930s. *truly furious*

more bullshit

But Grant-Taylor's most fabulous exploit was the one around which he built his training lectures. In the early part of the Battle of Britain, the German high command set up a school for pilots in a French town on the English Channel staffed by six of the best bomber pilots. The SOE decided it would be worth the effort to land a team by submarine and assassinate the six pilots. Agents reported that the men were spending every Thursday night drinking in a private room at one of the local hotels. The agents stole the building plans of the hotel from the town hall, and the British built a mock-up of it in a remote spot in Scotland. Six men were needed. Two would hide and guard their rubber boats. One would loiter at the front door of the hotel, one at the rear "to deal with emergencies." Two would go upstairs—one to guard the door of the private room and the other to go in and do the job. That man, the latter, was Grant-Taylor himself.

For weapons they chose pistols with silencers. Hand grenades or bombs, Grant-Taylor argued, were not reliable enough killers for such an important task. He pointed to the attempt on Rommel's life, when a grenade was thrown into his headquarters without effect. And Grant-Taylor's argument was later borne out by the failure of the 20 July plot on Hitler. The fact that the team would have to dress as French sailors to make their way unnoticed from the beach to the hotel ruled out submachine guns, which Grant-Taylor otherwise would have preferred.

They recruited several dozen likely prospects for the team, eliminating those who proved unsuitable during the training. One man had a tendency under stress to break into a run. The way such jobs must be done, Grant-Taylor argued, was at a fast walk. Another man tended to rock on his toes when firing, reducing accuracy. Others were eliminated as psychologically unsuited. To do this kind of job, Grant-Taylor said, "A man has to be without fear, without pity, and without remorse."

Finally, the team was trained and ready. The landing went off without a hitch, they reached the hotel without incident, and at last Grant-Taylor and his companion were at the door of the private room.

"As you open the door," Grant-Taylor would say at this point in his lecture, "keep your finger and thumb tightly grasped on the hem of the garment of Lady Luck—it might be guest night. And when you open the door, for God's sake don't stand there. Any fool can hit a door. Jump into the middle of the room." He did that, and found the six officers—along with two women, French prostitutes—seated at a table. One of the German flyers cursed, one slumped to the floor in a faint, and the others stared at him open-mouthed.

"Which one," Grant-Taylor would ask his audience, "do you shoot first?" Obviously the man who cursed should be high on the priority list, since he clearly had grasped what was hap-

145

pening. But the man who cursed should be second, not first. The officer who fainted might really have fainted. He also might have been quicker than the officer who cursed, not only grasping the situation but devising a counterplan. "You should shoot the one who fainted first," Grant-Taylor said, "the one who cursed second, and the others at your leisure."

Grant-Taylor never volunteered to say what he had done to the two prostitutes, but when asked he would admit that he shot them, too. The team needed time to get back to the beach, and they couldn't run the risk of anyone raising the alarm.

Grant-Taylor was in the room no more than two or three minutes, including the time it took him to take papers out of the officers' pockets. He and the man guarding the door picked up the other guards and were safely back at the beach before anyone at the hotel knew that anything had happened.

Almost as amazing as this story were the results Grant-Taylor got out of his training session. He took twelve of the least likely people in Fourteenth Army headquarters, people who were clerks and such because of one or the other physical disability, including poor eyesight. After two weeks, they could shoot the pips out of playing cards with either pistols or submachine guns, firing instinctively. Grant-Taylor rigged up a room of sandbags, put man-shaped targets in various places around the room, then had one of the trainees burst through the door and put two shots with a submachine gun in the heart of each target in less than twenty seconds.

★ ★

An Anglo-American Beer Party

Shortly after we arrived at Fourteenth Army headquarters, the monthly ration of twenty-four beers was issued. The custom at the front was to pick a quiet period, pull back half the troops from the line for twenty-four hours, and let them drink their case each. Then, two days later, after the first batch had recovered from their hangovers, the second half was pulled back from the line to drink. Our office/living tent was halfway between the area where noncommissioned officers slept and their mess, a convenient spot for Ziino's British friends to pause on the way home from this drinking spree. The trouble was they arrived about two or three in the morning and stayed until dawn.

Inevitably they ended up singing. Some of the songs were funny. One was about the ghost of Anne Boleyn walking the battlements of the Tower of London with " 'er 'ead tucked underneath 'er arm," how she caught cold in the damp and foggy night, and how awkward it was when she had to "blow 'er nose." Others were dirty ballads.

★ ★
The Fighting at Mandalay and Maymyo

It was not long before British forces arrived at the outskirts of Mandalay and the coordinating part of my job began again. The British-Indian Nineteenth Division was planning to send a brigade on an end-run to put a blocking position in at Maymyo, twenty-five miles east of Mandalay on the section of the old Burma road from Mandalay to Bhamo. At Maymyo the brigade could screen the flank of forces attacking Mandalay from the sizeable Japanese forces that were thought to be to the east. An OSS guerrilla group headed by Lieutenant Billy Milton was in the area, and it was important to coordinate their activities with those of the British forces. Milton and his guerrillas would try to improvise a strip for a light plane. I would be flown by light plane first to Nineteenth Division headquarters to get their plans and instructions, then to Maymyo, if the British brigade had succeeded in taking it, and then to the guerrilla group.

In Mandalay the Japanese had turned the old palace of the Burmese kings into a fortress, and when I arrived the Nineteenth Division was just about to begin its assault. The palace consisted of several acres of classical Burmese teak structures surrounded by walls about twenty feet high and just as thick.[1]

---

[1] The fighting lasted for weeks and only the walls of the palace remain. However, one of the old palace buildings had been moved off the grounds before the war and turned into a Buddhist temple. It can still be seen today.

I watched the artillery barrage begin with the division's chief of staff, a man named John Masters. He was full of stories, and he told them with great skill. Masters was a regular officer in the Indian army with the Gurkhas; he was, in fact, the fourth generation of his family to serve in India. He had been with the Chindits, rising to command a brigade, in their great rampage on the Japanese supply lines during the Battle of Myitkyina. Stilwell had totally misunderstood the purpose of the Chindits and the differences between the capabilities of a lightly armed, long-range penetration unit and a unit equipped and trained to take and hold ground. He had ordered the Chindits to form a permanent roadblock on the Japanese supply line rather than to ambush and raid, just as he had ordered the Marauders to attack Japanese pillboxes at Myitkyina without proper equipment. Like the Marauders, the Chindits did what Stilwell ordered; inviting attack by the much more heavily armed Japanese. They suffered terrible casualties. And like the Marauders, they had little love for General Stilwell.

I was impressed with Masters, with his professionalism as a soldier and with his storytelling ability, his way with words. In later years I picked up an autobiographical book, *The Road Past Mandalay*, by the author of *Nightrunners of Bengal* and *Bhowani Junction*, and discovered that the John Masters of the Nineteenth Division and the John Masters of the novels were the same person. At the time we were together watching the beginning of the Battle of Mandalay-Meiktila, John Masters didn't know he was a novelist either.

★ ★
Maymyo

Next day the brigade on the end-run reached Maymyo, and minutes later I took off in a light plane to join them. Mandalay is on the Irrawaddy River at the foot of the mountains. Maymyo is only twenty-five miles away as the crow flies, but since it is at an altitude of four thousand feet the distance is probably a hundred fifty by road. The town was an old British hill station, and the Japanese had quite sensibly put their headquarters in what had been the governor general's mansion on the outskirts. Equally sensible, the British decided that the mansion was where they would put brigade headquarters, as soon as the Japanese could be rooted out of it. My plane landed on what had been the old British race course, and I arrived at the mansion as the last of the Japanese defenders withdrew to the jungle.

At that moment I was overtaken by diarrhea. Behind the mansion was a fish pool and behind that was the privy the Japanese had used. It was in the Asian style—rather than seats, there were square holes in the floor. I proceeded to use it. To make it easier to draw my .45 I had cut the top off my holster, and as I straightened up my pistol dropped into the privy. This was the same pistol the sergeant had tried to take from me on the stretcher at Myitkyina, the guy I threatened to kill. Looking down, I could see it slowly settling in the thick accumulation of Japanese excreta. For a brief second I thought again about how precious a pistol was and how difficult it would be to get another. Down into the privy I went.

Once I emerged, I threw the .45 into the fish pond, stripped off my clothes, threw them in, and then jumped in myself. British soldiers setting up the headquarters paused in their hysterics long enough to give me some soap. I washed everything three times, taking the pistol apart down to the last screw.

When I was clean again I went down to the field where my plane had landed and where C-47s were now dropping supplies. I found a khaki-colored nylon personnel parachute that an airborne unit had used in the initial attack that morning and cut off a piece of one of the shroud lines. I tied one end to the eyelet on the butt of the pistol and a loop on the other end to go around my neck. And I wore the pistol that way for the rest of the war.

★ ★

Billy Milton's Group

The next morning I took a light plane to find Billy Milton and his group, who were about fifty miles due east of Maymyo.

Milton had parachuted into the area with thirty well-trained Kachins to conduct ambushes on a road network the Japanese might use to flank the British forces attacking Mandalay. The strip they had cleared was on the top of a hill about a thousand yards from the little village where they were dug in. We buzzed the village and got Milton's recognition signals, and the pilot made a pass over the field to inspect it. It was dirt rather than grass, but it seemed fine, so we came around and started the landing approach.

It was a tricky landing. To make it difficult for Zeros to strafe, Milton had left two tall trees on the approach to the runway. The pilot had to dip one wing to miss the first tree, then quickly dip the other to miss the second. We got past this obstacle and were settling in about ten feet above the runway when Billy came running over the crest and into the middle of the strip, waving to us not to land. The pilot gunned the motor and just barely got us airborne. Then we watched from the cockpit, open-mouthed, while Milton and his group disarmed a series of booby traps and dragged off the field some logs that had been concealed in the dirt.

Once more we dipped, first one wing, then the other. When the wheels touched the plane came to such a rapid stop it almost tipped up on its nose. Cutting the motor, the pilot turned around and said, "I hope we like it here, 'cause we're going to be here for a long time. This goddamned field has been plowed, and we'll never get up enough airspeed to make it out." We found out later that Milton had built the strip so a light plane could take out a Japanese prisoner for interrogation. He had then had it plowed to foil any Japanese search.

We did stay longer than we had intended, but it wasn't more than a few hours. Milton's entire group and the people from two nearby villages spent the next few hours systematically tramping up and down the strip until it was as firm as baked clay.

We went over the maps, noting all the intelligence that Billy and his group had gathered about the locations and strengths of Japanese forces and making plans for the group to gather more intelligence. That done, Milton's guerrillas gave us a meal of wild boar, venison, jungle fowl (the ancestor of the domesticated chicken), and wild peacock.

Billy's group had passed through the area of the Mogok mines, and every man had a little collection of gems he had traded for tobacco and parachute cloth to the villagers there. The pilot and I had brought a case of beer as a gift to Milton and his radio operator. They gave us some of their rubies and zircons.

At the time we thought this would make us wealthy, but in fact none of the stones was of any value. Almost all the 101ers carried Mogok gems around with them, usually in a old first-aid box about the size of a package of cigarettes. There was only one OSS man who came back with any gems that were valuable. He was on a PT boat that had dropped some agents in one of the bayou-like inlets on the coast, and on their way back the boat hit a mine and sank. This fellow got separated from the others but succeeded in making his way back, along the beaches, holing up and sleeping in the daytime and traveling at night. One night he stumbled and his hand broke into some sort of hollow at the bottom of which lay a pile of pebbles. He grabbed three of them and put them in his mouth to suck, an old infantryman's trick to alleviate thirst. When daytime came and he spit out the pebbles, he discovered that they were rubies, very fine rubies. The minute the war ended, he got thirty days' leave and spent it searching the beach he had passed over that night, to no avail.

★ ★

A Personal Decision

When I got back to Fourteenth Army headquarters, I decided that I had to make a decision about myself. Visiting guerrilla groups made me think that, dangerous though it was to be in a situation with no friendly troops nearby, at least a guerrilla leader could use his brains. At Myitkyna the Marauders had to attack on a hundred-yard front straight into machine-gun fire and hope that one or two men would still be on their feet to throw grenades. It wasn't brains that mattered—only luck.

151

A guerrilla leader, on the other hand, could keep constantly on the move. He could engage in deception. Since joining Detachment 101 I had thought a lot about how a guerrilla group should fight, the tactics it might use, and ways it could operate effectively with as little risk as possible to the lives of its men. As a liaison officer I had heard bullets again, and it made me realize that though they frightened me as much as before, I could manage combat because there was a chance that I would be able to affect the outcome. I radioed Ray Peers requesting that I be given command of a guerrilla group.

Peers radioed back that I could assume command immediately of a battalion being formed from two smaller groups then converging on a point in the mountains south of Maymyo. I felt much, much better about myself.

9

★ ★

Behind Enemy Lines

The guerrilla battalion I was to command was south of Maymyo. It was not so much behind Japanese lines as in a mountainous no man's land facing the right flank of the Japanese opposing the British and Indian troops at Mandalay. The British army was readying itself for what turned out to be the long and decisive battle of the Burma campaign. The battle area began along the Irrawaddy River at Mandalay and then, later, moved south to Meiktila. The Japanese main line of supply went south through Rangoon and points further before heading east to Bangkok over the route made famous by the *The Bridge over the River Kwai*. A secondary route ran from Meiktila to Heho and Taunggyi, thence over the Salween River and down to Bangkok. It was the territory around this secondary route that became my battalion's area of operations.

Several Detachment 101 groups had converged around a dirt airstrip carved out of an old rice paddy at the head of sharp-walled, narrow valley. The strip was about fifty miles south of Maymyo and seventy-five miles southeast of Mandalay. From Maymyo the road, which was nothing more than a rutted track wide enough for a bullock cart, ran south from Maymyo to the Namtu River. The OSS guerrillas had forded the river on bamboo rafts and elephants, which they had hired from a local entrepreneur and his mahouts. From the river crossing south, for twenty miles or so, the road was nothing more than a trail, barely wide enough for the men to go single file. Then it became a cart track again, running parallel to a north-south stream that swelled into a river about ten miles north of Lawksawk.

About twenty-five miles north of Lawksawk, the cart track

153

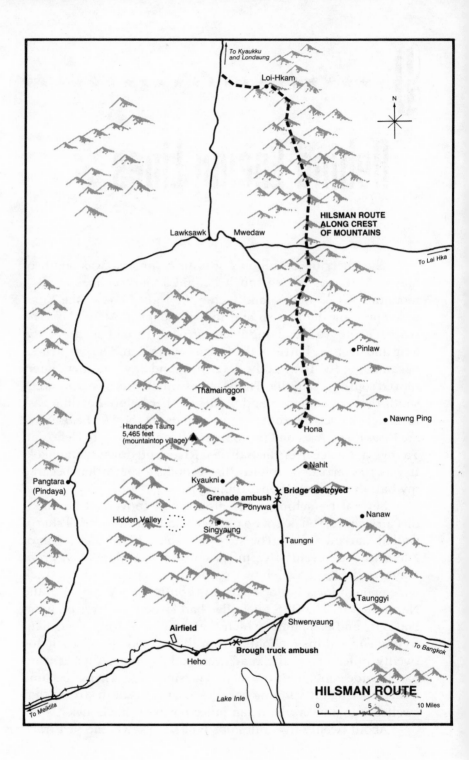

To Kyaukku
and Londaung

Loi-Hkam

N

**HILSMAN ROUTE
ALONG CREST
OF MOUNTAINS**

Lawksawk   Mwedaw

To Lai Hka

Pinlaw

Thamainggon

Nawng Ping

Htandape Taung
5,465 feet
(mountaintop village)

Hona

Nahit

Pangtara
(Pindaya)

Kyaukni   Bridge destroyed

Grenade ambush
Ponywa

Hidden Valley

Nanaw

Singyaung

Taungni

Nanaw

Taunggyi

Airfield

Shwenyaung

To Bangkok

Brough truck ambush

Heho

HILSMAN ROUTE

To Meiktila

Lake Inle

0   5   10 Miles

turned into a metaled road wide enough for a truck. Metaled roads were usable in the rainy season, when dirt roads turned into high, impassable rivers of mud. A Japanese force of regimental size, totaling something like three thousand men, was based at Lawksawk. It constantly patrolled the road to the north with company-size units. At that point, twenty-five miles north of Lawksawk, the Japanese had stationed an outpost in the minuscule village of Londaung. This was part of a Japanese battalion stationed about halfway between Londaung and Lawksawk.

Londaung sat off the north-south metaled road at the mouth of the narrow valley where the OSS groups were gathered. When guerrillas coming down the main road ran into Japanese at Londaung, they had pulled back, following sound practice, and found a trail over the ridge running parallel to the road. This they used to get to the next valley, hoping to sneak through the mountains and thereby move behind the enemy outpost. There they had found an abandoned rice paddy that was suitable as a drop zone for supplies and an airstrip for light planes.

Since the valley was so steep and narrow, they felt they could hold against any Japanese force at least until dark, when they would be able to escape. With the groups low on supplies and fatigued, the American commanders decided to stay a few days, getting supplies replenished by airdrops and evacuating the sick and wounded. The guerrillas were put to work building an airstrip out of the abandoned paddy field with their entrenching tools. The result made a good drop zone for C-47s, but it was not long enough for any planes except L-2s or L-5s—the military equivalent of a piper cub, able to carry one passenger in an open cockpit behind the pilot.

A day after the airstrip was made ready, I was flown in by light plane and introduced to my battalion. It was made up of one Chinese company, one company of Karens, and a scout platoon of Shans—a total of about three hundred men. The Chinese company consisted mainly of soldiers from the Chinese Fifth Army who had been wounded or left behind in the march out of Burma in 1942, and who had hidden among the villagers. There were also a few Chinese who had been born and raised in Burma.

The Karen company had been recruited from a settlement

around Maymyo. They were Christians, and it was the only guerrilla group I ever heard of that had its own chaplain. Before setting out on a patrol or an ambush the chaplain would gather the men in a circle for prayer. Lingering in my mind is that incongruous image of a ring of bareheaded men burdened with submachine guns, ammunition, and hand grenades kneeling in prayer against the serene backdrop of magnificent mountains and a clear blue sky.

The battalion included only three other Westerners—Sergeant William Brough, who commanded the Chinese company; Sergeant Albert Van Arsdale, his second-in-command; and Sergeant Edward Arida, the radio operator.

Bill Brough was an Englishman from Newcastle-on-Tyne. He had started the war as a conscientious objector, and although not a Quaker himself, volunteered to do alternative service with a Friends medical unit in China. The Quakers trained him in anesthesia and midwifery and taught him Chinese. When the war came to Burma, his job was driving supply trucks over the Burma road from Rangoon to the Quaker unit in Kunming, China. After Japanese Zeros shot two trucks out from under him, he started working with the American medical missionary Dr. Gordon Seagrave and his hospital group. Brough fell sick with cerebral malaria and was put on the last plane out of Myitkyina. When he recovered, Brough went back to the Quaker unit in China. But then Brough heard that Seagrave's hospital had been inducted into the American army, and he enlisted as a medical corpsman. Seagrave put Brough to work as an anesthetist, which was considerably more interesting than driving a truck. He stayed with Seagrave until the end of the Battle of Myitkyina, rising to be the unit's first sergeant. But, as Seagrave later wrote, "Bill still had a deep unrest in his soul." What Japan did to Burma and China, according to Seagrave, was beginning to tax the endurance of even the most sincere pacifist. So Brough requested transfer to a fighting unit, OSS Detachment 101, "since," he told Seagrave, "I'm not doing my share here."

As the horrors of war continued to weigh on Brough's mind, he wondered whether he had been right to be a conscientious objector. According to the story I was told, at about the time he was most troubled, his group tangled with the Japanese in the middle of a village. One of the guerrillas fell wounded in the village square. The Japanese left him there moaning as bait. After two attempts to pull the wounded man out failed, Brough's outrage overcame him and he made his own, single-handed attempt. He got the man out, and in the process killed one of the Japanese.

Forty-two years later, I sent the manuscript of this book to Brough, by then retired from a career as a physician and psychiatrist in Great Britain. His version of the story was a little different from the one I had heard. A few days before I joined them, he was with a platoon of Chinese OSS guerrillas about five miles south of the dirt airstrip. They ambushed a group of Japanese soldiers coming south down the trail, then made their way back to the airstrip. In the meantime, the Karen group ambushed some Japanese near or at Londaung.

On their way back, Brough's group saw C-47s circling over the airstrip and parachutes coming down. When they arrived at the strip they found that among the parachutists was a news correspondent, a man named Nathan Latham, from one of the two newspapers the army sponsored in the China-Burma-India theater, *The Stars and Stripes* or *The CBI Roundup*. Latham was determined to interview the inhabitants of Londaung about what life was like under Japanese occupation. Against Brough's express orders, he persuaded a local tribesman to act as guide and an Anglo-Burman guerrilla as interpretor. The ambushes, of course, had prompted the Japanese battalion further south to send out patrols. Latham was promptly captured.[1]

What happened, to use Brough's British understatement, was that "the Karen platoon had one man killed and another wounded through the thigh, whom I pulled out of the ambush."

In any case, at some stage Brough went through a difficult time, whether after he killed the Japanese soldier, as I had heard it, or before, as he remembers. Either way, he wrestled with his conscience for some time, and when he had worked it out he applied for transfer to regular combat status. He distinguished

---

[1]The only thing we were able to find out about Latham's fate came from village gossip, which was that the Japanese had carted him around tied up for a week or two to extract any intelligence he might have had and then executed him.

himself in combat, and 101 headquarters put him in for a battle-field commission as a second lieutenant in the U.S. Army. It was after our particular group had been behind enemy lines for several weeks that the approval finally came through.

Brough was as brave a man in combat as I have ever known, yet he never lost the concerns that had made him a conscientious objector. One incident, which occurred much later, will illustrate. A Japanese foraging patrol visited a village called Hona, where our battalion had stayed one night and whose people we knew. The Japanese, unaware of our connection with the village, and without any cause that we could discover, had butchered a priest and three other villagers, including a woman. Some weeks later, our group arrived in another village far from there and surprised an AWOL Japanese soldier in bed with his girlfriend. Our guerrillas took him prisoner and brought him to me with his arms tied behind his back. They pushed him into a kneeling position for questioning. I was sitting on a raised platform in the *pongyi kyaung*, the priest's house, in front of a huge statue of Buddha, cleaning my boots with a dagger.

The Japanese rarely surrendered. Those the Allied troops captured were usually wounded and unconscious. When they did surrender, they seemed to feel that doing so irrevocably severed them from their people, and that they were under no restraints except to obey their new masters. Perhaps more importantly, the official attitude of the Japanese military was that since soldiers must never surrender or be captured, there was no need to train them for such a contingency. Allied soldiers were taught to give their name, rank, and serial number, nothing else. As a result, Japanese prisoners almost always talked without hesitation—it might be better said that they talked with abandon.

I asked the man the name of his unit, and when he told us I recognized it as the one from which the Hona patrol had come. I asked him if he had been on that patrol. With what seemed to me unmitigated arrogance, he said that he had indeed been on that patrol. My temper snapped. I think I would have struck him with my dagger if Bill hadn't put his hand on my arm and brought me to my senses.

Although I didn't realize it at the time, it turns out that

Brough and I had met prior to our guerrilla assignments. When I was wounded at Myitkyina, Brough was the first sergeant of Gordon Seagrave's MASH unit. He had been in charge of the litter detail and escort platoon that had taken me and the other wounded from the perimeter at the Y back to the airstrip.

Van Arsdale, Brough's second-in-command, was an American. Where Brough had deep philosophical concerns about war and about life, Van was oblivious to anything beyond the immediate. Where Brough was brave because he had overcome fear, Van was brave because he didn't experience any fear beyond immediate danger. I had known men like him among regular-army enlisted men between the wars, the kind James Jones wrote about in *From Here to Eternity*.

Van had been a merchant seaman, and the year 1942 found him in Singapore engaged in some questionable adventure ashore. When the Japanese arrived, unexpectedly coming down through the jungle of Malaya rather than attacking by sea, as the British had expected, Van served in the hastily organized militia. When the defense collapsed, he stole a Malayan outrigger canoe and made his way across the straits to Sumatra, in the Dutch East Indies. He departed just ahead of the Japanese, on a ship to Rangoon. He was still in Rangoon when the Japanese hit Burma. Bowing to the inevitable, he enlisted in the British army. When the Americans arrived in the China-Burma-India theater, he transferred to Detachment 101 as a sergeant. After the war I saw Van periodically. He told me that he had stayed in Southeast Asia when the war ended, acquired a surplus PT boat, and smuggled arms to various independence movements before the colonial authorities threw him in jail. Then he spent time flying illegal immigrants into the United States from Mexico in a light plane. Next he acquired a well-digging rig and drilled water wells for suburbanites in the northwest. Then he drifted back to the merchant marine. He finally retired on his pension, bought himself another surplus PT boat, and the last I heard was catering to scuba-diving parties in the Caribbean.

Van was a great favorite with the Chinese guerrillas. He wore a pair of camouflage pants with suspenders and no shirt, only a khaki towel around his neck to wipe away the sweat. He carried one of the fancy 9-millimeter submachine guns that the

OSS had obtained from the Dutch, and a Chinese orderly trailed behind him with a high-powered sniper's rifle that had telescopic sights. Van used both weapons with such enthusiasm that Brough and I had to keep special watch to see that he didn't start firing before the order was given.

The other officers of the Chinese company were a Chinese lieutenant, who spoke nothing but his native tongue, and a Chinese who spoke some English. Everyone called him Fenigwan, and I assumed that Fenigwan was his name. After the war I learned that it meant translator, and indeed we did use him in that role.

The officers of the Karen company were Captain Dennis Htun, a Karen who held a king's commission in the Burma Rifles, and a Burmese lieutenant, Arthur Toh, who was also from the Burma Rifles. Htun enjoyed authority more because he was something of a political figure than because of his military background and training; Toh was actually better trained. In any case, I put my own command post with the Karen company whenever it was involved in combat operations.

Eddie Arida was our radio operator and code clerk. Eddie was from Brooklyn, and he seemed to have few interests other than poker. In the evenings Brough and I would be poring over maps, plotting our next moves; Arida and Van played poker. The battalion had been issued a bag of silver rupees to pay the villagers for labor and supplies we had to buy from them. When we first started out, before we had bought anything, the bag was so big two men had to carry it suspended between them on a bamboo pole. Van and Arida used the rupees for chips. One of them would win for a while, piling up huge paper winnings. Then the other would. In the end I think they simply agreed to forget the whole thing.

Eddie's equipment was a radio specially built by 101, a telegraph key, and a hand-operated generator. One of the Karens carried the generator and pumped it when Eddie was sending and receiving. Our code was what was called a one-time pad. Somewhere in Washington a machine ground out random five-letter groups in duplicate. Pages of these were glued together to make two identical pads. One pad was kept at headquarters, and one was with us. Each letter of one of our outgoing messages would be written on top of a letter on the one-time pad. Suppose the letter of the outgoing message was *F* and the letter in the one-time pad was *D*. A chart on the first page of the one-time pad gave a list of all possible three-letter combinations. You would look up *FD* in the chart and send over the air whatever the third letter was. I remember that the third letter in the *FD* combination was *R*—because *FDR* were President Roosevelt's initials. At headquarters, they would receive *R*, write it on the proper place on their copy of the one-time pad, which would be over the same *D*. Looking at the same table under *DR*, they would get *F*—the letter of the the message. It was called a one-time pad because once a page of five-letter random groups was used, it would be destroyed.

★ ★
Arms and Equipment

The rules of war specify that guerrillas who wear a standard uniform must be treated the same as regular troops, while those in civilian clothes may be treated as spies. None of us believed that a uniform would make any difference. We expected that anyone who fell into Japanese hands would be summarily shot. As I mentioned, the only one who did fall into enemy hands was Nathan Latham. As far as we knew, he was executed in a matter of days. But there were better reasons for wearing a uniform. First, it was a lot easier logistically to furnish uniforms. Second, our guerrillas had had very little training, and like all untrained troops they were trigger-happy. Wearing a uniform lessened the chances that we would be shot by one of our own people. So we all wore jungle green or camouflage nylon trousers and shirts.

The standard footwear was jungle boots. As footwear for the rough terrain we were moving through, they were an abomination. They had no arch or ankle support, and a long march always resulted in foot problems. What was worse, the damn things wore out in two or three weeks of heavy marching—and heavy marching over difficult terrain was what kept a guerrilla group alive. Whenever we could scrounge them, we got paratrooper boots for ourselves and our troops. These were regular-army marching shoes with the Munsen last that went back to the nineteenth century and with heavy leather tops that, like the jungle boots, came to just below the calf.

Detachment 101 had abandoned steel helmets early on. A helmet made it difficult to hear the noises of the jungle, and being able to hear those noises was the difference between life and death. Also, when a helmet brushed against a twig it made a terrible clang that no enemy could fail to hear. In need of protection against sun and rain, we adopted the Australian or Gurkha hat. It was a wide-brimmed hat similar to an American cowboy's with one side pinned up to the crown. The Burmese jungle was full of wild peacocks—the peacock is almost a symbol of Burma—and a peacock feather stuck on the upturned side of this hat became the 101 badge.

The only training we had time to give our guerrillas was how to use their weapons. It would have been the height of foolishness to use our people to take or hold ground. They were best used for gathering intelligence, ambushing, and blowing up bridges and other installations on the enemy's supply line. Brough and I decided that their weapons and equipment should be appropriate for these missions and nothing else.

The weapons, in other words, had to be simple and easy to use. Since safety for a guerrilla lies in keeping on the move, they also had to be light. Our solution was to organize each of the companies into four platoons. Each platoon in turn was made up of three light-machine-gun squads and one 60-millimeter mortar squad. One of the eight to ten men in a machine-gun squad carried a Bren gun, a British light machine gun; one carried a sniper's rifle with a silencer on it; and the others carried the British Sten gun, a submachine gun that was very light. They all carried ammunition for the Bren.

In the mortar squad, the chief mortarman carried the mortar tube and the number-two man carried the base. For personal protection both of these men carried .45 pistols. The rest of the squad carried Sten submachine guns and ammunition for the mortars.

Most of the men also carried a *kukri*, the curved Gurkha knife about the size of a machete. Originally it was a fighting weapon, and the Gurkhas were said never to draw it without taking some blood—which meant they had to prick their finger every time they wanted to cut some bamboo or sharpen the *kukri* itself. We used *kukri*s to cut paths through the jungle, to chop bamboo, to build huts against the rain, to split coconuts, or any one of a thousand other housekeeping tasks.

In an ambush, we would use Bren guns as the principal weapon, for they could engage the enemy with accurate and rapid fire at a distance of fifty to a hundred yards. The submachine-guns would be used to protect the Bren gunners from a flanking attack or in case of surprise. After the latter had fired their magazines of thirty rounds, the submachine-gunners would lay down fire to protect them while they pulled back. They in turn covered the withdrawal of the submachine-gunners. This sort of rearward leapfrogging would continue until the guerrillas were out of sight and could fade into the jungle.

Mortars would be stationed behind the first rise, and they would begin firing to provide cover the minute the ambushing party began to pull back. The rule was that no engagement would be allowed to last any longer than it took the Bren gun to fire a thirty-round magazine and start to pull out—thirty or forty seconds.

When the mission was to blow a bridge or some other installation, the Bren guns would be stationed to protect the demolition party, which was usually Brough, Van Arsdale, and myself. The submachine-gunners' role would be to protect the Bren guns. The mortars protected the withdrawal if it had to be made under fire.

In raids, our idea was to sneak a Bren gun within range of an enemy camp, shoot it up, and run, again using submachine guns and mortars to cover our withdrawal.

The men armed with a sniper's rifle, a telescopic sight, and a silencer were to be used in a variety of special circumstances—to harass an enemy installation from a distance, for example, or to pick off an enemy machine-gunner in covering a withdrawal.

The general rule for 101 guerrilla groups was that they should keep moving, never spending two nights in the same place. But if, in spite of every precaution, a group was surrounded, it would need much heavier equipment to defend itself than it could carry. Accordingly, each group made a list in advance of what it would like to have in such an emergency. The equipment was packaged with parachutes for an airdrop and placed in a special warehouse at the C-47 airfield. If a group got into trouble, the heavy equipment could usually be dropped within a matter of hours. The list for our battalion included half a dozen heavy machine guns, four of the large, 81-millimeter mortars, and two recoilless rifles, all with ample ammunition.

★ ★
Airdrops

Food was also a problem. We all carried enough K-rations for two days. These consisted of concentrated tea, coffee, milk, a can of Spam or something that was supposed to be a ham omelet, some bad-tasting crackers made of wheat concentrates, and the like. Our main food was rice, soy sausages, and canned tomatoes. We were supplied by airdrop; C-47s would freedrop the rice, fifty pounds in a hundred-pound sack, as they had at Myitkyina, and parachute cases of number-ten cans of soy sausage and tomatoes. After a drop each squad would be issued its share and would divide the load equally between men. For the first few days after a drop we would also try to hire coolies from one of the local villages. Otherwise each man would be carrying, with ammunition, close to ninety pounds, and most of our men didn't weigh over one hundred thirty pounds themselves.

Rice was the native staple, and the soy sausage was as good or better than what little meat the guerrillas might get at home. The airdrop would include big chunks of rock salt and bags of curry powder, and with these and a few other spices that could be traded with the villagers in exchange for parachute cloth, the men were reasonably happy.

The big problem was the tomatoes, which they found strange and unappetizing. But tomatoes were the only source in our diet of vitamin A. It was essential to eat tomatoes, but most of the troops found ways to avoid them. After a few weeks,

Brough and I realized that he, Van Arsdale, Eddie Arida, and I were the only ones in the whole damned outfit that were not afflicted with night blindness—the worst possible affliction for guerrillas. The doctors at the base arranged for our next airdrop to include powdered fruit juice. Our guerrillas found this just as strange and almost as repugnant as tomatoes, but once a week thereafter we lined the whole outfit up and made each and every one drink the juice while we watched.

Airdrops included tobacco, which was rationed out to everyone, whether or not they smoked. Those who didn't smoke could trade the tobacco for other things.

A pound or two of crude opium also arrived in the airdrops. Sometimes we purchased it in the villages as well. The Chinese company included four addicts, and part of their "contract" was that they be supplied with a rupee's weight of opium every week. The opium came in a ball that looked like a dirty-white piece of crude rubber. I carried it in my own pack, and once a week I would dole it out to the four addicts in a little ceremony. We would cut a stick about two feet long, fix a rupee to one end with a piece of adhesive tape, and tie a string in the middle, moving the string until the rupee and the weight of the long side of the stick balanced. I would then take the rupee off and cut slices of opium off the ball and mold them onto the end of the stick until it balanced again. The addicts smoked their opium at the end of the day in traditional Chinese opium pipes. A few puffs made up a day's ration.

Most of our opium went to our four addicts, but sometimes we had to use it for two other purposes as well. Because of their experience with worthless Japanese paper money, the villagers we occasionally hired to carry ammunition and other supplies at first refused to accept anything but rupees, which were heavy for us to carry. After a while, however, we discovered that they much preferred parachute cloth. White cotton parachutes were used to drop food. The more valued red, blue, and orange rayon parachutes were used for weapons and ammunition. The villagers, who hadn't seen manufactured cloth since the beginning of the war, were delighted with the parachutes. But when the job was to carry heavy loads over mountains, they demanded that their pay also include a ration of opium. Tragically, the only

165

way even the unaddicted among these poor, malnourished, usually diseased people could do heavy work was with the aid of opium.

The second purpose that opium served was as a medicine. Once we had to give it to the entire battalion. The Japanese had sent a large force to chase us down, and they kept after us so steadily that it was too dangerous to pause even for an airdrop. About that time almost the entire outfit came down with bacillary dysentery, not uncommon in those parts. We ran out of sulfa and radioed the doctors at the base for advice. They prescribed a thumb-sized chunk of raw opium for each man in the outfit, which temporarily wiped out our supply. I didn't get a high from eating the opium, but it stopped the diarrhea.

★ ★

The Language Problem

Language was not as great a problem as one might have expected in such a polyglot force. Complicated general orders, of course, were issued in English and translated into Chinese, Karen, Shan, Kachin, and Burmese. Brough had more practical Chinese than he claimed, Van Arsdale had a bit, and then we had the Fenigwan, the Chinese translator. Dennis Htun and Arthur Toh spoke English perfectly and translated into both Karen and Burmese. In fact, at least one man in each squad in the Karen company spoke passable English. And a couple of both the Shans and Kachins spoke some English.

But most of what we had to communicate to each other was not all that complicated. Mainly what we had to talk about concerned food, ammunition, and other supplies. We also had to give instructions about the line of march for the day, which mainly involved showing the company and platoon leaders the trails on a map. And we used a map to designate places where we would try to regroup if the Japanese surprised us.

We quickly developed our own patois, based on pidgin English. "This fella, he bad hat," for example, meant that the man being discussed was either a criminal or, more likely in the war,

166

that he was in the pay of the Japanese. Around the pidgin we developed our own specialized vocabulary that included some Chinese, some Karen, some Burmese, some Kachin, and some Shan. Because of the British military's influence in Burma, our patois also included some Urdu. Thus most of the men understood that *saf karow* meant "wash" and *tanda pani* meant "drinking water," or water that had been boiled if it came from a village well. Orders for simple tactical manauvers, such as "Take your squad around to the right and protect our flank" were delivered with a lot of hand motions and a few simple words in this patois.

We also became rather accomplished pantomimists, acting out what we wanted to say. However, like the game of charades and the sign language of the deaf, some hand and body motions became standardized. Some came from American military hand signals. A clenched fist raised in the air and pumped up and down rapidly meant "on the double!" Others were just natural. If the lead scout on the trail dropped to the ground, and then held his arm out palm down and pushed toward the ground, no one needed to be taught that he meant "down!"

Bill Brough recalls that his Chinese soldiers were pleased to help him add to his vocabulary at every opportunity. But after one engagement he overheard one of his Chinese soldiers saying to the others: "There we were being fired at and Brough told me that under fire I should use words he already knew and not try to teach him new words." Brough says that the other men thought it terribly funny. The truth, however, probably was that the soldier had been just as scared as Brough during the fight and was not really trying to conduct a Chinese lesson but was using ordinary words without thinking about Brough's limited vocabulary.

Brough also recalls that one of the big differences between us and the Japanese was that when we were in a fire fight we were as quiet as we could be. But if a Japanese unit was ambushed, the senior officer would start bellowing orders at the top of his lungs, usually to spread out and take up a formation from which they could attack. We avoided doing this on the assumption that yelling would draw fire to the person shouting the orders. Also, we didn't need to do much yelling, because we had a very simple standard operating procedure in such circumstances. Each man fired all the rounds in his Bren gun or sub-machine-gun clips and then retreated as fast as possible under the cover of our back-up 60-mm mortars and Bren guns, which commenced firing as soon as the operators no longer heard our weapons. Brough says that he reckons he was the most soft-spoken company commander in the U.S. Army, but the rest of us would not concede the title readily.

The biggest problem was dealing with the villagers. Buying food or hiring coolies to carry ammunition and supplies was not too difficult. But communication became more complicated when the subject was intelligence information on the Japanese and information about local trails. We quickly learned that in the hinterlands of Southeast Asia, you never ask a question that can be answered by either yes or no. Asian politeness requires that you be given the answer you want to hear. So if you ask, "Does this trail lead to Hona?" the answer is always "Yes." The way to ask the question is, "Where does this trail lead?"

When we went into a village, our first question was always, *Japani shee dith la?* or "Are there any Japanese?" *Muh shee bu* meant that there were no Japanese about. If the answer was a vigorous nodding of the head, we didn't really need to understand the words "Japani shee der." Although I have forgotten the Burmese and Shan words, we would than ask, "How many?" When we didn't understand the words for the numbers they gave, both the villagers and we would resort to using our fingers.

Burmese is a tonal language, and this can lead not only to enormous misunderstandings but sometimes to situations that become ridiculously funny. I remember standing with a village headman on a mountain looking over a valley. Map in hand, I asked him where various villages were, starting with the one the map showed was the nearest. "Ho naw," he said, pointing, with the "Ho" at a slightly higher pitch than the "naw." "Over there," is what he was saying, with the slightly higher pitch indicating it was a little ways. As I named each town further away, the pitch on the "ho" had to rise to indicate that it was a little farther than the previous village. By the time we got to the fifth or sixth, his voice was cracking as he stretched for what was beginning to come close to high C.

★ ★

The Theory of Guerrilla Warfare

None of us, not even we Westerners, knew much about the theory of guerrilla operations. Arida could fire his submachine gun; beyond that his skills were those of a radio operator. What training Brough, Van Arsdale, and I had had was in the handling of weapons, simple infantry tactics, laying booby traps and demolitions, and jungle lore. The Americans shared school-boy stories of how British troops in the French and Indian War had fired volleys from close-order drill formation while the Indians skulked behind trees, and Indian tactics seemed appropriate for guerrillas. But beyond the need to skulk behind trees we didn't know much.

During my months as liaison officer to the Fourteenth Army I had thought about guerrillas tactics and developed a few ideas. My first idea was obvious—guerrillas should never try to take or hold ground. Untrained as they were, they couldn't stand up for two minutes to Japanese veterans. Moreover, these mountain villagers were used to raids, fighting and running. Our rule, already mentioned, that no engagement should last more than the time it takes to fire one thirty-round magazine from a Bren gun, suited their tradition. Our motto was fire and run.

My second idea was equally obvious—guerrillas should never spend two nights in the same place. The Japanese had trucks and, we suspected, at least one unit equipped with horses. If we stayed too long in a place and they spotted us, they could quickly dispatch enough regular soldiers to annihilate us.

Westerners think of Asia as densely populated, and parts of both China and India are. But Southeast Asia—Burma, Thailand, Malaysia, Indonesia, Laos, Cambodia, and Vietnam—are crowded only in the fertile lowlands. Often we would march for days over mountainous back trails—made not by man but by deer, tigers, and elephants—without seeing any signs of human habitation. Safety lay in movement.

My third idea seemed to me to be equally obvious, but as I had seen in The Arab's outfit, it wasn't followed by all the 101 guerrillas. The idea was to do everything we could to stay on the good side of the natives. The country around Myitkyina had been Kachin. The Kachins were friendly to the British and, thanks to the missionaries, equally friendly to Americans. They were anti-Burmese and, because of the way the Japanese had behaved when they first arrived, anti-Japanese. But we were now in Shan country, where it verged on Burmese and Karen land. At the beginning of the war, politically active Burmese were anti-British and pro-Japanese. By 1944 they were anti-Japanese, without really being pro-British. The Shans had also become disenchanted with the Japanese, but because of their historical fear of the Burmese they were not really anti-British. Their attitude was essentially neutral.

In the face of this complex network of attitudes, it seemed best to keep the civilian populations we encountered at least neutral, if not sympathetic. I made it an absolute rule that none of our men could have relations with any village female. Second, we would commandeer rice, tobacco, and labor from villagers only in case of dire need, and when we did we would pay for it handsomely. If we took rice and the villagers wanted rice in return, we would pay them back more than we had taken, twice as much if feasible. And when we paid back in kind, we added both money and cloth.

My final idea was not so obvious. If a group operating behind enemy lines got into trouble—if, for example, the enemy detached troops from the main line to chase a guerrilla band and the pursuit got close—the natural human instinct was to run. But heading for your own lines, I concluded, would be a dangerous mistake. The closer you got to your own lines, the denser the concentration of regular enemy troops. On the other hand, if you went deeper into enemy territory, you met fewer troops.

What you met deep in enemy territory were police. Unlike troops, they were trained to fight one on one, or at most in teams of no more than a dozen. A military force equipped with such specialized weapons as Bren guns, mortars, rifles, and submachine guns and only slightly trained to fight as a team could easily defeat several times as many individuals armed with nothing but individual weapons. Two platoons of Japanese regular soldiers could have defeated my whole battalion with no difficulty. But one of our platoons of forty men could have defeated a force of over one hundred policemen. And our battalion could have taken on a police force of close to a thousand for at least several hours. My conclusion was that if we got into trouble we would head south, keeping to lightly populated mountains and jungles but going deeper and deeper into enemy territory. As we got farther away from concentrations of enemy troops, we would be likely to meet only police.

★ ★

Taking Command

When I took command, the groups making up the battalion were camped on the ridge east of the airstrip near Londaung. The mountains in that part of Burma were steep. The trails, where they existed, ran either along the bottom of valleys, where the villages were, or along the crest of one of the razor-backed ridges. Standing on a ridge trail, you could look down on both sides.

What makes the memory of this particular ridge so vivid was that elephants were being used to bring supplies from the airstrip. Slowly, ponderously, swaying from side to side, one of these behemoths would come up the trail straight at you, staring with his beady eyes. That elephant wasn't going to stop. It was like facing a robot tank. With steep slopes on either side of you, getting out of the way was difficult—but there was no choice, even if you had to hang over the slope from a tree.

Sleeping on the ridge was also a problem. With no flat places to put a blanket down, you had to sleep in a reclining position with your feet downhill or sideways, braced against a tree.

The day after I took command I made a little speech, first to the Chinese troops and then to the Karen. I sketched the strategic situation and our general mission—to gather intelligence, harass the Japanese, ambush, and disrupt enemy supply lines however we could. I also threw in some standard American stuff about the officers' determination to be fair, the standards of conduct and responsibility the officers expected the men to meet, and what an honor it was to be fighting for human rights and liberty. Brough described the scene in a letter written over forty years later:

171

I have a hilarious memory . . . of you being overcome—good American that you are—with the need to say something inspiring to the Chinese and of using me to interpret. My Chinese was . . . at the best bread and butter stuff, and I had difficulty with words like "liberty" and "freedom," which I had never learned. So I told them you were using words I was not able to translate. It turned out to be a liberal translation governed by the extent of my Chinese vocabulary—which gave you a mistaken view of my linguistic abilities and entertained the men.

When I got to know the Chinese soldiers better, I realized that the notions I was expounding would have sounded completely outlandish to them, and I began to worry just how much of a fool I had made of myself. Brough assured me that he had exercised extraordinary license in his translation. This was one time I was grateful for his not following orders.

★ ★

The Strategic Situation

The battalion I commanded was one of four groups clustered in the hills around the airstrip under the general direction of Major Patrick "Red" Maddox, an Anglo-Burman officer who had been with 101 from the very beginning. The question was what these four groups should do next. The Battle of Mandalay-Meiktila was just beginning and would last several weeks. The Japanese supply line ran south to Rangoon, further south to Moulmein, then east over the bridge on the River Kwai to Bangkok. A secondary supply road climbed east from Meiktila up through the mountains to Heho, then through another range of mountains to the valley of Inle Lake. From there it snaked its way up the escarpment to Tuanggyi, which sat on the shoulder of a very large mountain. "Taung," in fact, means "mountain," and "gyi" means "big."

From Heho and the valley below Taunggyi, two roads ran north on each side of another mass of mountains, meeting at Lawksawk. Here about 3,000 Japanese were stationed, screening the Meiktila-Thailand road. About twenty-five miles up the road leading north from Lawksawk, a narrow valley branched off to the northwest. A trail only wide enough for men to go single file led up this valley through Londaung, then on up to our dirt airstrip.

The heavily populated, flat country from Mandalay to Rangoon offered no cover for guerrillas, but if one or two of our battalions could get into the mountains overlooking the Heho-Tuanggyi road, we could do the Japanese a lot of damage.

The decision was that two of the four groups would stay facing the Japanese based in Lawksawk and form an intelligence screen. The third was to get behind Lawksawk by going around it to the west, and our group was to go around it to the east. Once behind Lawksawk, we would be in a position to ambush, blow bridges, and harass the Japanese in any way we could.

Brough and I pored over the aerial photographs and large-scale maps, looking for a way around both the enemy roadblock and the main Japanese position at Lawksawk. The ridge trail we were camped on continued to the Kyaukku-Lawksawk road. For the fifteen to twenty minutes it would take to cross the road, we would be at risk. A Japanese force might suddenly appear on trucks. But once across, we could follow narrow trails south with relative safety until we got south of the roadblock. But then the valley narrowed and the sides were so steep that for about five miles the only way south was along the metaled road. The rule of thumb dating at least from the days of the Roman legions is that troops in good condition carrying arms, ammunition, and their food (a total of about seventy to ninety pounds), marching fifty minutes and resting ten, can make three miles an hour—about twenty-five miles in a day—and be able to fight at the end. Troops carrying only arms and ammunition on a forced march can make five miles an hour, making about forty miles in a day, and still be able to fight. So from the time the head of our column started down that road until the rear of it cleared, at least an hour and a quarter, we would be exposed.

Once off the main road, trails led up into the next north-south range running parallel to the Kyaukku-Lawksawk road. From the air photos it looked as if there was an animal trail along that ridge line, and it would be reasonably safe to follow that trail south until we hit the road that ran east from Lawksawk to Lai-Hka in the next valley. Once over that main road, we would be in the relative safety of the mountains and jungle.

At dawn the next morning we started off, single file. Our scouts having traveled back and forth over the trail in the preceding days, we were virtually certain that we wouldn't meet a sizeable Japanese force. But this was my first time out, and the thought of being behind enemy lines was disconcerting. Soon, however, the physical strain of climbing a mountain trail with packs and ammunition claimed all my attention. The aphorism about war being long periods of boredom interspersed with short periods of sheer terror should be revised to include long periods of physical discomfort.

We grew tense again as we neared the north-south road. We sent scouts ahead and then moved forward ourselves with great caution. Shortly, we met some villagers, and when they reported that no Japanese had been seen for three days we felt better. We found the trail paralleling the road south, went up from that into the mountains, and spent a restful night. Going south on the trail would be less dangerous than the road.

We developed a pattern of operations that became standard. Two- and three-man patrols from the Kachin-Shan scout platoon fanned out to the rear as well as ahead and on our flanks. We made it a practice of sending men dressed in local costumes "to market," equipped with things to sell. We also tried to recruit temporary agents from villages we made contact with. Because this was risky, we held people from the same village, preferably relatives, in protective custody.

The next day was the dangerous one, when the valley narrowed and we had to spend an hour or more on the main road itself. Scouts north and south reported no signs of life. We started out. Walking down that road seemed like a death march. Any moment I expected to hear the dreaded trucks. An hour of fast marching passed, and the head of the column reached the spot where the trail led off to the left. Another twenty-five minutes and we were clear.

By that night we were at the foot of the north-south ridge, at the tiny village of Loi-hkam, twenty-five miles north of Lawk-sawk and about five miles in from the road. Even if the Japanese found us and got a force in position to attack, we could make it to the mountains. We issued instructions about how to withdraw in case of attack, contacted headquarters by radio to report our position, ate a hurried meal, and fell into an exhausted sleep.

★ ★
A Raid on Lawksawk

We were set to head straight into the mountains at dawn, but the radio contact with headquarters changed our minds. The British had received intelligence reports that the Japanese were assembling a large force at Lawksawk, large enough to suggest a possible flank attack on the British fifty miles away, near Mandalay. We were ordered to send agents to the market in Lawksawk. We dispatched several groups of two men each and patrols on all the trails and waited. By nightfall all our agents were back. They had no information. Japanese outposts had been set up on every road and trail outside Lawksawk. No one was allowed in or out.

We reported this information to headquarters, and the next morning got orders couched in apologetic language. Headquarters realized that guerrillas were ill-suited to the mission, but there was no choice. Air reconnaissance had been as fruitless as our agent probes. Headquarters had to find out if something big was going on at Lawksawk. They wanted us to take a fighting patrol—a full company is what they suggested—and probe the outskirts of the town. The idea was to attack a Japanese outpost on one of the trails leading toward town and take a captive. If we failed to take a captive, they wanted us to lay down an ambush and wait to see what kind of force the Japanese sent out to investigate. From the nature of the enemy's reaction, we should get some clue as to the kind of force assembled there.

Bill and I thought the assignment was suicidal, but we had no choice. We decided to take one platoon from the Chinese company and one from the Karens, leaving the rest to dig a strong defense around Loi-hkam. We also notified headquarters to ready the emergency drop in case we needed it.

The outpost we chose was at Mwedaw, a tiny hamlet on a trail into Lawksawk. We started well before dawn and made the twenty-five miles to the outpost in five hours, arriving in mid-morning. The outpost was at the top of a round grassy hill. It was deserted.

It would have been much better for us if the outpost had been manned. We could have overwhelmed it and obtained unit identifications. Now about the only thing we could do was wait and see what kind of reaction our attack would provoke from Lawksawk. We deployed the Chinese platoon on the right, at the military crest of the hill, giving them a field of fire in the direction of Lawksawk. The Karen platoon we deployed on the left.

The response came more quickly than we expected. Brough, Van Arsdale, Arthur Toh, and I had gathered in a shed with a wooden floor, a roof of nipa leaves, and no walls. As we studied the maps and munched our K-rations, a burst of machine-gun fire passed just over our heads through the roof, raining bits of leaves down on us. In the next instant all four of us were crawling under the floor. We must have looked totally ridiculous. We couldn't have been seen from below the military crest, where the Japanese had come into contact with our men. They were aiming at those troops, not us.

Recovering ourselves, we ran down to see what was happening. At that moment someone in the Chinese platoon must have decided that the Japanese patrol was vulnerable. He jumped up and charged, firing his submachine gun. Then the whole Chinese platoon took out after him, firing and shouting, *"Sha! Sha!"* (Kill! Kill!)

The Japanese must have been startled, but not nearly so startled as Brough, Van Arsdale, and I. Such foolhardiness was bound to end in disaster. The Japanese disappeared, and the Chinese charge petered out. When we got to where the Chinese were, Brough and Van Arsdale started herding them back to their original position.

The Japanese were regular soldiers; they hadn't run, but had gone around to our right flank. When we got about halfway back to our positions, a machine gun raked the trail. I threw myself to the ground and rolled into the ditch, with Van Arsdale beside me. My right arm was numb and tingling, the same sensation I had had after being hit at Myitkyina. I remember cursing and thinking, The very first action I see after Myitkyina, I get hit! I rolled up my sleeve, expecting to see a shattered elbow. Nothing. In diving for the ditch, I had hit my funny bone.

Soon a mortar shell exploded on the other side of the trail, followed by others at intervals of a few seconds. Van said, "After this next one goes off, let's break for it." We did, and made it back to our original positions.

I got about ten yards behind the Karens and tried to see what kind of force was attacking us. But the next thing I knew, all the Karens had pulled back beside me. Every time I moved, the Karens followed like puppies after their master.

First the Chinese charge and now this! All I could think was how absolutely absurd it was to carry out this kind of operation with guerrillas.

It was obvious that if we stayed a minute longer, both platoons would be destroyed. I yelled at Brough and Van to break contact and get the hell out. We didn't have to urge haste. We covered the first five miles in considerably less than the hour traditionally allotted for a forced march. Miraculously, no one had been hit. We made the twenty-five miles back to Loi-hkam in about four hours.

★ ★
Braced for Disaster

Night was falling when we arrived, exhausted. It was clear that the force in Lawksawk was substantial. They wouldn't be far behind us, and we had to be ready for a full-scale attack at dawn. We got on the radio and asked that heavy machine guns, mortars, and ammunition be dropped at the very first light.

At dawn two beautiful C-47s came roaring out of the sky. Within an hour we had the machine guns and 81-millimeter mortars in place. But no attack came. Patrols sent out in every direction found nothing. To this day, I can't understand why the Japanese didn't attack.

We had to get into the high mountains, quickly. The problem was all that heavy equipment. We spent several precious hours disassembling pieces and lugging them to the jungle, where we had to abandon them.

177

Finally, we got going. If my theory was correct, that when in danger go further behind enemy lines, the thing for us to do was get south of Lawksawk, where the main Japanese forces were based. That was what we would attempt.

The trail followed the ridge line of a spur going up to the main north-south ridge. My plan was to get up to that ridge in the hopes there would be an animal trail along it. For the first hour or so, I was consumed with anxiety that the Japanese might launch a flank attack. Stretched thin as we were, we would have little chance.

As dusk began to fall, the long file of men came to a standstill and a messenger from Brough, who was at the head of the line, said that he had ordered a halt for the night. I was furious. I stormed up the trail until I reached Brough and demanded to know why this outfit couldn't march at night. Brough argued that he was afraid of missing the trail south along the crest. The terrain was so steep now, he said, that we need not fear an attack from the flank. And the men were exhausted. The truth is, he was right on all three counts. I had been so preoccupied with keeping the column moving that I hadn't noticed the change in terrain. It was the only time Brough and I were ever angry at each other.

We hurried down the trail to make sure the rear guard took up a good defensive position. Then we chose a spot where the sides were particularly steep and there was a clear field of fire for a good two hundred yards along the trail below. Not even a full Japanese battalion of five hundred regulars could have done us much harm. Relaxed now, the adrenaline ebbing, I found it an enormous struggle to climb back to where Arida, the radios, the food, and my bedroll were. That night I slept without even a dream to interrupt me.

Periodically over the next few months, I fretted about all that equipment we had abandoned in the jungle. It must have amounted to several thousand dollars. As time went on, I realized that it was precisely the fact that the United States had the wealth and resources to afford that kind of lavish support for its troops that was making the difference in the war. American troops went into combat knowing that logistical backup would not be stingy. That knowledge gave them great confidence. It

West Point, 1940. Hilsman's class (June 1943) would soon suffer more casualties than any other, before or since, in the history of the Academy.

The Philippines, 1941. Dinner for the author's father, Colonel Roger Hilsman (in background, wearing pith helmet), and the men he led across Mindanao after the defeat at Davao. He eventually surrendered as ordered by General Wainwright and began a captivity that would not end until his son's OSS team freed him three and a half years later.

The author, typically armed with a .45 pistol (cover of holster cut off for easy access) and a 9mm submachine gun fitted with a silencer.

An official Japanese photo of the author's father's surrender on the island of Negros. From the left: Japanese Colonel Ota, Colonel Hilsman, Major Ed Mason (his adjutant), and an unidentified Filipino officer.

The command group of Hilsman guerrilla unit. From the left: Eddie Arida, radio operator; Hilsman; Sgt. Albert Van Arsdale, second in command of the Chinese company; Lt. Arthur Toh, the Burmese lieutenant; Capt. Dennis Htun (back turned), a Karen who held a King's commission in the British Burma Rifles; then Sgt. Bill Brough, commander of the Chinese company; and "Fenigwan," the Chinese-English translator.

The Hilsman guerrilla battalion on the march about 125 miles behind Japanese lines.

MESSAGE (SUBMIT TO MESSAGE CENTER IN DUPLICATE) (CLASSIFICATION)

No. THREE   DATE 2-MAY '45.

To Tex :

Now at NAWNG PING L M
6046. Hit JAP FORAGING PATROL
AT LM 6245 AT 15.00 HOURS. WOUNDED
ONE. CAPTURED ONE PISTOL. ⊙ JAPS RAN
OFF TO SAMKAI ⊙ INFO C.3. ABOUT FIVE
HUNDRED JAPS AT KONTHA AREA ⊙ WE ARE
MOVING SOUTH TOMORROW. DIFFICULT TO
CONTACT YOU WHEN RAINING. WE MAY BE
ATTACKED TONIGHT— DON'T WORRY.

Bill. 1645

OFFICIAL DESIGNATION OF SENDER.   TIME SIGNED

AUTHORIZED TO BE SENT IN CLEAR | SIGNATURE OF OFFICER | SIGNATURE AND GRADE OF WRITER

U. S. GOVERNMENT PRINTING OFFICE : 1942   16—27880-1

A message from Bill Brough to Hilsman. "Tex" was Hilsman's code name.

Myitkyina airfield, March 1945. Lt. Billy Milton briefing his men just before they parachuted in to set up ambushes on roads leading to Mandalay during the British 14th Army's long battle for the city.

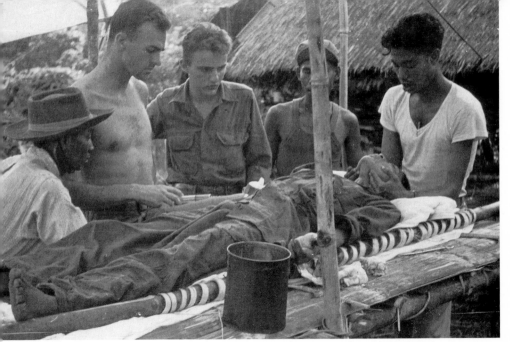

The OSS's "parachuting surgeon," Dr. Charles G. Hutter, operating on a wounded guerrilla. Photo taken shortly after Hutter had made his first jump—with no training whatsoever—into Red Maddox's battalion north of Lawksawk. The battalion had suffered heavy casualties, and Hutter operated steadily for three days until an airstrip could be built.

Albert Van Arsdale looking through field glasses at Japanese-held Lawksawk. Headquarters had asked Hilsman to probe the town with two platoons to find out something about the size of the force there. They soon learned it was an entire regiment.

Hilsman and Bill Brough celebrating the end of the
Burma campaign in June 1945 by firing 81mm mortar
flare rounds. Hilsman is wearing a *longyi*, traditional
attire for Burmese men.

Mukden, Manchuria, the day after the Japanese there were notified of
their country's surrender. Soviet soldiers are chatting with the two
American pilots who brought in Hilsman's OSS team, but the convivial
atmosphere deteriorated rapidly.

Colonel Hilsman and Captain Hilsman at Mukden. The author's father had kept an extra uniform, clean and pressed, for the day of his liberation.

The family reunites in San Francisco. The long war is over.

Pleiku, South Vietnam, 1962. First as director of intelligence and research at the State Department and then as assistant secretary of state for Far Eastern affairs, Roger Hilsman was one of President Kennedy's chief advisers on guerrilla warfare.

meant that when supplies and equipment tipped the balance, the advantage would be to the Americans. It was prudent to expect an attack that morning, I kept telling myself. If I hadn't ordered the emergency drop and an attack had come, we would have been destroyed.

The next morning things looked much brighter. We found the crest trail—not exactly on the crest, but a few hundred yards down the other side. Once on it, we were again in control. We spent the second night strung out on the ridge with no worries. No one could mount much of an attack up those steep sides, and an attack on either end of the column along the ridge line would have to be on a front about five men wide. We were well above four thousand feet, so the nights were cool. We slept very well.

★ ★
An Encounter with the Palaungs

The next day we took a crosstrail down from the ridge to find water. It ended up in a little pocket of a valley between the main ridge and a spur, at an altitude of about three thousand feet. There we found a tiny hamlet of Palaungs, the primitive mountain people whose women stretch their necks from childhood with rings of brass. Sometimes they can be seen in circus sideshows. They told us they had never seen a Japanese—ever— and that they hadn't seen a white man since the British district officer had departed in 1941.

The headman invited several of us into his nipa and bamboo hut. The floor was dirt. On one side was a raised sleeping platform covered with woven raffia mats. In the back of the hut a tiny cooking fire burned under a black iron pot sitting on a tripod. In the front, another small fire was placed between two wide sitting boards of mahogany, polished by years and years of sliding human bottoms. We gave him gifts of rayon and cotton parachute cloth and rock salt. The salt was needed, for some of these mountain people had goiter from lack of iodine. He offered us a clear and powerful beer made from glutinous upland rice, and boiled rice with a curry of wild boar. We spent the night camped beside the village.

Back on the ridge the next day, we reached a high point from which we could see Lawksawk about seven miles away. Van swore he saw Japanese military vehicles through the field glasses, but no one else did. That night we positioned ourselves for a quick dash across the east-west road from Lawksawk to Lai-Hka.

We started out well before dawn and arrived at the crossing at first light. We put one squad with its Bren gun in an ambush position about a hundred yards east of the crossing point, and another hundred yards west. We then ordered the Chinese company to cross the road and set up a defensive position a few hundred yards down the ridge facing south. Another squad then crossed the road to take up an ambush position one hundred yards east on the other side of the road, and another one hundred yards west. Only then did the rest of the battalion cross the road. Then the two squads in ambush position on the north side of the road crossed. The rear guard followed, sweeping the road with pine branches to cover our tracks.

We were now truly behind enemy lines, in a mountainous, sparsely populated area within striking distance of the Japanese lines of supply, not only those from the south to Lawksawk, but also—much more important—those from Bangkok through Taunggyi and Heho to the main Japanese forces fighting the British at Mandalay and Meiktila. We could start behaving as guerrillas should, running intelligence patrols and networks of agents, ambushing, blowing bridges, and harassing the enemy.

10

★ ★

Guerrilla Operations

The terrain was not so mountainous in this area, nor was it so heavily forested. In dozens of places, all we would have to do to make an airstrip for a light plane to evacuate wounded would be to fell a few trees on the approach. But for now this was no advantage. Being well behind Japanese lines, the terrain made us feel much more exposed than we had in the high mountains.

The airdrop of heavy equipment had included very little food, and we were beginning to run short. It was difficult for three hundred men to live off the land when the land was so poor and so sparsely populated. The first night we put in a defensive position, ate cold K-rations, and slept beside our firing positions. The second night we came to a hamlet of about six houses that had been deserted some time ago in obvious haste. Every house had in its storage room two or three huge baskets, at least five feet tall and four feet in diameter. Each could hold as much as ten to twenty bushels, and most were half full of unhusked rice. Carrying it would be no problem, but if we did we would also have to bring the grinding stones. I felt uneasy about spending the night in the village, but the men were hungry and in the two days since we had crossed the east-west road we hadn't seen a single human being. We sent patrols out on every trail to set up ambushes and put the rest of the battalion to work pounding rice to remove the husks.

A troop of monkeys was raising a huge chatter in a nearby grove of trees. I gave one of the snipers permission to shoot a few with his silencer on. It was the last time I did that—I hadn't known that a wounded monkey screams like a frightened child. For those of us squeamish from the screaming, one of the patrols on the trail provided an alternative. They sent a man back with a python they had killed that must have been fifteen feet long and weighed as much as one hundred pounds. The thought of eating snake bothered me. I got some comfort from remembering that during my father's march across Mindanao, he and his group not only ate monkeys and pythons but also grubs picked out from rotting logs. The python, it turned out, when cut into chunks and cooked with curry powder, looked and tasted like chicken.

★ ★

The Pattern of Guerrilla Operations

The next day we were on the move by dawn. We followed back trails, taking up a defensive position each night and sending out agents and patrols in all directions. Each day produced intelligence on Japanese installations and troop movements, which we radioed back to headquarters. Our pattern of operations was not to keep the whole battalion together, but rather to send out the Chinese company, which numbered about a hundred men, to the east, say, to lay ambushes on each of several trails, and to send half of the Karen company, again a total of about a hundred, to the west, leaving still another hundred men to defend the headquarters group with the radio and heavier supplies. For the next few weeks, this pattern of activity produced a substantial amount of intelligence about Japanese installations and troop movements. It was used to guide Allied bombing raids and by British intelligence in keeping track of the Japanese order of battle.

Twice a day at specified times, usually when we were on the march, Eddie Arida would set up his dah-dit radio and send the intelligence we had gathered in coded messages. Requests for airdrops of food and ammunition went the same way. Base headquarters maintained an open emergency channel twenty-four hours a day, which we could call for an emergency drop if we were surrounded.

The Japanese at the time were sending out foraging patrols to various villages for food for supply-line troops along the Meiktila-Thailand road. Several of the patrols walked into our ambushes. The groups were small, enough men to commandeer supplies and carry them. Although our ambushes were reasonably successful, the Japanese were seasoned troops. Taken by surprise, they often managed to break contact with our guerrillas and pull back in the orderly fashion of veterans with long combat experience.

We continued to operate in the area east of the Lawksawk-Shwenyaung road, working our way south to the Heho-Taunggyi road, sending out patrols and agents, and reporting the intelligence they gathered to headquarters. We got to within twenty miles of the Heho-Taunggyi road, near the village of Hona, but concentrations of Japanese farther south were too heavy for us to risk operations in that direction. The mountains in the Heho-Lawksawk-Shwenyaung triangle would have been ideal as a base of operations, but the villagers of Hona—who had had particularly bad experiences with the Japanese and who were therefore eager to help as agents—reported that truck convoys between Lawksawk and Shwenyaung were frequent. We dared not risk crossing the north-south road.

The terrain southeast of the road we had crossed coming south was mountainous jungle for about half the distance to Taunggyi. The mountains were not so high as those north of the Lawksawk–Lai-Hka road, along which there was fairly heavy Japanese traffic, but the jungle was thick and offered us ample protection. South of this heavy jungle the terrain turned into rolling hills of pasture, dotted with villages and patches of jungle, especially along the streams. Since Taunggyi was a big town for this part of the world, and on the secondary supply route from Meiktila to Thailand, it had to be an important intelligence target. We headed east, continuing in jungle.

The date was 15 April. We had been in operations for one month. We had been commended for the intelligence we had supplied, we had inflicted a few casualties on the Japanese, and we had suffered none ourselves. We were feeling much more confident about ourselves.

We spent the next several days in this jungle, sending patrols and agents out in all directions. They came back with detailed information about enemy forces in and around Taunggyi

183

and about their convoys and supply dumps. This kind of information was just what the air corps needed, and they used it to good purpose in guiding their bombing missions. But with so little Japanese movement through the jungle, there wasn't much opportunity for ambushing. Various elements of our group had a few skirmishes with Japanese foraging patrols. Brough and the Chinese ambushed one large patrol, inflicting several casualties without suffering any of their own. What particularly pleased them was that—according to a message from Brough scrawled on a scrap of paper I still have—they captured an officer's pistol. But that was about all.

We edged south toward Taunggyi and finally came to a hamlet of about ten houses where the rolling hills began. Taunggyi sat on the shoulder of the mountain ridge off in the distance. To go farther south would be enormously dangerous. Yet we had gathered just about all the intelligence we could in this area. We couldn't go east without infringing on the area assigned to the OSS guerrilla battalion commanded by Major Bob Delaney. Thus we planned to go north into the heavy jungle, head west and then south, and find a place to cross into the mountains of the Lawksawk-Heho-Shwenyaung triangle. From that position, we could gather intelligence on the Japanese at Heho and Taunggyi, and we could ambush on all three roads that formed the triangle.

★ ★
Airdrop North of Taunggyi

In the meantime we needed an airdrop, and for that, a clearing. This was essential, first, to allow pilots to spot the identification panels, and second, to keep parachutes out of the trees. The panels helped the pilots get the right drop to the right group.

In spite of such precautions, C-47s frequently searched for a group in vain—so frequently, in fact, that if a C-47 couldn't find its assigned group and stumbled on another, it was to go ahead and drop. Either the extra supplies would come in handy, or they could be used to ingratiate the group with villagers.

North of us was nothing but thick jungle. Neither maps nor air photos revealed a suitable drop zone nearer than a three-day march. We decided to take the drop here, in the open pasture beside the village. The Japanese would see it, but by the time they mounted an attack we would be long gone.

The procedure for an airdrop was standard. After locating a suitable drop zone, the guerrilla group would radio the map coordinates to base. A C-47 could carry six thousand pounds, so one plane was enough for a routine drop of food and ammunition for our group of three hundred men—twenty pounds per man. If we had spent the preceding week or so gathering intelligence rather than fighting, only about five pounds of the twenty would be in ammunition. Supplemented by rice and other items from the villages, fifteen pounds of food would last about a week. If the work had been ambushing, or if the group had not been in a position to receive a drop for two weeks or more, two C-47s would be needed. When we heard the C-47s droning overhead we would lay out the panels, made of the white-cotton parachutes from previous drops. Our recognition symbol was an H for Hilsman.

As soon as the pilot recognized the panel, he would waggle his wings and go around for a drop run. He would come in as if for a landing, level off at an altitude of three hundred to five hundred feet, and cut the throttles to a speed just above stalling. All the planes used for airdrops had had their doors at the left rear removed to facilitate drops. If the drop zone was large, the aircrew would stack the bundles of supplies in a line along the floor of the cabin, with the static lines from the parachutes hooked to a steel cable running along the top of the cabin. At a signal from the pilot, part of the crew would start shoving bundles out the door, while the rest pushed the other bundles down the cabin to them. If the drop zone was short, the crew stacked as much as they could in the door, and the plane made additional runs. In any case, at least two passes were needed—one for the supplies being parachuted and one for those, largely rice, falling free.

After putting out their panels, the guerrillas would take shelter. Not only was free-falling rice dangerous, but the parachutes on the heavier bundles would often break. At the instant of the drop, the plane would be going about seventy-five miles

185

an hour. In three hundred to five hundred feet of free fall, the bundle would accelerate to perhaps twice that speed. A case of number-ten cans of tomatoes—not to mention a case of ammunition or a machine gun—going one hundred and fifty miles an hour can do a great deal of damage.

We radioed our coordinates and waited. The monsoon had begun and the clouds made finding us difficult. Each morning would start out at least partly clear. Then the clouds would gather and about mid-morning it would rain in sheets. When it stopped, the clouds would thicken again, and in late afternoon the downpour would come again. The first day after we called for the drop, we heard some C-47s in mid-morning, but the clouds were too thick and too low. The same thing happened the second day.

★ ★
A Japanese Spy

How long could we stay there waiting for a drop without the Japanese discovering us? The evening of the second day three Shans appeared from the south. They were each on their way north on personal business, they said, and had met on the trail. One of them seemed unusually curious about us, asking questions about where we had been and where we were going and about our equipment. The Shans in the scout platoon were particularly suspicious. Finally, they seized the fellow and searched him. Rolled up inside one of the cigarettes he was carrying was a note of instructions from the commanding officer of the Taunggyi Kempei Tai, the Japanese secret police. The man had been sent to locate our group and report on its size, equipment, and mission. Without urging, the man confessed, giving details of the Kempei Tai's personnel and operations.

Having a prisoner on our hands posed a dilemma. If we had been in a safer area and near a place suitable for an airstrip, we would have ordered a light plane to take him out. We were far from any such place, and taking men out of operations for several days to escort a prisoner increased the risk for all of us.

186

On a long march there was also a chance that the prisoner, who now knew a lot about us, would escape. If he had been someone with a great deal of intelligence, such as a Japanese officer, we would have been justified in making the several days' march. But this man was just a local, a flunky quisling, with no special knowledge at all.

Commanders had the right to try soldiers under their command for minor offenses and, when the command was isolated, as ours was, for more serious offenses as well. But they didn't usually have the authority to try persons for offenses that required a general court martial, such as spying or treason, since those carried the penalty of death. But it was the understanding among OSS guerrilla leaders that the senior Allied commander in any particular district had the authority to hold a general court and that they, the guerrilla leaders, were by definition the senior Allied commanders. It was only after the war that I learned that authority was vested in the senior Allied commander of flag or general rank. None of the guerrilla leaders was aware of this, and almost all on one or two occasions exercised the authority they thought they had.

Weighing the pros and cons, I decided it would not be right to put the lives of three hundred men at risk simply to return for civilian trial a man whose guilt as a spy was beyond doubt. Accordingly, we proceeded with a proper trial—very short, but proper—and sentenced the man to death by firing squad. We carried out the sentence the next morning.

After the war, I asked myself if I would do the same again. To this day I am uncomfortable that I had a man executed on my own authority. But I would do the same again. The sense of responsibility a commander feels for the lives of the men placed in his charge is strong, and I have no abiding feelings of guilt at having taken a life to reduce the risk to theirs.

★ ★
The Drop

The fact that the Japanese Kempei Tai had sent an agent looking for us confirmed our fears. If we didn't get a drop on this, the third day, we would have to do without. We decided on a dramatic measure to attract the C-47s' attention, in spite of the danger that it would also attract the Japanese. Most of the mortars we carried were 60 millimeter, designed for light infantry. But we had been lugging along one 81-millimeter mortar. One man carried the tube and another the base. And for emergency use we also carried several flare shells among the 81-millimeter ammunition. These were somewhat like the rockets used in Fourth of July fireworks displays. They would go straight up for several hundred feet, burst into a parachute, and ignite a bright flare that would float down, burning, for almost a full minute. We readied the 81-millimeter mortar and the flare shells and waited for the drone of the engines.

The planes came early in the morning, right on time. But again the clouds were so thick they couldn't see us. The minutes stretched to an hour. The planes kept droning, but they were getting low on gas and we began to think we would not get a drop at all. Suddenly a patch of blue showed through the cloud cover. We fired our shell straight at it, and the flare burned bright and lovely.

The next instant C-47s began diving through the hole in the clouds, more C-47s than I had seen at any one time since Myitkyina. Two planes had been scheduled for us. Four others had obviously failed to find their assigned groups, and since they were low on gas they were following the procedure of dropping to any group they could.

None of the six planes wasted time. The sky filled quickly with parachutes. It was like a bombing attack without the explosions. One case of ammunition with a broken parachute went through the thatch roof and raised bamboo floor of a village house and splattered on the ground beneath, where the pigs and chickens lived. None of the ammunition exploded.Then came the free-falling rice, gunny sacks half full. By this time every man in the outfit and all the villagers were either in slit trenches or behind trees in the jungle. After that, one C-47 made a final run, dropping two yellow parachutes. This was the beer ration and mail for Brough, Van Arsdale, Arida, and me.

We had little time to lose. We kept the outposts lightly manned against an attack and put the rest of the men to work

188

gathering the supplies and packing them for our departure. There was a lot to do. We had thirty-six thousand pounds to dispose of. One third of each plane's load was rice. I had the bags of rice piled in a stack—twelve thousand pounds makes an impressive hill—and I climbed on top to direct the operation. The mail was put at my feet, and the Americans kept stealing glances at it as we worked. We couldn't take the time to open it until we were ready to depart.

We hired villagers as porters for the ammunition we couldn't carry ourselves and sent runners to neighboring villages with invitations to come and get food. Some of the food would still probably go begging.

Within an hour and half we were ready to go, and Bill, Van, and Eddie gathered around for their mail. Each received a letter, which he gobbled up. The rest of the mail was disappointing. Mail drops usually brought a package or two from home with the things we liked; families remembered our favorite foods and did their best with the rations they got to send them to us. This time I was the only one to get a package. With the others watching anxiously, I stood on top of a pile of twelve thousand pounds of rice and opened the package. Inside I found one can of chili con carne, a favorite of mine, and a one-pound bag of rice. So we had twelve thousand and one pounds of rice.

★ ★
Probing for a Crossing

We started north immediately, moving as fast as we could and by trails through the deepest of the jungle. Three days later, we turned west and marched to make contact with another OSS group in the mountains south of the Lawksawk-Lai-Hka road and east of the Lawksawk-Shwenyaung road.

One of the groups under Maddox's direction had gone around Lawksawk to the west and was operating south of it, as we were. We would see something of them later. But the others, whose mission had been to form an intelligence screen opposite enemy forces in Lawksawk, had actually engaged in a conventional battle. They had probed Japanese positions and dug in for

189

the counterattack, which came in some force. They had inflicted considerable casualties on the Japanese but, being neither trained nor equipped for regular operations, had suffered very high casualties themselves. The group with which we made contact had been formed only recently. Maddox had sent it to ambush on the roads leading into Lawksawk from the east.

The commander was a lieutenant who had had a lot of combat experience in Italy, but none as a guerrilla. He was nervous about the fact that there were no friendly forces around, and his reaction was not to keep moving, but to dig in.

He had been impressed with the defensive capabilities of this particular village. Being only a few kilometers from the Lawksawk-Shwenyaung road, it had been visited frequently by the Japanese and almost as frequently bombed by the Allies. In response, the villagers had built themselves a second village near the stream bed in the densest jungle. The canopy of vegetation was so thick that nothing grew beneath the towering trees, where it was perpetual dusk. They had cleared away rotting leaves three feet deep, exposing the bare earth, and between the trunks had built huts for all the village functions. They followed what amounted to a military routine. While they worked in the fields around the real village, lookouts were posted for airplanes. A temple bell would sound an air-raid alarm whereupon the natives would take shelter in the hidden village. They also had scouts posted on all the trails leading to the village and a separate set of alarms to signal the approach of Japanese patrols. The OSS lieutenant decided to take advantage of what they had done. He turned the village itself into a strong point, with dug-in gun positions roofed with logs, then stationed part of his force in the secret village. From there they could attack the rear of any Japanese force that was itself attacking the village on the hill.

We told the group about our recent adventures, stressing that the Japanese could be expected to send out fighting patrols looking for us. The OSS lieutenant was confident. They were so well dug in, he thought, that they could hold against any Japanese force. Because of the trap they had planned, the lieutenant actually welcomed an attack.

A Japanese fighting patrol did find them a few days later,

190

hitting them hard with the professional efficiency of battle-hardened veterans. The untrained OSS guerrillas broke and ran. But the lieutenant and his guerrillas were lucky. The attack came in late afternoon, and night came soon enough to permit most of them to escape. They crawled out by ones and twos.

★ ★

Skirmish at Hona

Our battalion headed south, looking for a safe way to cross the Lawksawk-Shwenyaung road into the Heho-Lawksawk-Shwenyaung triangle of mountains. But the traffic on the road was too heavy to risk a crossing. Finally, late one afternoon, we reached the southernmost point of our earlier stay in this area, near the village of Hona.

Just as we started to set up a defense position for the night, two villagers from Hona came hurrying up the trail. A strong Japanese foraging patrol was pillaging the village. These two had succeeded in slipping out to the jungle, but not before they had seen the Japanese shoot a priest, a woman, and two other villagers who had tried to run away. They thought the Japanese wouldn't be finished their looting for another hour or two.

Although it was risky, Brough and I figured we had a good chance of getting a force into a blocking position on the trail the Japanese patrol would probably take on the way out. Brough led with the Chinese company. I followed with Arthur Toh and two of the Karen platoons. The plan was for Brough and the Chinese to put in the block. Then I would put the Karens into an ambush position forward of the point where the Chinese branched off from the main trail. This would protect their withdrawal.

Night fell rapidly, as it does in the tropics, and by the time we reached the place for Brough and the Chinese to branch off, it was very dark. The Karens designated to keep contact with the rear of the Chinese column lost it, so it was impossible to determine just where the Chinese had branched off.

Night actions are extremely difficult even with well-seasoned regular troops. The risk that these untrained guerrillas

191

would end up shooting each other was high. I disposed the two platoons for an ambush. Shortly, heavy firing broke out from the other side of the village. I couldn't distinguish any that was clearly Japanese—it sounded like British Bren guns and American submachine guns—and I feared the worst, that one of the Chinese platoons was actually firing at the other.

In any case, when the Chinese came up the trail toward us they would be unnerved and trigger-happy. The Karens would be just as jumpy. The danger that the Japanese could get themselves organized fast enough to catch up to Brough and the Chinese began to seem much smaller than the danger of a clash between Chinese and Karens. I pulled out the Karens and chased them up the trail to the main camp as fast as possible.

Brough and the Chinese arrived half an hour later carrying a wounded sergeant. The Japanese patrol, which had started for home as the Chinese were getting into position, walked right into the ambush. Those Japanese not killed by the initial burst of fire had bolted into the jungle without firing a shot.

The sergeant didn't have his squad in position when the firing started. Instead of stopping the squad where they were, he had continued to move it forward, and they had walked right into the crossfire from another squad. He had been hit in the thigh by a bullet from one of our own submachine guns.

The Karen platoons at headquarters had thrown together a bamboo and nipa hut while we were gone to shelter the radio and other supplies from rain, and we used it as medical station. Immediately after the man had been hit, Brough put a tourniquet around his upper leg to stop the bleeding. Now, by lantern, we could see that the thighbone had been shattered.

Bill thought his medical training was extensive enough to enable him to tie off the blood vessels that had been damaged. This, he said, along with plasma injections and morphine, would stabilize the man for two or three days. That might be enough time to get him to a hospital by light plane. I held a flashlight and, as Brough directed, sponged away the blood with pads of gauze while he tied off the damaged vessels.

There were few suitable places nearby to carve out an airstrip, and with Japanese out looking for us, bringing in a light plane would be dangerous as well. We thought of the area south of where we had crossed the east-west road. It was a two-day march, but the only choice we had. We radioed headquarters the coordinates with an urgent request for a plane two days later. Well before daylight, one of the Chinese platoons was on its way, carrying the wounded man in a litter. The platoon would rendezvous with us three days later.

The rest of us moved out shortly after daylight. Van wanted to go back to Hona and get identification papers from the Japanese dead. Searching for bodies in the dark would have been difficult and too time-consuming for the wounded sergeant's safety, so they hadn't attempted the night before. Chances were that the Japanese would be back with a stronger force that day. Intelligence people were always pressing for papers; this time it hardly seemed worth the risk. But Van was determined, so I made him swear to spend no longer than ten minutes in the actual search. When he caught up to us on the trail, he was grinning broadly and waving a bundle of papers.

★ ★
On the Run

Over the next few days the Japanese began to send out stronger patrols, designed for fighting rather than foraging. When one of these hit an ambush, it was our guerrillas who broke contact and pulled back—in our case, at a dead run. Evidence mounted that some of these patrols were looking specifically for us. We maintained the practice of never spending two nights in the same place, and kept agents and soldiers dressed in local costume on all the trails around us.

Reports from our agents confirmed that Japanese patrols of platoon size were fanning out over the trails in the area. They also reported a strong force of battalion size equipped with trucks at Taungni, on the north-south road midway between Lawksawk and Shwenyaung. The force was clearly alert and ready to close with us once one of the platoon-size patrols made contact. When the Chinese platoon that had littered the wounded sergeant to the airstrip rendezvoused with us, they brought additional reports of platoon-size patrols.

By now we were long overdue for an airdrop. Again food was short. We were also out of tobacco, which for our soldiers was almost as bad as being out of food. For several days we had been on the trail ten hours a day, each man carrying about seventy-five pounds of equipment, arms, and ammunition. Ambushes left on the trails behind us had been sprung twice. The Japanese had found our general location, and would soon pinpoint us.

We sent agents ahead to scout the area and readied ourselves to slip across the north-south road by laying ambushes on both sides, the technique we had used when crossing the road from Lawksawk east.

The agents reported the trails immediately ahead of us clear, and we made it across the road without incident. That night we spent in the deserted village of Thamainggon, about three miles from the main road and at the foot of the ridge of the Lawksawk-Heho-Shwenyaung triangle. The command group had their blankets on the floor of the the priests' house. Arida spun the radio dials as we ate K-rations, the last food of any kind that we had.

After a few minutes, Arida looked up and said in a weary voice, "This is V-E Day. The Germans have surrendered." I went out on the porch, called the troops not on outpost together, and made the announcement. If there was any response, it was one of irony. Our chances of getting out of the trap we were being herded into seemed small.

We were on our way at first light, over a trail climbing steadily into the mountain triangle. Unlike the trail to the high ridge we had taken after the raid at Lawksawk, which followed a spur of the main ridge, this one simply went up and up over terrain that was like a tilted jungle plain. Finally we came to the foot of a very steep face, the base of the high mountain. The trail went up this face for two or three miles, making hairpin bends as it went. My hopes rose. Although the terrain didn't offer the safety of those razor-backed ridges we had followed from Lawksawk, it might have its own advantages.

After much climbing we came to the foot of a sheer cliff. Carved out of the face of the rock was the trail. It was wide enough only for a pack pony. Every twenty or thirty yards there was more space, so that a pack pony coming in one direction could squeeze aside while another passed in the opposite direction.

When we got to the top of the mountain, we all stared in amazement. It wasn't jagged, but rounded, like two halves of a melon, one slightly higher than the other and connected by a saddle about five hundred feet long and no more than a hundred feet wide. And here on the twin tops of this mountain was a *pongyi kyaung* (a priest's house) and a village of about twenty houses. The village sat on the lower mound and the *pongyi kyaung* on the higher. The British army map I carried had a scale of one half inch to the mile, and it showed a mountain, Htandape Taung (*taung* is the Burmese word for mountain), 5,465 feet high with a pagoda symbol on it, but no village. The mountain itself was the highest in that part of the range. Its northern and western faces were cliffs like the one we had just climbed on the east. The west face had also had a trail cut into the living rock, but only climbers equipped with ropes, pitons, and hammers could have gotten up the north face. To the south, behind the *pongyi kyaung*, the ridge narrowed until two hundred yards further south it turned into a razor back, so narrow that a man could look down both sides.

The significance of this unique village and its location gradually sank in. Two Bren guns, properly sited and sandbagged on each of the two trails cut into the cliff faces, could hold off a vastly superior force indefinitely. Two more Brens on the razorback, with the help of mortars, could hold off just as large a force attacking from the south. The Japanese had earmarked a couple of battalions to hunt us down, but they certainly weren't going to augment that force with enough more troops to root us off this fastness. Even if they did put two or three battalions against us, it would be impossible for them to mount coordinated attacks on all three approaches at once. If they came at us from one direction, we had two secure escape hatches. If they somehow managed an attack on two of the approaches, we still had the third. A few hours before we had felt trapped. Now, suddenly, we felt marvelously safe.

195

11

★ ★

Holidays Behind the Lines

For several days our only food had been rice boiled with extra water to make a porridge—what the Chinese call congee rice. No one had had any tobacco. But that night on top of an impregnable mountain, we feasted. Except for shortages of cloth and several other goods that came from the outside world, the village had not been touched by war. The people grew upland rice and tobacco in the little *cwms* that hung on the side of a mountain. These were scattered about the range, some as far as three or four miles away. The villagers had two dozen ponies trained to carry pack baskets. And it was the first *pongyi kyaung* we had seen where the furniture and religious trappings were in place and the Buddhist monk was in residence. He spent his days performing ritual prayers in front of three Buddhas, and each day a different woman of the village brought him two meals, morning and night.

The headman said that the only villagers who had ever seen Japanese were the three or four delegated to make a monthly trek to the market at Lawksawk. He was delighted to supply us with all the rice and tobacco we wanted in exchange for parachute cloth and the promise of an extra airdrop of rice and tobacco.

An airdrop would be problematic. Since the two mountain-tops were occupied by buildings, the only place for a drop was the narrow saddle. This was very small for a drop zone. Then there was the approach. The village houses and the *pongyi ky-aung* would prevent planes from coming in over the long axis of the rectangle, and if they came in over the short, hundred-foot axis, we could lose most of the drop. So the drop had to be made

197

on the diagonal, the plane coming over the saddle with the village on the right, about level with the plane, and going out with the *pongyi kyaung* on the left, a bit higher than the plane. The pilots who came were skillful flyers, but even so we lost about a fourth of the drop over the far cliff.

After the drop, Brough and I agreed that the position was so safe and the troops were so in need of a rest that the rule about not spending two nights in the same place was off—a decision that brought cheers from the guerrillas. We ended up spending almost a week there resting, and using the village as a base headquarters for another four days after that.

The command group used the porch of the *pongyi kyaung* as quarters, slinging jungle hammocks between the wooden columns well away from the Buddhas and the *pongyi* inside. The view was spectacular. Over the roofs of the village below we could see the far mountains over which we had come stretching north toward Maymyo. To the west we could see the valley and the road from Lawksawk descending to Heho; to the east, the valley and road going from the junction east of Lawksawk to Shwenyaung. At night, cooking fires blinked here and there in the villages. Monsoon clouds would roll in and it would rain in late morning, clearing a bit in early afternoon. Showers would come again just before the sun began to set. The sunsets were extravagant.

Arida and Van spent their days in a nonstop poker game, using what was left in the group's bag of silver rupees as chips. Brough and I spent our time poring over maps plotting our next phase of operations.

We also started a volleyball tournament in the flat area in front of the *pongyi kyaung*. The command group was quickly eliminated, and the Karens and Chinese battled it out, with the Chinese the overall winners.

A Bengali who had been cooking for the command group asked for a bag of flour in the airdrop. He thought he would like to try his hand at baking a cake. A sack of flour was included in the next drop. It was put inside one of the gunny sacks used for rice and free-dropped. Upon impact the flour sack burst inside the gunny sack, so we had a cake filled with gunny-sack fibers.

We bought a water buffalo, the nearest thing to beef that

was available. The troops cut their share into bite-sized chunks for curry, but the command group wanted steak, preferably filet mignon. The problem was that no one in the group knew anything about a cow's anatomy. Arida was from Brooklyn, I was an army brat who had lived mainly in cities, Bill was from Newcastle-on-Tyne, and Van couldn't help. The consensus was that steaks came from the rump. What we got was awful, tasteless and tough. It was only after the war that I learned that filet mignon came from the area near the long muscle that runs along the spine. The thought of all that filet mignon going into curry still annoys me.

★ ★

Trouble in Paradise

It turned out that staying more than one night in the same place brought dangers other than a siege by the Japanese. Our Karens were Christians, but they were also mountain tribesmen. So were the Kachins and the Shans. Some of the Chinese were coolie laborers in civilian life and some farming peasants. All came from subcultures in which power was the arbiter of behavior toward the powerless, and all carried Bren or submachine guns. The villagers carried *dah*s. The only thing resembling a rifle in the entire village was an old hunting gun that was only one generation removed from a flintlock. The headman had inherited this gun with his office to be used against man-eating tigers. With three hundred men of such differing backgrounds, idleness was bound to breed trouble.

The Chinese were inveterate gamblers, and an enterprising villager had set up a continuous card game in his hut. One night we heard screams of pain from the village. When Brough and I tracked it down to that particular hut, we found the villager strung up by his hands to the rafters and three or four of the Chinese soldiers beating his bare back. They accused him of cheating and stealing a .45 pistol—one of the Chinese was a mortar man, and he carried a pistol rather than a submachine gun because the mortars were enough of a burden. We turned the villager over to the headman, and the pistol was duly returned. The Chinese we fined a week's pay for taking matters into their own hands.

That was only the beginning of the trouble. The next day we got an airdrop, this one including basic items such as new uniforms and jungle boots. The boots were particularly needed, since the constant marching had put holes in most of our tennis-shoe soles and reduced the nylon boot tops to rags. We divided the various items between the Karen and Chinese companies and each retired to its own part of the defense perimeter for the distribution.

Brough and the Chinese lieutenant were supervising the distribution to the Chinese. As Arida and I sat on the porch of the *pongyi kyaung* having a cup of tea, Brough unexpectedly appeared at the foot of the stairs, dragging the Chinese lieutenant by the collar and holding a .45 pistol in his hand. White with anger, Brough handed me the pistol, pushed the lieutenant in my direction, and in a barely contained voice said, "This bastard pulled his .45 on me." The lieutenant, he reported, had started to help himself to a new pair of boots. Brough, preoccupied, told him to wait until the men were taken care of. The Chinese objected, Brough shut him up, whereupon the lieutenant drew his gun and threatened Brough with it.

In the best of circumstances, the authority of four Westerners over this polyglot group of guerrillas was tenuous. The cultural chasm between us and the troops was a deep and convoluted as the Grand Canyon, and between the Chinese and the Karens almost as great. Nor were our guerrillas subject to the network of laws that soldiers in an American, British, or Chinese army would have been. They were contract soldiers, probably with no legal obligation to obey orders. We maintained authority only to the extent that we continued to command the respect of the majority of each of the ethnic groups. If we violated the mores of any particular group, that group would turn on us. On the other hand, if we failed to exert the authority we claimed to have, they would obey only the orders they wanted to obey, and then only after debate and negotiation. Down that path lay military disaster for all.

The members of the Chinese company quietly began to gather below us in front of the porch, looking up expectantly with their tommy guns in hand. I quickly appointed a court of inquiry consisting of myself as presiding officer, Van Arsdale, Lieutenant Toh, the Chinese translator, and two of the best Chinese sergeants. We heard the evidence, conferred with each other, and agreed that the lieutenant would be relieved of his command, fined a week's pay, dismissed from the group, and dispatched for Maddox's base as soon as possible. From there he would be transported back to his home village near Maymyo. Those of us in the command group and the court of inquiry picked up our weapons and lined ourselves up along the edge of the porch. Looking down at the Chinese assembled below, I made the announcement in a voice as firm and no-nonsense as I could muster. The Chinese soldiers glanced at each other, hesitated, and then mumbling their approval began to wander back to their fires.

That night I decided that holidays were more dangerous than action. We weren't ready to move south yet, but we had to do something to keep the troops occupied. The next morning I sent half of the Karen company to lay ambushes on the Lawk-sawk-Shwenyaung road, and Brough and the bulk of the Chinese company to see if they could blow a bridge on the Lawk-sawk-Heho road.

My plan was to move the whole group south two days later, as soon as these missions were complete. But we were delayed by a radio message from Maddox. The group that had gone around Lawksawk to the west had operated for weeks in the mountains west of the Heho-Lawksawk road, using the same guerrilla tactics that we had used. In the past two weeks they had detected no Japanese movement on the road and their agents reported that there were no longer any Japanese in the villages along the road. Emboldened, the group came down into the valley. No Japanese appeared so they spent several nights in a small town on the main road.

One noon, a motorized Japanese column arrived so suddenly that their outposts were overwhelmed and the main group was pinned down by fire. A number of those still alive at nightfall crawled out and were making their way to our mountaintop stronghold by ones and twos. In no shape to go on with us, they stayed in our mountain fastness for some time after we left. The disgraced Chinese lieutenant, a Karen terminally ill with TB, and the chaplain to care for him remained with these men and then guided them back to Maddox's position over the razorback ridges we had used coming south.

★ ★
The Move South

Japanese fighting patrols were still looking for us from Lawksawk south to Shwenyaung. We went south on the razorback and when the terrain became impassable we cut west, through the smaller mountains on the Lawksawk-Heho side of the main ridge.

At Heho the Japanese had an airfield for Zeros. From the mountains we watched them taking off and landing. Allied bombing attacks seemed ineffective against them. Forty years later I visited the area and found out why. The Japanese had constructed camouflaged underground revetments for the Zeros, a remarkable feat.

We followed a narrow valley the villagers said had been only rarely visited by Japanese, even though it was easily accessible from the main Lawksawk-Heho valley that paralleled it. The *pongyi kyaung*s were operating as if in peacetime. But we did not linger. We took the first trail we could find that cut back into the high mountains.

Once in the higher mountains, we began to feel safe again. The maps of this area of Burma were dotted with the notation "Many sinkholes." The mountains are largely limestone, and millions of years of monsoon rains have riddled them with caves. A sinkhole results when a cave collapses. But every now and again, the rains work to produce a hidden valley. We stumbled on one of these the next day. The trail came into the head of the valley atop a ridge and went twisting down a steep slope, making hairpin turns every few hundred feet.

In the monsoon season a stream began from springs about halfway down the slope, swelling as it went until by the time it reached the valley floor it had become a respectable brook. The valley was only a mile and a half long, and midway through it the stream had become a small river. Then, at the end of the valley, the river made a sharp turn and disappeared into a cave. The sides of the valley were steep. Only three switchback trails led in and out—the first down the steep entrance, the second down the eastern side, and the last down at the other end.

Although the valley was not nearly so safe as our mountaintop fastness, it wasn't likely that we would be attacked on all three trails simultaneously, and an attack on any one trail could be defended long enough for the main group to escape on one of the other two. We put two Bren guns on each of the trails, protected by tommy-gunners and backed up with a 60-millimeter mortar. The Brens could hold off a force of company size for ten to fifteen minutes and then leapfrog back, protecting each other by mortar fire. With our agents going back and forth constantly and our active local patrolling, Japanese forces probably wouldn't be able to sneak up on us, certainly not from three directions at once.

The valley did have one disadvantage, which almost spelled disaster. A drop had been scheduled for the day after we arrived in the valley, before we were fully aware that it lacked an entry or an exit for a plane. Our radio description described it only as narrow and deep. When the C-47 arrived for the drop it dove down to five hundred feet for the first pass. We watched in horror as the pilot realized that the valley had no exit. He managed to climb over the cliff at the end, but only by banking between two huge trees. The rest of his passes he made from above the valley rim. The drops were scattered and some of the rice bags burst, but we were content.

There was nothing to indicate that the Japanese had any clue of our presence here. Unescorted convoys of trucks were traveling frequently over the Heho-Taunggyi road, less frequently going partway up the Heho-Lawksawk and Shwenyaung-Lawksawk roads. We were finally in a position to gather intelligence, harass the enemy, and perhaps ambush a foraging patrol and a truck convoy full of supplies.

Our agents reported that trains were no longer running between Heho and Shwenyaung and that with Allied bombing so frequent the Japanese had taken to sending their truck convoys at night. A night ambush was safer than one in the daytime. We thought this might be an opportunity. Our headquarters was in a central position near the top of a mountain forty-five hundred feet high and about six miles north of the Heho-Shwenyaung road. The Karen platoons were ordered to set ambushes on each of the approaches to headquarters, and Brough took the Chinese company to see if they could set a night ambush on the road from Heho to Shwenyaung.

When Brough and his group reached the road, they found it narrow and twisting as it made its way through the pass in the ridge. Since the road was macadam, however, convoys could move fairly fast. Brough set Bren guns to command a stretch of the road, and almost immediately heard the sound of vehicles laboring up the grade. Four Japanese trucks appeared with their lights on. Brough let them go past the first gun and then opened fire with both. One fired west from a point about ten yards ahead of the convoy, one east from a point about fifteen yards behind its tail. The lead truck crashed into the trees at the side of the road. The second crashed into the tail of the first. The third stopped, burning, and the fourth stalled, its lights continuing to burn. A wounded Japanese soldier slid out of the back of the third truck and, caught in the lights of the last truck, staggered toward the side of the road. One of Brough's Chinese yelled, "Hey, Japani!" and the man stopped and looked. The Chinese soldier cut him down with a burst from his tommy gun, while the rest of the platoon raked the trucks with fire. They rifled the dead Japanese for identification papers and began to pull out, leaving one man to toss a final grenade into the back of each truck. The whole ambush had taken no more than five minutes.

★ ★
Blowing a Bridge

Just after we arrived at the valley, headquarters radioed that the British were concerned about the possibility of a Japanese attack on their flank. They had driven the enemy south from Mandalay and Meiktila, and the major fighting was now between Meiktila and Rangoon. The Japanese, it was feared, might bring forces from Thailand through Taunggyi and Heho for an attack on British supply lines now running through Meiktila. There was also a possibility that the Japanese would mount a raid of some sort from Lawksawk, since they still had a regiment of about two thousand men based there.

Our plans to ambush and harass along the area's roads were exactly what was needed, headquarters said, but first priority should be given to blowing up the bridge where the Shwenyaung-Lawksawk road passed over a deep gorge near Ponywa, five miles north of Taungni. There the Japanese had about three hundred men. If the bridge was knocked out, they would have a hard time reinforcing the Lawksawk garrison for a raid. Even if they didn't try a raid from Lawksawk, taking out the bridge would hamper their efforts to bring the Lawksawk garrison and its artillery down to support the Taunggyi-Heho areas.

The air corps had tried several times to bomb the bridge, but accurate bombing was impossible against a structure nestled so far down in the river canyon. Studying the air photos, Bill and I thought we could blow the bridge and at the same time lay an ambush on the road. I had been thinking a lot about how to make ambushes more effective. This would give us a good opportunity to try out a new idea.

We already had the supplies we needed. They included plasticene, a powerful explosive that could be molded and shaped like clay, dynamite caps, and the plunger, wire, and other equipment needed to set off the charge. We also had a supply of primacord—a new invention that had given me an idea for ambushes. Primacord was a special kind of explosive in the form of rope. We had found it useful for getting rid of trees when we built airstrips. All you had to do was wrap the primacord around the tree, put a dynamite cap on one end, run some wires to a flashlight or the plunger, and *bam!* down the tree would go.

Brough and I took our supplies and two platoons of Karens, each bolstered by a 60-millimeter-mortar squad, to blow the bridge. We brought along all the primacord we had, about two hundred yards, and about a hundred hand grenades. As part

205

of my plan for the ambush, we had unscrewed the detonating mechanism, pin, and spring from each grenade, stuck the end of a three-foot piece of primacord in its place, and taped it down.

We started off well before dawn, slipping and sliding up muddy trails to the edge of the hidden valley, then down to the valley floor below. The bridge was twelve miles away as the crow flies, but about twenty-five on the twisting mountain trails. It took us five hours of forced marching. We reached the bridge between eight and nine in the morning.

The bridge was pretty much as we'd imagined. The road was macadam, barely wide enough for two jeeps to pass, and after three years of war badly in need of repair. It was full of potholes from the torrential rains and, near the bridge, bomb craters, which the Japanese had filled in with dirt and gravel. The ground sloped steeply down the hills on either side for about two hundred yards before it reached the edge of the gorge itself, with the road winding down the slope to the bridge in a lazy S. It was these steeply sloping sides that had hampered the air corps in its bombing. The bridge spanning the gorge was narrow, permitting one-way traffic only. It consisted of four steel I-beams, about seventy-five feet long, laced together with smaller crossbeams. Heavy wooden planks lay across the top of the upper two beams to make the roadway, which was bordered by iron railings.

My first thought was that it was almost exactly like the bridge the guerrillas blow up in *For Whom the Bell Tolls*. For Hemingway's guerrilla band, blowing the bridge is extraordinarily dangerous because an enemy force might appear on the road at any moment. So it was for us. Part of the Japanese force at Lawksawk might unexpectedly be ordered south. Or the commander of the three-hundred-man force at Taungni might decide to send out a fighting patrol to check on the bridge. In either case, our guerrillas would be no match for the Japanese. At best they could delay the Japanese force for a few minutes. Those of us working on the bridge wouldn't have time to get to cover unless the Japanese were exceptionally careless.

We positioned half of the Bren guns, protected by a squad of tommy-gunners, north of the bridge, where they could fire at any troops coming from Lawksawk. The other half we positioned south of the bridge so that they could fire at troops coming from Taungni. We put the two squads of 60-millimeter mortars just over the hill, with observers at the crest to direct the mortar fire at troops coming from either direction.

Then Brough and I took a closer look at the bridge. Almost immediately, Brough discovered a brass plaque saying that the components of the bridge had been manufactured in Newcastle-on-Tyne, his home town. The first thing he did was pry off the plaque and store it in his pack.

Whoever said things are always more difficult than they appear was right. All four beams would have to be severed, and the only way this could be done with the explosives we had was by setting one charge on the western side of each beam and another, slightly offset, on the eastern side. This would provide a scissors effect, throwing the northern half of the bridge to the west and the southern half to the east. It would work only if we wired all eight charges to blow simultaneously. This meant all eight had to be connected, with a dynamite cap in each charge. So it was a good thing we had the plunger; a flashlight battery could set off one dynamite cap, but not eight. Even so, we couldn't be certain that the plunger would generate enough charge. As a backup system, we would also have to connect all eight charges with primacord.

And that was not the end. Even if the charges all blew, and blew simultaneously, they still might not have enough force to cut the beams. We would have to pack each charge down with mud, directing the force of the explosion toward the beam and not in the air.

All this would take a lot longer than we had bargained for. Brough and I would have to climb out on the lower beams to do the work. First, the plasticene, wire, dynamite caps, and primacord would have to be passed down to us from above. Then we would have to place the charges, pack them, set the caps, and wire the whole lot together. Hanging onto beams during the work was an additional handicap. Some of the work could be done while our legs were gripped around a beam. But we would have to stretch to do most of it, holding on with one hand and doing the work with the other. As if this weren't time-consuming enough, the men helping us would have to climb down three hundred feet to the stream bed below and bring mud back up in their Gurkha hats for packing the charges.

As it turned out, the job took us two long hours. It was terrifying to think of being shot at while hanging on these beams attending to the seemingly endless details of setting charges. I can remember cursing Hemingway, whose hero set and blew his bridge in about fifteen minutes.

But when we finally made the last connections and pushed down the plunger, there was the compensation of a marvelous explosion. Debris catapulted into the air and then came raining down over a wide expanse. A couple of huge planks landed only yards away from us. When the last of the debris had landed, we rushed to the brink of the gorge and there at the bottom were the two sections of the severed span, one pointing upstream and one, downstream.

★ ★
The Ambush

We didn't waste time gloating. It was time to set the ambush. The plan was to put it in about a half a mile south. At that point, the road curved around the breast of a hill. The upper side of the road cut into the hill, producing a bank about three feet high that was overgrown with weeds and bushes. Behind this growth and from above, we laid out one hundred yards of primacord. Every three feet we put grenades, hanging them near the edge of the bank under leaves and bushes, and taped the primacord from each to the hundred-yard strip. We taped a dynamite cap to one end of the long strip, ran two wires to an observation post on the hill above, and fastened the two ends to the plunger.

One of the two platoons and both of the mortar squads would man the ambush. We put two Bren guns twenty yards from each end of the primacord and well up on the hill above it. One gun of each pair was aimed at the road the Japanese would be on. The other would rake the road running alongside the primacord. Tommy-gunners were positioned to protect each

208

of the Bren guns, and the mortars were placed on the other side of the hill.

It was now well past noon. Taking the other platoon, Brough and I retraced our steps along the hidden valley trail for about a mile, then stopped to have our first meal since two in the morning. We had slid over mountain trails for five hours. We had labored frantically for two blowing up the bridge. And we had worked just as quickly for another hour setting the ambush. Now we had an hour to rest and eat, then another twenty-five miles to go before getting back to the valley. When we finally returned, we had been gone for over twenty-four hours, pushing our bodies hard the whole time.

Although we didn't know at the time, the next day the Japanese garrison at Lawksawk was ordered to move south to Shwenyaung. The first to depart was a force of at least three battalions of infantry, totaling perhaps a thousand men. They marched down the Lawksawk-Shwenyaung road in a column of twos along the right side of the road. Two scouts led the way, followed a hundred yards behind by an advance guard of around two hundred men. This was in turn was followed by the main body. The column reached the bridge at mid-morning and apparently didn't realize how recently it had been blown. After making their way down one side of the gorge and up the other, they resumed their march in the same formation.

The Karen lieutenant in charge of our ambush let the scouts go by. Then when the advance guard, still in a column of twos and marching not twenty-four inches from the bank, came opposite the line of grenades, he pressed down the plunger.

One hundred grenades blew simultaneously, scything the road with steel fragments for the whole hundred yards. The two Bren guns in front of the primacord raked the melee of wounded Japanese scrambling for cover, and the Bren gun aimed north fired one continuous burst at the head of the main body, which deployed to each side of the road and after a short delay began to return fire. The two mortars opened up from behind the hill on the deploying column to deter it from making a rush, while the platoon fled over and around the hill toward the hidden valley trail.

Some weeks later, the headman of the nearby village of

Ponywa gave us an accounting of the casualties. The Japanese had dragooned his village into lending ox carts to carry the wounded and men to dig graves. The headman didn't know the number of wounded, only that his village had supplied twenty oxcarts to carry them. But he did know the exact number of dead. A Japanese officer had cut off the right thumb of each corpse to be sent back to Japan for cremation, and the bodies had been put in a mass grave. The total was 104.

12

Final Burma Days

The Japanese undoubtedly followed the Karen platoon that sprang the ambush far enough to find the area where we were based. So in keeping with our rule that when in trouble, move deeper behind enemy lines, the next day at first light we moved south again.

We set up headquarters in a central position near the top of a mountain forty-five hundred feet high and about six miles north of the Heho-Shwenyaung road. Then we set ambushes on all the approaches.

By now it was clear that the Japanese in Burma were defeated and had no alternative but to fight rear-guard actions as they slowly retreated to Thailand. The British had pushed the main Japanese forces down to the outskirts of Rangoon, leaving a blocking force on the Meiktila-Heho road. As a result, the Japanese in our area were effectively cut off from their parent force, although their lines to Thailand were still open. They continued active patrolling and raiding to harass the British, but it was clear that they were not capable of a major offensive.

As a consequence, our guerrilla group found itself in a peculiar situation. We were behind the enemy as they faced the British roadblock on the Meiktila-Heho road front. But since the Japanese force had been withdrawn from Lawksawk, the area north of the Heho-Shwenyaung road, where we were operating, was in a kind of no man's land, not behind enemy lines. This made me very uneasy, and I bombarded headquarters with radio messages asking for permission to shift to the area south of the road, in the mountains either east or west of Inle Lake. There, if we got into trouble, we could go south again without

211

having to pass through areas where Japanese troops were operating. After some indecision while headquarters contacted Stilwell's and Mountbatten's commands, we were told that this area had been assigned to Force 136 of the British SOE. We had to alter our tactics. Since we were operating on the flank of the Japanese rather than behind them, we had to be prepared to see our ambushes triggered by much larger fighting patrols than those we were used to when properly behind the Japanese lines. And as we moved about on the trails, we were much more likely to walk into ambushes laid by the Japanese.

★ ★

Alliance with the Burma National Army

Early in the war the Japanese had trained and equipped the Burma National Army, made up of Burmese anticolonialist nationalists. Some of the BNA had fought against the British in the Arakan and at Imphal and Kohima, but in our area they had been used only as guard troops at airfields and supply dumps. The fact that the Japanese had been defeated and that it was only a matter of time until they were driven out of Burma was as obvious to the Burmese as it was to us. So as the Japanese fell back, BNA leaders had contacted the Allies about changing sides. An agreement was reached that BNA units would place themselves under the nearest Allied commander. Headquarters radioed me that a BNA company whose assignment under the Japanese had been to guard the Heho airstrip would be coming to join us—and they had been given our coordinates. With some trepidation, we sent runners to contact the BNA as they marched in our direction. We had no choice but to guide them to where we were.

For both our guerrillas and the command group, the adjustment was strange. We were joined by about a hundred ethnic Burmese wearing Japanese army uniforms with Burmese national markings and armed with Japanese weapons. Their commanding officer was Bo Tha Shwei. Every morning at dawn, he would assemble the company and lead them in calisthenics to Japanese military commands.

No one in our group slept as well as before. The individual BNA soldiers and officers seemed friendly enough, but the Japanese uniforms and drill commands made us nervous. As a test, we decided to send them out on an ambush. They went, they came back a few days later saying that the ambush had been sprung on a Japanese motorized patrol, and that two Japanese had been killed. Our agents confirmed their report. Gradually we came to accept them.

Our battalion now consisted of one Englishman, three Americans, about one hundred and fifty Chinese, another one hundred and fifty Karens, a couple of dozen Kachins and Shans, one Bengali, two Sikhs, and now about one hundred ethnic Burmese in Japanese uniforms. We must have been a strange sight.

★ ★

Visitors

The British finally decided that the time had come for them to start pushing up from Meiktila toward Heho. The mountain pass between Heho and Shwenyaung being the obvious place for the Japanese to make their stand, we decided to go east of the Shwenyaung-Taunggyi road, where we could harass the Japanese supply line. We slipped across the road at night and after a two-day march took up a position east of Hona, in the jungle near the open land north of Taunggyi.

By this time, the story of our ambush had become known outside of Detachment 101, and headquarters radioed asking if we would be willing to have some visitors. Specifically, someone at either Mountbatten's or Stilwell's headquarters saw a political opportunity. It wasn't just the fact that we were still operating behind what was technically enemy lines; our company of Maymyo Karens were the only Karens in the war. They wanted to send in two signal corps photographers to take pictures of the Karens and our operation. Also, a Pulitzer Prize–winning war correspondent named George Weller wanted to come in, by parachute if we couldn't manage to fix up an airstrip. The photographers could come immediately. Weller was in Delhi and wanted to come about a week later. Flattered, we agreed.

The photographers arrived in an L-5 light plane without incident. At first we were pleased to be the focus of attention, but over the next few days they became an obnoxious burden. They complained about the food, about having to sleep on the ground, about having to march so much, and especially about the risk they were running. Within two days they had all the pictures they needed, and they wanted out. We explained that we couldn't waste time finding and preparing an airstrip just for their convenience, and that they would have to wait until we had a prisoner, a wounded man, or a lull in the war. This news brought loud complaints.

★ ★
A P-38 Attack

Our command group, as I said, was in the jungle in the mountains above Hona. A Karen platoon was in an ambush position to the east. Brough and the Chinese company were in the village of Hona, where we had had the skirmish with the foraging patrol, about five miles to the east. They also had an ambush position just south of the village. The strong Japanese force at Taungni, south of where we had blown the bridge, continued to send out fighting patrols in all directions.

In the meantime, headquarters had persuaded the air corps to put a squadron of P-38s at the disposal of Detachment 101. They were at a strip somewhere south of Lashio, and a radio channel was kept open twenty-four hours a day waiting for our calls for an air strike. We were accustomed to supplying the intelligence for bombers, but having a whole squadron of P-38s at our beck and call for close air support was a heady thought. All of us looked for opportunities to call for a strike.

To our delight, Brough contacted me on the walkie-talkie to report that a force of one or two Japanese platoons—at least fifty men—had moved into the village of Nahit, five miles south of Hona. He suggested that this was a perfect opportunity for the P-38s, and I radioed base immediately. The P-38s, they said, would be there within an hour.

Three of the headmen of nearby villages had been conferring with me about supplying agents and coolies, so I invited them to come with me to the ridge overlooking the valley. The opportunity to impress them with the power our guerrillas could wield was too good to miss.

The P-38s arrived right on time. They made magnificent banks and turns, dived, pulled out, and dived again. We could hear the distant explosions. Great columns of smoke rose from the valley below. Unless the Japanese had moved out within that one hour—and they had no reason to—they would be suffering heavy casualties. I was as proud as one of the Burmese peacocks strutting by.

Then I noticed that the columns of smoke seemed to be a little north of where I thought they ought to be. I got out my compass, took a sight on the smoke, and transferred the line to my map. It went five miles north of Nahit, right through the village where Brough and the Chinese were!

I tried to get Brough on the walkie-talkie, with no success. Then I sent runners and readied the rest of the battalion to move out on a rescue mission. We would have to litter Brough's wounded to the north, to a safe light-plane strip.

The runners came back just as we were about to move out. Having witnessed the work of friendly bombers in the past—particularly at Myitkyina—Brough understood the problem of identifying targets when you are traveling three hundred miles an hour. Therefore, as soon as I had confirmed that the P-38s would launch a strike on Nahit, Brough had pulled both the Chinese and the villagers out of Hona and withdrawn them deep into the jungle—where sadly they watched bombs tear up the buildings of that friendly village.

★ ★
Evacuating a Casualty

The bombing attracted Japanese attention. Agents reported fighting patrols of platoon strength coming our way from

Taungni on every trail. One ran into an ambush Brough had set. Another ran into a Karen ambush, and one of the Karens was wounded. I decided that we had better move north. This would force the Japanese patrols to travel farther to find us and thereby increase the number of places we could set ambushes. It would also put us closer to our mountaintop fastness if things got too hot.

We started north immediately, looking for a place to put in an airstrip as we went. All that day we marched and searched in vain. At dusk we came to a place where sunlight reached the ground—that is, a sort of opening in the jungle canopy that permitted brush to grow ten to fifteen feet high. We couldn't risk the noise of dynamiting large trees, but we could cut the brush with our Gurkha *kukris*. The problem was that the field would be perilously short, and because of the tall jungle all around, a plane's approach would have to be very steep. An L-5 definitely could not make it. The rough equivalent of a Piper Cub, the L-5 had a cruising speed of about sixty miles an hour and a landing speed of about thirty-five. It needed a field of at least a hundred yards with a good approach. The only plane that could possibly make this strip would be an L-1—a very light plane, with a wing spread so great in relation to its overall weight that it flew, the pilots said, like a kite. It had a landing speed as low as fifteen miles an hour. Its one flaw was that if it was caught in a crosswind on takeoff or landing, it was likely to float downwind almost sideways.

We radioed base and they said that an L-1 would arrive early the next morning. We cleared the field by torchlight.

The L-1 arrived right on time and touched down with only feet to spare. The pilot was not as discouraged as I thought he would be. He supervised the topping off of several trees on the approach, and said takeoff would be no problem—so long as we helped him with some "special arrangements."

An L-1 could carry three passengers in a pinch. In spite of the short field, the pilot said he would take three. The wounded Karen had first priority. Then we had two sick men and the two signal corps photographers. I thought we could give the sick men a ride on one of the bullock carts we had dragooned to carry extra food and ammunition. I didn't think they were so sick that their lives depended on early treatment, although by a peculiar twist this turned out to be a flawed judgment. The two photographers were growing more and more belligerent in their demands to get out. Thinking an appeal to their sense of responsibility would be the way to handle the problem, I left the decision up to them. If they would agree to let the sick go on the plane, I said, we would guarantee to get the two of them out in no more than a week. They chose to take the plane and let the sick men stay.

Then came the special arrangements. We hand-wrestled the plane over to the extreme edge of the strip until its tail was well into the jungle. Six of our guerrillas held on to the trailing edge of one wing, six held on to the other. Four men held the tail. The pilot revved the engines to full power while the sixteen men restrained it with their heels dug in. After a minute or so the plane began to move in spite of their efforts. The pilot dropped his hand and the men began to push. The L-1 spurted forward, was lazily airborne within a few feet, yawed right and left as it drifted higher, and cleared the trees nicely.

The signal corps photographers had kept saying how grateful they were for having been given a choice and that they would show it by sending us the best collection of pictures we could imagine. We never saw a one.

★ ★

Incident at Pinlaw

We made our way to Pinlaw, a tiny hamlet several miles east of the north-south road in the midst of medium-sized mountains covered with thick jungle. From there we sent out platoons to put ambushes on every trail the Japanese would be likely to use, keeping only fifty men to defend the headquarters.

Positioning the Bren guns for defense in that thick terrain was a problem. There was no way to cut fields of fire short of the monumental task of chopping down the jungle itself. We finally built gun platforms twenty feet up, in the forks of trees, hauling sandbags up bamboo ladders.

The dozen houses of the hamlet were perched on a hillock, from which the underbrush and a number of large trees had

217

been cleared to allow sunlight in. We chose the highest hut for the headquarters group, looking down on the other huts below.

The next morning Brough and I were eating breakfast at a rude table in front of the hut when a .45 pistol went off in the large barracks-like structure below us. We were on our feet and running before the echoes stopped. One of the two sick men left behind so the photographers could go home had committed suicide.

When a Westerner decides to commit suicide with a pistol, he usually puts it to his temple or in his mouth and blows out his brains. But a Karen villager, experienced only with knives, uses a pistol to cut his throat. The soldier had fired at his jugular. The bullet had cut the vein and blood was rhythmically pumping out of the wound in a bright-red fountain. Brough and I lifted the man's head to see if there was anything to be done.

The U.S. Army adopted the .45 pistol in the early 1900s after the Philippine insurrection. Apparently a man shot by the old .38 pistol would often live long enough to kill the person who shot him. In those days the Americans were fighting the Moslem Moros in Mindanao, and a lot of stories circulating in the army about the inadequacies of the .38 were about the Moro *juramentados*, the oath takers. A Moro would take an oath to win himself a place in heaven by going on a killing rampage that would end in his death and take a number of unbelievers with him. In a ritual ceremony his body would be strapped with strips of wet bamboo. As the bamboo strips dried, they would constrict. The combination of religious fanaticism and pain would spur the *juramentado* on to fantastic feats of endurance, inducing a state of killing frenzy much like that of the old Norse berserkers. As the bamboo strips constricted they would also act as tourniquets, so that even if the *juramentado* were wounded he could go on fighting longer than normal.

I remember hearing as a child the story of one *juramentado* whose feat was supposed to have been influential in getting the .38 replaced. One quiet Sunday, he appeared in an American camp on a rampage and tore down the company street killing several soldiers with his three-foot *kris*, a wavy-edged sword. A lieutenant who was one of the army's best pistol shots was cleaning his .38 in his wall tent—about six feet by ten—when he heard the shouts. He loaded his pistol and just as he started for the street, the *juramentado* appeared at the door. The lieutenant emptied his revolver at the man and killed him, but the *juramentado* also killed the lieutenant. All six shots had hit the *juramentado* in the chest, one actually nicking his heart. According to the story, there were twenty-seven *kris* slashes on the lieutenant's body.

In any case, there were enough verified examples of the .38 failing to stop a man for the army to look at alternatives, specifically a pistol with a bullet that, in the words of the army's specifications, "on hitting a man whose bayonet had already pierced your tunic, would lift him up, and throw him back." The heavy .45 bullet, almost as big as a man's thumb, would do just that. A man hit in the hand by a .45 would be spun around and knocked down. I've seen a man with a neat round .45 bullet hole in his forehead, oozing purple, the back of his head entirely gone.

When we lifted up our poor Karen, the hole in the back of his neck was big as your fist, with pieces of his backbone scattered around the edges. He was past even the help of morphine; it took him no more than a few seconds to die.

★ ★
A Karen Bad Hat

The next day one of our agents came in with a report that the Japanese had called in all their regular collaborators to persuade them to serve as agents. They were to fan out over all the trails with the express mission of locating exactly where we were. And the following day the Karens brought in a Karen they had stopped near one of their ambushes. They said he was a notorious bad hat, a collaborator who had taken an active part with the Japanese in the impressment and torture of his own people. Knowing that Brough and I would require independent proof, they brought with them the headman and principal *pongyi* of a village near the main road that had been the victim of Japanese atrocities. Both confirmed that the man was a quisling and that he had been responsible for the death of several Karens.

219

We had another trial. The evidence was overwhelming, and in what seemed to be an Asian custom, the accused man freely admitted his guilt. The sentence was death, to be carried out at dawn the next day. One man in each Karen squad was a regular soldier in the Burma Rifles, as mentioned earlier, and a delegation of these regulars came to us shortly after the trial to request that the execution be carried out in true military style— with the traditional last cigarette, the offer of a blindfold, and a proper coup de grâce. It would be done as they wished, we said.

In the middle of the night, Brough and I were wakened by what was obviously the sound of torture. We investigated and found that the Karens had added their own punishment to the sentence. It was not a pleasant sight, and Brough and I tried to argue against this behavior. After all, the man was to die in a very few hours. The Karens quite coldly made us understand that this man was a Karen, that we British and Americans might have our customs in such cases but that the Karens had theirs. It became clear that we were on the verge of overstepping the bounds of what the Karens—Christians and loyal allies though they were—thought was acceptable behavior.

This was potentially more dangerous than the confrontation with the Chinese lieutenant over the combat boots, and Brough and I had no choice but to retire to our hut. The only thing we could do was to carry out the sentence of death promptly at dawn. It also seemed essential that we not neglect our promise for a proper ritual. We carried out the execution to the letter.

The only incongruous note was the firing squad selected by the Karens themselves. I had assumed they would pick the regular soldiers among them for the job, arm them with sniper's rifles, and go through the traditional drill of presenting arms, aiming, and firing. Instead they arrived at the execution site with a raggle-taggle lot armed with a Bren gun and half a dozen tommy guns. After I had ordered the cease-fire and stepped forward for the coup de grâce—the traditional pistol bullet through the head—two of the tommy gunners fired another burst, as if for emphasis. I was halfway to the ground before I recovered enough to carry out my part of the ritual with what dignity I could manage.

The whole episode is one that I still find distasteful. Brough and I should have known what the Karens would do to one of their own people who had turned traitor. We should have ordered that the sentence be carried out immediately after it had been pronounced.

★ ★

The Japanese Ruse

I decided that we had better get to our mountain fastness as quickly as we could. Reports of heavy Japanese patrolling continued to come in throughout the day. We spent the night at Thamainggon, the village where some weeks earlier we had heard that it was V-E Day.

Then the next morning, just before we started off to continue our flight to the mountain fastness, one of our agents arrived with a report that the large Japanese force at Taungni had pulled out and was headed for Taunggyi. If so, the patrolling and agents hadn't been a concentrated effort to locate us, but a feint to cover their withdrawal. This was a favorite stunt of the outlaws of the American West. After robbing a bank, they would go on a rampage shooting up the whole town. People thought they were going to continue the raid, robbing every store in town, while in fact they were keeping people's heads down to cover their withdrawal.

Over the next few hours other agents came in with the same report. Sheepishly we started south, spending the night not in our mountain fastness but in the village of Kyaukni.

The next day we continued south, ending up in Singyaung, a village at the foot of the mountains that contained our hidden valley and just opposite the bridge we had blown. It was here that we captured the AWOL Japanese soldier in bed with his girl-friend, described in Chapter 9—the one who had been on the patrol to Hona that had butchered a priest and three villagers and at whom I was so enraged that Bill had to stay my hand. He was a superior private of the Third Company, First Battalion, 114th Regiment of the Eighteenth Division, which had been reconstituted after its virtual destruction at Myitkyina. The soldier confirmed that the Japanese were pulling out, at least from Taungni. We sent out a strong patrol and found out that Taungni was, indeed, deserted.

He also confirmed that the enemy had suffered about 140 to 150 casualties in our ambush south of the bridge. The intelligence people at base would be anxious to interrogate him, so it was a high priority to build an airstrip to fly him out. We moved across the road—with relative confidence this time—and approached the village of Nanaw, a little south of Nahit, the village we had tried to have the P-38s bomb, and ten miles north of the Shwenyaung-Taunggyi road. Near the village was a nice, flat, well-drained field that needed to have only two trees blown out of the way to make a strip. The next morning an L-5 arrived to take out the prisoner.

There were exceptions to the rule that Japanese taken prisoner were always eager to talk. Some tried to escape, more often tried to commit suicide. Because he was already disaffected enough to go AWOL, we were afraid this is what our prisoner would do. I remembered a case of attempted suicide from my days as liaison officer with Fourteenth Army. A British officer stopped a jeep that had a badly wounded Japanese officer spreadeagled on the hood, legs, arms, and head tied down. His right leg was shatterted. The British officer was outraged at the idea of treating anyone so severely wounded so badly, enemy or not. The two Gurkha drivers explained that the man had tried to kill himself by ripping off the bandages with his free hands. When they tied him down, he tried to rip them off with his teeth. Our L-5 pilot, who had also heard such stories, was determined not to have a raging Japanese in the cockpit behind him. We wanted to get the prisoner back alive for interrogation, but we could take no chances that he might try to commit suicide by taking the plane and pilot with him. We put him on the floor of the rear cockpit and bound him hand and foot in a kneeling position. Then we put one of our sick men on the seat holding a drawn .45 pistol and instructed him to knock the prisoner out with the barrel at that first sign of resistance and, failing that, to shoot him.

★ ★

George Weller

The L-5 that took the prisoner away had brought in George Weller, war correspondent for the *Chicago Daily News*. Where the signal corps photographers had been a pain, Weller was a delight. He was of the old school of war reporters, tough, bold, and enterprising. He had won a Pulitzer Prize for his reporting in Greece in the early days of World War II. He had finagled his way into taking parachute training, and he had jumped into combat several times with airborne units. He marched with the troops, slept in foxholes, and happily ate K-rations.

Years after the war, Weller was still doing much the same kind of reporting. Once, he was covering some troubles in Afghanistan and the only transportation he could find to take him through the Khyber pass was a local bus crammed with passengers. There wasn't any standing room. So Weller, by this time well into his sixties, rode over the pass on the roof. And unlike our signal corps photographers, he never complained. Or at least never about hardship. He did complain about our capturing a Japanese soldier just when he was about to join us. If the L-5 hadn't had to land, he said, he would have been able to make another parachute jump.

The command group was in another *pongyi kyaung*, and under Weller's friendly and interested questioning we told our war stories hour after hour, drinking local rice beer as we did. About two in the morning all of us—Weller, Brough, Van Arsdale, Arida, Htun, Toh, and I—stepped out on the balcony to relieve ourselves. We were lined up, still talking, when over the trees about a quarter of a mile away arched a silent green signal rocket. It was the Japanese.

We had been following our usual routine of sending out agents and patrols. Our men were in their usual defensive positions. Outposts were in place. Still, the fact that the enemy had been pulling back had bred overconfidence. Somehow a patrol had slipped by our people and was in position not a quarter of a mile from our perimeter. The rocket, we were sure, was a signal to another Japanese patrol. And it might well be the signal to attack.

Cursing myself for permitting the men to slacken off, chagrined and angry that we had come so close to the end of the Burma campaign only to fall into this silly trap, I set about as quietly as possible to wake the troops and ready them for an attack.

But it never came. We stood to for the rest of the night, and at dawn we sent out patrols, cautiously. Later we learned that a Japanese patrol had indeed penetrated our screen of agents and patrols and had scouted out our position. But it had been a small scouting patrol, not a fighting one. Having decided that we were battalion strength, it had quietly withdrawn.

I spent the night in anxious self-recrimination, more tense than if there had been actual fighting. But Weller reveled in it. He was actually disappointed that the Japanese hadn't attacked.

The day after the Japanese patrol probed our position, Brough took the Chinese company east and then south, scouting the northern approaches to Taunggyi. They encountered and exchanged fire with a large Japanese patrol, but both sides withdrew almost immediately. Shortly thereafter, Brough met an entire village on the march. They were Karens who, like our Maymyo Karens, were living outside their native areas in the midst of the Shans. Throughout the war, they had had a bad time at the hands of the Japanese because they were Christian and hence pro-Allied. With the war in Burma winding down, they were afraid the Japanese might take some final vengeance before departing. When Brough returned to Nanaw, he was herding about seventy-five men, women, children, and their animals and ox carts along the trail. We gave them a guide to safer territory in the north and radioed to have some rice dropped to them.

★ ★
Winding Down

In the meantime, the British were slowly advancing up the Meiktila-Heho-Taunggyi road. Headquarters radioed us to start making our way to Lawksawk, which Maddox now occupied. There we would disband and pay off the troops. After the episode with the Japanese patrol, I wasn't going to let our guard down. We followed our usual standard operating procedures.

At the first bivouac, we got a radio message that Brough's commission as a lieutenant in the American army had come through. Some friends at headquarters had included a set of lieutenant's bars in an airdrop that same day. They were badly tarnished, so Van and I used cigarette ashes to polish them up. Then we had a little ceremony. High in the mountains of Burma, this Englishman from Newcastle-on-Tyne swore to uphold the Constitution of the United States and protect it from all enemies foreign and domestic. Bill maintained his allegiance to king and country, but said that he had no misgivings. After all this, he said, he couldn't conceive of there ever being a conflict between England and America. So I swore him in and pinned the shining gold bars on the lapels of his nylon green shirt.

The Chinese troops put on a feast to celebrate. The main course was *jiao zi*, a meat dumpling much like a ravioli. The flour they used was full of gunny-sack fibers, and the meat was water buffalo, tough even after it had been laboriously minced. We sat at tables they had rigged up in an open place in the middle of the perimeter. To make the celebration special, we fired off our last few rounds of the 81-millimeter flares.

After Maddox radioed that the C-47s scheduled to take our men out of Lawksawk would not arrive for several days, we declared the coming Sunday a holiday. We sent to the surrounding villages for rice beer, which duly arrived in three-inch diameter bamboo tubes with hot chili peppers placed over them so the beer wouldn't get watered down when it was carried over a stream. And we scheduled a series of competitive games—a volleyball tournament again, foot races, arm wrestling, and singing contests. Everybody except the men on outpost and perimeter duty got a little drunk.

When we got to Lawksawk, orders were waiting instructing us in the procedure for paying off our troops, which was to be done in prewar silver rupees that headquarters had flown in. British civilian authorities were worried that our men would take their weapons home with them and use them in a future rebellion against British rule. As a consequence, elaborate precautions were to be taken, including field inspections of the men's belongings. Thinking of the heavy weapons and ammunition we had dumped in the jungle not twenty miles from Lawksawk and how easy it would be for out men to make them operational again, Brough and I were amused. But we carried out the orders.

As a way of forestalling trouble when the weapons were taken away, Colonel Peers had sent us a lot of stuff to give to the more deserving of our soldiers as presents. This included a supply of handsome shotguns, which would be useful for hunting birds and the like, but not for revolution. So we had a sentimental ceremony.

One sour note was that because the airfield at Maymyo had been reported as unfit, the C-47s had to shuttle discharged troops to either Myitkyina or Lashio. This was fine for the Chinese, who had been recruited mainly from the area south of Myitkyina, but hell on our Maymyo Karens. Lashio was about a hundred and fifty air miles from Maymyo and well over two hundred on the serpentine mountain roads. I took one of the pilots aside, told him the problem, and said that if he could make it into Maymyo we would load him down with Japanese swords, carbines, and pistols that we had captured along the way. This along with a first-aid box full of Mogok rubies and sapphires for each of his crew. The pilot buzzed the Maymyo strip on his next shuttle run to Myitkyina and reported back that it would be a piece of cake. I never told Colonel Peers.

★ ★

Holiday in India

After the last of our men were dismissed and on their way home, Brough, Van Arsdale, Arida, and I flew to Myitkyina to report to Detachment 101 headquarters, which was in a village outside Myitkyina. I borrowed a jeep and drove out to see where I had been wounded and to look at the temporary cemetery where the Marauders lay, under crosses decorated with their helmets and dog tags. I paused a little longer where McKnight lay buried.

226

A letter was waiting for me from Millie, the nurse at the Twentieth General who had taken care of me when I was wounded. A friend in 101 had kept her informed of my whereabouts, and she knew I had a leave coming. A bunch of nurses and their friends, mainly doctors, had booked all ten rooms in a small hotel at a beach resort on the coast south of Calcutta, and I was invited to join them. It was July. The memory of Calcutta the previous summer was vivid, but headquarters couldn't cut me orders to Darjeeling. So I radioed Millie I would meet them in Calcutta, and then went to the paymaster and drew ten months' back pay, less deductions for war bonds. Lieutenants only made $135 a month, captains just a bit over $200, but that much money would go a long way in India.

We swam, we went on a fishing boat and got seasick, we ate a lot, drank some, played hearts, and tried not to think about what was going to happen next in the war.

I got back to Detachment 101 headquarters at the end of July. Colonel Peers said he hoped that I had had a good time, since I would be departing for China and another job immediately. He sounded glum. Japanese forces in China, Manchuria, and the main Japanese islands appeared to be as strong as ever, and no one doubted their determination to fight to the last man. Peers agreed with the slogan the GIs in the China-Burma-India theater had thought up: The Golden Gate in '48.

13 ★★★★★★★★★★★★★★★★★★★★★★

A POW Rescue Mission

What Peers had in mind for me in China was a short-term liaison job. Two OSS guerrilla groups had begun operations behind enemy lines in the south, where none had been operating before. The Chinese regular army had just begun an offensive, and there had been some failure in coordination that left both the OSS people and the Chinese angry. Peers felt that the situation required someone who had experience in liaison work. I was the only one in the outfit who had any. I was to fly to Kunming immediately, be briefed, and report to Chinese army headquarters without delay.

Peers said the job would last only a few weeks, and I took the opportunity to say that if we had any operations in Manchuria in the future, I hoped he would consider assigning me to one. I had done some checking with the intelligence people. Their information was that all the higher-ranking American officers captured in the Philippines had been taken out of the camp in Taiwan, where they had been sent from Manila, and shipped to camps in and near Mukden in Manchuria. I had received a Red Cross message from my father that had been written in 1944 saying he was a prisoner and in good health. It seemed likely that if he was still alive, he would be in one of the Mukden camps. Peers said that he would not forget my request.

In Kunming the first person I saw was Morris Swadesh, and he spent the evening drumming into my head ten basic sentences in Chinese on which, he said, I could build enough of a vocabulary to get along.

The next day, 4 August, I hitched a ride on a C-47 south and reported to Chinese headquarters. On 6 August the atomic bomb was dropped on Hiroshima. On 9 August another was dropped on Nagasaki. Over the next few days messages were exchanged between Washington and Tokyo. Then on the fifteenth Emperor Hirohito spoke to his nation on radio, announcing Japan's surrender.

Sometime near the end of July General George C. Marshall, seeing that the war might end sooner than expected, became concerned about what local Japanese commanders might do to American prisoners if a sudden surrender created panic. He sent a message to General Albert C. Wedemeyer, who had replaced Stilwell as commander of the Chinese-Burma-India theater, asking for his suggestions.

General Marshall's fear was well founded. A number of local Japanese commanders did butcher American prisoners of war, most notably at Fukuoka, where captured B-29 crew members were tortured and beheaded on three separate occasions, even in the hours immediately following the emperor's broadcast.

Most of the POW camps were over a thousand miles away from any Allied troops. It would take weeks to get a combat force near them. The only hope seemed to be to parachute small teams into each camp, confront local commanders with a demand to release the prisoners, and hope that the audacity of the move and the confusion that would inevitably accompany Japan's fall would do the trick. At least, it would demonstrate that the United States cherished its men and would punish any action to hurt them. This decision to parachute teams into the POW camps had been taken during the period when the atomic bombs were dropped in Hiroshima and Nagasaki. On 11 August, responsibility for developing plans for the rescue missions in China was assigned to Colonel Richard Heppner, head of OSS in China, and his new deputy, Ray Peers.

The OSS intelligence sections assembled data on the location of the camps and on suitable drop zones nearby. The plans called for the teams to take off from an airfield at Hsian,[1] in

---

[1]Hsian, in the Wade-Giles spelling, or Xian, in the pinyin spelling now used in mainland China, was the capital during the Ch'in dynasty (221 BC–207 BC), the first to unify China, and the place from which the name China comes.

north central China, in B-24s equipped with extra gasoline tanks for the long round trip. The OSS station at Hsian was given responsibility for assembling the radios and other equipment the teams would need.

On 15 August I got a radio message from Colonel Peers. I was to fly to Kunming as soon as I could get a plane, take a physical exam to make sure my belly wounds would stand a parachute jump, and then make my way as quickly as possible to Hsian. An OSS team was being assembled to parachute into the Hoten POW camp just outside Mukden, Manchuria. I had been assigned to the mission.

It was a Kafkaesque journey. It began in the dark with a wild jeep ride to the airport during which I kept thinking how ironic it would be to get killed in an accident now that the war was practically over. Then it took me twenty-four hours to find a plane to Kunming. Next came the physical exam, which consisted mostly of strapping me up in a fourteen-inch girdle of medical adhesive tape—just in case, the doctors said.

OSS headquarters also decided that I needed two additional pieces of equipment. One was a medical kit heavily stocked with sulfa pills and morphine syrettes, which a lot of the POWs would probably need. The second was a money belt loaded with gold napoleons, most dating from the 1920s. I might have to buy food and other things for the POWS, and no one knew what attitude the Manchurian Chinese might have toward paper currency. But peasants the world over understood gold. It was so heavy I began to worry what might happen if my parachute landed in a river or lake.

I spent that night trying to sleep on a pile of parachutes at the airport, along with a sergeant assigned to the mission as a photographer. Every time I turned over, the tape would catch and pull out some of the hair on my chest. No planes were going to Hsian, and we had no authority to commandeer one. Finally we caught a plane to Chungking, and after an additional long wait, another from Chungking to Hsian.

I spent the long hours repeating the questions about my father and our relationship. Why had he been a distant parent? How had he come to be the person he was—romantic and sentimental, with a fantasized self-image of the soldier?

★ ★
Mukden and the POW Camp

When the sergeant and I finally arrived in Hsian, we found that the team had left without us. Washington, knowing that Japan's surrender was imminent, had ordered teams to the camps on 16 August. Another B-24 was ready to drop us at Mukden the next day.

The members of my group that had gone ahead were Major James Hennessy, in command; Major Robert Lamar, a doctor trained as a parachutist; Sergeant Edward Starz, a radio operator; Sergeant Harold Leith, a Russian interpreter; Sergeant Fumio Kido, a nisei who would be the Japanese interpreter; and a Chinese nationalist, Major Cheng-shi Wu, who would be the Chinese interpreter. They had been dropped in a vegetable field just outside the gates of a camp at Hoten, on the outskirts of Mukden.

Upon landing, Hennessy, Lamar, Leith, and Kido started for the prison camp about a quarter of a mile away, while Starz and Cheng set to work gathering up the supplies that the B-24 had dropped on its second pass. Hennessy and the men with him were met and taken into custody by a Japanese platoon double-timing toward the drop zone. Starz and Cheng were taken by another platoon coming from the other direction.

The Japanese had heard of the surrender but were not convinced. They stripped the members of the team and forced them to kneel. They were particularly puzzled by the presence of Kido, the Japanese-American. At various times over the next few hours different members of the team were beaten, especially Kido. The Japanese soldiers beat him down to the ground with their rifle butts. Kido braced himself and struggled up to explain that the war was over and that the team had come only to establish contact with the prisoners. Then they beat him down again. Kido must have known when he volunteered for this mission that it was much more dangerous for him as a Japanese-American than for the others. It took extraordinary courage.

Finally an officer arrived on horseback and the team was taken to Japanese military police headquarters. They were no longer mistreated. The next day they went to the prison camp to see its commanding officer, but they weren't allowed to talk with the prisoners. That night the Japanese installed the team in the Yamato Hotel, the best hotel in Mukden, but kept them under guard. The guards were there to protect them, not to imprison them, they were told. The following day they returned to the prison camp, still under guard, where they were allowed to tell the prisoners that the war had ended.

The next day, a group of Russian officers flew in to Mukden to discuss the Japanese surrender. While the negotiations were going on, one of their staff officers went to the prison camp with half a dozen soldiers and ordered the Japanese guards to turn over command of the camp to the Americans, along with their weapons. The OSS team, still in the Yamato Hotel, established radio contact with Hsian.

It was at this time that our B-24 arrived over Mukden. B-24s had dropped supplies twice since the team had been delivered, but no American planes had yet landed. The plan was for the sergeant and me to parachute into the vegetable field outside the gates of the Hoten camp. The OSS team had radioed that there was one camp on the outskirts of Mukden, and three other camps each about a hundred miles away. General Wainwright was at one of these distant camps. The team had passed a message to the Hoten camp that I was coming to find my father, but so far there was no information about him.

As we were readying ourselves to jump, the pilot called me forward. There was a Russian plane on the airfield outside Mukden. He said that he and the crew would be willing to land at the strip and wait until I found out if my father was at Mukden or some other camp. If it was some other camp, they would take me to it. It was extraordinarily generous of them, and I was very grateful.[2]

In the waiting room under the control tower, a Russian general with two aides was conferring with a Japanese general. I interrupted to tell them my story. One of the Russian aides, a

---

[2]As it turned out, the pilot and crew paid a high price for their generosity. Uneasy about the presence of Americans, the Russians slashed the tires on their plane, and it took about two weeks for them to get replacements.

female major, spoke English. The Japanese general said that the OSS team was at the Yamato Hotel, and surprisingly he offered me his limousine and driver.

When I arrived at the Yamato Hotel the OSS team was on the steps preparing to depart for the prison camp. They were astonished to see an American OSS captain climb out of a long black limousine that was flying the three-star flag of a Japanese lieutenant general. I offered the team a ride and we all arrived at the prison camp together.

When we got to the gates of the camp, I asked an American POW on guard if he knew a Colonel Hilsman. He did, and he pointed out the barracks where I could find him. Once in the barracks, I saw him from across the room, sitting on his bunk. My father was a small man, five feet six at the most, and he had never weighed more than 140 pounds. Now he was no more than 100. When I had last seen him, his hair was salt and pepper. Now it was white as snow. But when I called to him, he stood up, smiled, and started walking toward me.

★ ★
My Father's Story

During the early days of August, my father and his fellow prisoners had noticed that the Japanese guards were tense. They deduced that something important was happening. Rumors were flying about a German surrender, about an American invasion of the Philippines, and about an attack being mounted on Japan. Many of the prisoners assumed that they would suddenly and without warning be moved to some other camp, as they had been moved from Taiwan. Most packed their few possessions to make sure that they would not be left behind. But the Japanese told them nothing, not even on 15 August when the emperor broadcast his surrender message.

On 16 August they saw some parachutes fall in the nearby field, but they had no idea who the parachutists were. When the six members of the OSS team were brought to the camp a few prisoners caught a glimpse of them. My father's diary records that the men were wearing green shirts and trousers made of some unfamiliar material, and leather boots that came halfway up their calves. He was disappointed; if they had been Americans, he wrote, he would have recognized their uniforms and equipment.

Japanese guards continued their watch in the guard towers, but none came near the prisoners. It was not until the next day that they were told the war was over. The OSS team appeared before the assembled prisoners and gave them the bare facts about the end of the war. Judging from my father's diary entry, an even more important event for the prisoners was that the Japanese guards then distributed most of the remaining Red Cross supplies that were ordinarily doled out bit by bit. They also gave the prisoners mail that had been denied them for weeks and perhaps months.

Wild rumors circulated among the prisoners about what would happen next, including one that American combat troops were marching to Mukden from the sea.

The next day the Russian staff officer appeared and ordered the Japanese to turn over their weapons and command to the American POWs. The Americans immediately marched their former guards to nearby vegetable fields to dig potatoes for the camp kitchen.

It was the next day, 23 August, just before I arrived in the camp myself that my father was given the radio message that I was trying to find him.

★ ★

The Meeting

As my father started toward me, I rushed to meet him. We embraced, but things seemed anticlimactic. I asked him how he was. He asked me how I was. I said I wanted to thank him again for the present he had given me when he came to visit at West Point before going overseas. He said he had always been a little ashamed that an aluminum cigarette case was his only farewell gift—he just had not had time to do any shopping. So I showed

235

him the case and the bullet hole and told him how it had saved my life. He was clearly pleased.

Then with almost childlike curiosity he examined my uniform and equipment. My shirt and trousers were jungle green nylon and he kept reaching out to finger the material. Compared to the flat dishpan helmets of World War I that he knew, my helmet must have looked as if it belonged to a man from Mars. And I was carrying an officer's carbine, a weapon that had not been invented at the time he surrendered. The only equipment he recognized was my .45 pistol and my canteen. He had particular difficulty grasping the size of the war and how huge the American war effort had been. When he surrendered, the U.S. Army numbered fourteen thousand officers and perhaps a half a million men. That America's armed services now numbered well over a million officers and twelve million men amazed him. "Son," he said, "I'm very glad to see you. And I'm grateful that you came. But it's been a terrible three and a half years. What," he went on hesitantly, "took you so long?"

14

★ ★

Encounter with the Soviets

The POW barracks were two-story brick buildings that must have been built as Japanese army barracks. From the outside, they looked like the barracks in old American army posts like Fort Leavenworth in Kansas or Fort McNair in Washington, D.C. Inside, however, they were quite different, very Japanese. Each floor had a long open hallway that ran down the long side of the building, higher than an American would expect and much wider, probably to provide space for indoor drills in bad weather. Off this central hallway on each side were what might be described as open bays. Extending the length of each bay was a sort of well, about two feet below the central hallway and six feet wide. In the middle of the well was a large coal stove for heat in the winter. Some traditional Japanese restaurants have a similar arrangement, each table set over a circular well in the floor where glowing charcoal is kept in small metal canisters.

In each of the bays and on the same level as the hallway were a series of posts supporting a sort of balcony, which may have been temporary, with ladders going up to it. Along the partitions between bays, on both floor and balcony level, the POWs had their bedrolls or—for the few who were either lucky or good traders—cots. The men on the lower level had less climbing up and down to do, but dust and dirt falling through the cracks from the top level were an annoyance. My father's bedroll was on the lower level. He had spent a lot of the idle hours stuffing paper in the cracks above it.

At mealtime, details of two or three POWs would bring food from the main kitchen in large canisters to each of the bays. In the winter, when the stove was burning, the canisters could

237

be kept warm, and throughout the day the men could heat water in their canteen cups for tea. In any case, each man's portion would be dipped out into his mess kit, and the men would eat sitting on the lower level, their feet dangling in the well.

The toilet facilities were in an adjacent building, connected by a corridor. The latrines consisted of holes in the floor over a ditch, through which water was occasionally flushed from some central location. The flushing was so occasional that the stench was overpowering.

I spent the first night with my father in the camp, improvising a bedroll out of my emergency parachute. I wasn't allowed to go to sleep until every POW on the floor had inspected my camouflaged nylon, which they had never seen. The lights were kept on in the central hallway, and all night long a stream of POWs afflicted with dysentery or just plain restlessness trooped back and forth to the latrines. The traffic made sleep difficult, but even worse were the fleas. The barracks were swarming with them. They jumped all over you, pelting your face so steadily that it felt like a gentle rain. They also bit. Filial piety can ask only so much. As a member of the OSS team, I was entitled to a room with a bath at the Yamato Hotel, and the next day I moved.

★ ★
Treatment of the POWs

After having listened to wartime propaganda for three and a half years, we were surprised to find the POWs better housed, better fed, and better treated than any of us had expected. They were also in remarkably good condition. My father was particularly so. His slight, wiry build was probably one reason for his good health. He didn't require as much food as a large man. Another reason was his will power and self-discipline. One of his best friends among the POWs was a doctor, and my father followed his advice to the letter. On the ship that transported his group from Taiwan to Manchuria, they had had less food than in any other period of the war. Before the voyage was half over they were frantic with hunger. The ship had been used to carry sugar, and there was sugar in every nook and cranny of the hold. The doctor told them to eat no more than one handful of this a day. My father followed his instructions to the letter, but many of the POWs didn't, and some even gorged themselves on sugar. The result was terrible, dehydrating diarrhea. Many died.

Another reason my father was in better condition than most was probably the fact that, although he was only in his mid-fifties, he had a full head of snow-white hair. Age is respected in Asia, and this seems to have affected the way the Japanese guards treated him. Some officers my father's age who were bald were beaten. My father never was. On the contrary, he had been treated kindly and with respect by Colonel Ota, to whom he surrendered, and at least decently throughout the rest of the war.

We found a small group of American civilians in Mukden, interned in the compound of what had been the U.S. consulate. They, too, had been treated correctly. They had been permitted to make arrangements with civilian shops to deliver food and other necessities to the compound, and for doctors to visit them. The only thing they had been denied was new civilian clothing. As their clothes wore out, the Japanese supplied them with what must have been captured British army pajamas and hospital bathrobes, heavy winter ones. The compound looked like a British military hospital with lots of patients but no doctors or nurses.

After seeing the camp and condition of the POWs, I came to the conclusion that the Japanese had not behaved anywhere near as badly as Allied propaganda would have it. Surrendering to any army is a risky business. In the heat of battle, soldiers of every race and nationality expect a trick and tend to shoot at any sudden movement. Also, after a battle soldiers are keyed up and angry, having seen their friends killed and maimed. For several days anger can flare up over slight provocations. The captors may feel that they are too shorthanded to take men from the battle line and escort prisoners to the rear—that escorting prisoners puts their own people too much at risk. But a deliberate decision to kill prisoners rather than spare the men to escort them to the rear rarely happens at levels higher than the squad or platoon, where relationships are close and emotional.[1]

Of course, on occasion the Japanese acted in a manner that can only be described as barbaric. The Bataan death march was indeed a death march. The risk of taking fellow soldiers from the battle line cannot explain the way the Japanese behaved toward their prisoners. Neither can Japanese behavior be explained by the fact that surrendering is tricky, dangerous, and tied up with emotions generated by the heat of battle. In the Bataan death march the beatings and shootings of unarmed POWs went on too steadily for too long a time.

Although none of the POWs in the Hoten camp at Mukden or the nearby camps were involved and we in the OSS POW rescue mission heard nothing about it, evidence was brought out after the war that not far from Mukden the Japanese maintained a secret experimental station for biological warfare where they conducted experiments on prisoners of war.[2]

What is particularly difficult to understand are the incidents of deliberate torture and execution of POWs, as at Fukuoka. One is tempted to ascribe such incidents to cultural differences—that a nation's attitude toward its own soldiers who surrender affects its attitudes toward enemy soldiers who surrender. The Japanese resisted capture with fanatic zeal, and their attitude toward surrendering must have made them less considerate of enemy soldiers who surrendered.

But then one has to remember that German actions could be equally barbaric. Take, for example, the massacre by Waffen SS troops of over a hundred Americans who surrendered at Malmedy in the Battle of the Bulge. The motive for this seems to have been ideological, in some way related to the self-image of the SS illustrated by its death's head insignia. And though German POW camps in which Americans and Britishers were

---

[1]At My Lai during the Vietnam War, an American lieutenant killed a substantial number of unarmed civilians during a sweep of a village suspected of being hostile. However, since the lieutenant's unit was not under fire at the time, his behavior cannot be explained as concern about taking men away from the battle. To many veterans the only explanation of the lieutenant's behavior is that he suffered from an extreme form of xenophobia.

[2]See Peter Williams and David Wallace, *Unit 731, Japan's Secret Biological Warfare in World War II* (New York: The Free Press, 1989).

kept in general conformed to the standards of the Geneva conventions, camps for Russians did not, and there were a number of incidents in which the Germans treated Russian POWs as badly as the Japanese treated Americans on the Bataan death march. Finally, of course, there were the Nazi death camps, which make anything the Japanese did pale in comparison. Over six million Jews were killed in the camps and another six million gypsies, Slavs, and others.

I have been told, although I cannot verify the information, that of American POWs in World War II about 1 percent died in German camps during captivity, and about 40 percent in Japanese camps. These statistics are questionable. Many of the Americans POWs who died in Japanese hands were on ships that were sunk by American submarines.

★ ★
An Airdrop by B-29s

Though conditions at the Hoten camp were much better than we had expected, food was short. One of the first things the OSS team did was to radio for an airdrop of food and medicines. The problem was that the workhorse C-47s couldn't make the round trip to Mukden, no matter how many extra gasoline tanks were installed in them, and there were only two or three B-24s that had extra tanks. The latter made some drops. Someone who must have had no experience whatsoever with drops ordered one made by B-29s, the big Flying Fortresses. Either the planes couldn't fly slow enough or the pilots didn't understand the need to slow down, but in any case the B-29 drops were a disaster. When those of us in the OSS team who had had experience with airdrops saw the B-29s and realized they were going to drop supplies, we tried to get the POWs under cover. Our fears were justified. The drops were apparently aimed not for the vegetable field but for the camp itself. And almost all the parachutes burst their panels. Cases of number-ten cans of food came crashing through the roofs of the barracks, even demolishing one of the Japanese staff cars. Canned tomatoes made up a large part of the delivery, and at first glance the smashed tomatoes looked a lot like blood. It took us half an hour to determine that none of the POWs had been hit.

Before the air drops, in fact the day after I arrived, we commandeered a Japanese army truck and set out to find a village that was interested in gold napoleons. Only a few miles out of the city, villages were plentiful. and they seemed prosperous. But despite our assumption that gold broke all cultural barriers, these Chinese villagers were not at all interested in napoleons. After more than an hour of arguing, they agreed to take about a thousand dollars' worth of napoleons for about two hundred dollars' worth of food. But we were glad for the exchange. We bought a full truckload of fresh vegetables, enough to keep the whole camp supplied for two or three days. It had been a long time since the POWs had seen fresh vegetables. In addition, we bought pigs, chickens, and enough eggs to give each man in the camp at least one.

Next we took the truck to a Japanese army supply dump and loaded it with canned goods, especially milk.

Once the OSS team got the camp well stocked with food, the next highest priority turned out to be dental equipment. There were two army dentists among the POWs, but they had had almost no equipment, medicine, or dental tools to work with, and the POWs' teeth were in very bad shape. We made a tour of Japanese army hospitals in the Mukden area and carted away two dental chairs, medicine, and samples of every dental tool we could find.

★ ★

American Arrogance

As members of the OSS team, we had both the right and the duty to see that POWs got the things that they needed and had been denied. Looking back, what I am ashamed to admit is that in taking them, we were arrogant and contemptuous. When we arrived at a supply dump or one of the hospitals, we didn't just tell the Japanese what we needed; we lined officers up at gunpoint and made our demands by needlessly brandishing our weapons. And we confiscated their samurai swords for souvenirs.

The fact that they let us get away with it testifies to the discipline of the Japanese people and their obedience to the emperor. On one occasion, a young Japanese lieutenant came close to not letting us get away with it. A Japanese division with all their arms and equipment was coming down the road to Mukden to surrender to the Soviets. Some of us on the OSS team were going out of town on an errand in the opposite direction. There was a tie-up, and we got out of the jeep and ordered a couple of Japanese trucks to make way so we could proceed. The lieutenant was sprawled on top of the load in one of the trucks. He made a vulgar, disapproving gesture. We drew our weapons and ordered him to climb down off the truck. He, too, was armed, and I realized then that he was debating whether or not to obey. I wondered what we four high and mighty victors might do if he resisted. Would we fire? If we fired, what would the rest of the Japanese division do? Four men standing there with drawn weapons facing fifteen thousand?

★ ★
Waiting for Evacuation

At the Yamato Hotel, the OSS team lived on ten-in-one rations brought in by the B-24s. My father and Ed Mason, who had been his adjutant on the island of Negros, would come to the hotel for meals as often as they could, and I was surprised not only at how much they ate but at the fact that they were so undiscriminating. Here was my father—who had been so picky about his food that my mother in despair had finally fallen back on a standard menu of steak, chops, or roast beef; potatoes or rice; and a green vegetable—eating anything he could lay his hands on. He particularly relished a concoction of canned milk, fresh eggs, and cocoa. Before prison camp, he would have found such a drink nauseating.

There were not enough B-24s to carry all the POWs to Hsian, so the bulk of them were to go by train to Port Arthur,

243

whence the navy would take them to Okinawa for flights home. General Wainwright, who had arrived from one of the outer camps, flew out on a B-24 in time to take part in the formal surrender ceremonies aboard the battleship *Missouri*. The sick were also flown out, first to Hsian, then Kunming, and then Manila, where first-rate hospital facilities were available. Others more fit were flown to hospitals in the States. Officers who had commanded islands or large units, along with one or two of their former staff officers, flew to Manila so they could be debriefed on matters such as claims arising from the fall of the Philippines. Since my father and Ed Mason were scheduled to fly to Manila anyway, it was easy for OSS to arrange for me to go with them—if they were willing to wait until my assignment was completed. They were, so OSS cut me orders to accompany my father all the way to San Francisco. A point system determined when you were rotated back to the United States, and I had accumulated enough to have been sent back weeks before, at the end of the Burma campaign, but it took time to push the paperwork through.

★ ★
Encounter with the Soviets

These arrangements took about three weeks. In the meantime, we continued to buy food from the Chinese villagers and to commandeer it from Japanese supply dumps. We went on a couple of shopping expeditions to bargain for presents to bring back to the United States and once to have our pictures taken by a Chinese photographer working with glass plates. We also spent our time watching the POWs stuff themselves.

In the days following my landing at the airfield and meeting the Russian and Japanese generals, a few more Russians also came in by air. But the main body marched down from Siberia through Harbin and then down to Mukden. The center of the modern city of Mukden was a park, circled by a road with other roads coming into it like the spokes of a wheel. One day we heard the tramp of troops marching and rushed out to the balcony fronting our rooms. Down one of the roads from the north we could see a column of troops. As they neared the circle, they straightened ranks, and began to sing their famous World War II song—"Meadowlands." It was an impressive—and touching—moment. We fell silent with the warm thoughts of their brave stand at Leningrad, Stalingrad, and the outskirts of Moscow and of their long fight, yard by yard, to reclaim their country and defeat the Nazis.

But our euphoria did not last. For the first few days we could not go anywhere without Russian soldiers hugging us, pounding us on the back, and insisting that we share a drink of vodka. But then orders must have come from Moscow. In addition to watching the POWs gorge themselves, we also watched the Soviets systematically loot Manchuria.

Being trained to gather intelligence, the OSS team realized the importance of reporting what the Soviets were doing. We understood that the Yalta and Teheran agreements specified that Manchuria and its industrial potential, which were essential to China's recovery from the devastation of war, belonged to China. If this was correct, then the Soviets were violating the accords. First, the contents of Japanese warehouses—civilian and commercial as well as military—were loaded on freight trains and dispatched to the Soviet Union. When that was done, the Soviets went into factories, unbolted the machinery, and shipped it north as well. The OSS team reported all this to headquarters, and in return got orders to make photographing and reporting on Soviet activities our first priority after taking care of the POWs.

The Soviets gradually became aware of what the OSS team was doing. We had expected them to notice, and not to like it. But we didn't know what kind of reaction they would have until an incident in a Japanese restaurant.

My father had come to the hotel for lunch that day, but he was not feeling well and decided to go back to camp early. Three of us on the OSS team and one of the civilian internees, dressed in his British pajamas, decided to go to a Japanese restaurant for a change. We were tired of ten-in-one rations. We had reservations made for a private room at what the hotel said was the best Japanese restaurant in town. Not only was the food good, but it was also served by a staff of geishas, who would entertain us with song and dance.

The private room was on the second floor of the restaurant. The ground floor was crowded with Russian soldiers, drunk and happy. As we filed through the lobby on our way upstairs they cheered us—three Americans and, they thought, because of the British pajamas, one Englishman.

The meal was exactly as advertised, delicate Japanese dishes served by doll-like girls with rice powder on their faces. They took turns playing some sort of stringed instrument and singing songs. Between the language barrier and their custom of dissolving into semi-hysterical tittering behind their fans at any attempt at a jest, conversation with them was almost impossible. But we were enjoying ourselves.

At one point an argument broke out among the Russian soldiers on the floor below. The shouting got louder but the voices grew fewer, until we could hear only two. Then everything went quiet except for one voice, loud and strident. This voice declaimed something, and punctuated the declamation with a pistol shot. The shot was fired in the air, but it went right through the floor beside us and out the ceiling. Another declamation and another shot. A third declamation and still another shot. By this time we were all huddled together on the floor along the walls trying to guess where the floor beams might be thick enough to stop a bullet.

We heard new voices, some harsh commands, and things got quiet again. Shortly after we returned to our meal the door burst open. A Soviet sergeant and two soldiers jumped into the room, tommy guns leveled and pointing toward us. They gestured for us to raise our hands.

Over the next few minutes we tried to argue with the sergeant, to explain that we were Americans and their Allies. But he would have none of it. The man was very drunk. He slung his tommy gun, directing the others to keep theirs pointed at us, and proceeded to take our pistols, our watches, and our wallets.

Then, demonstrating that he had understood at least some of what we had been trying to say, he launched into a tirade against the three of us who were OSS men. Truman and Americansky, or words to that effect, were prominent and accompanied with several vivid and vulgar gestures of disapproval. He then turned to the civilian internee in his British pajamas and launched into another tirade with gestures just as vulgar. We caught the name Atlee, which showed the sergeant was up to date, since Churchill had been ousted in the election following V-E Day.

The sergeant then unslung his tommy gun and prodded us down the stairs and into the lobby.

I began to worry. By this time it was obvious that the sergeant was in fact commanding a military police detail that had come to the restaurant in response to the shots. He was drunk on duty, a felony in anyone's army. He had also robbed Allied officers at gunpoint. It appeared to be dawning on him that what he had done was serious. If he took us to military police headquarters, all would be well for us, but maybe not for him. Suppose he decided to solve his problem by getting rid of us instead? It would be all too easy to take us out to the alley behind the restaurant, shoot us, and claim that we had tried to escape on the way to the station.

As we were prodded through the lobby, I tried to find someone who spoke English, German, or French. A Russian captain responded to my pleas by saying that he understood German. Bad as my German was, it was not difficult to get him to understand that we were on an official U.S. mission, sent to Mukden to help American POWs. I also lied a little. These Soviet troops had been transferred from the German front, so I said that I, too, had spent most of the war in Europe, fighting Germans, and that I couldn't understand why our Soviet *Kamaraden* had turned against us. The captain intervened with the sergeant. They argued. Finally, the sergeant asserted his authority as patrol leader. The Russian captain looked at me with a sad expression, and shrugged his shoulders as if to say that he had done his best.

The sergeant took us outside, then around the house to the alley in the rear. It was a Chinese alley, no more than six feet wide, with high wooden fences on each side. There was no way to escape that narrow shooting gallery. I said to the others in as flat a voice as I could manage that if the sergeant started shooting, we should try to run for it.

247

It was one of the longest walks of my life. But nothing happened. Once we reached the end of the alley and rounded the corner into the street, we headed for the hotel in a very fast walk. The next day we warned the other members of the OSS team not to go out at night and passed similar word to the POWs.

★ ★
Soviet Harassment

The next morning all of us on the OSS team, including the Russian speaker, presented ourselves at Soviet army headquarters to protest. As we entered the building, a guard stepped forward and threatened us away with a tommy gun. It was the same sergeant, sober but no less hostile.

Broad daylight made a difference. We brushed past him and asked the aides outside the office of the commanding general, who knew us, for an appointment. We only had to wait ten minutes before being ushered in.

With the general was the English-speaking Russian who had interpreted for me at the airport when I first arrived. We told our story, and she translated. When we had finished the general said that if we could identify the sergeant, he would be tried and punished. We said that he was on guard right outside the general's office. "Good," said the general. "He'll be arrested, tried, and—if proven guilty—executed."

We would have been content with less drastic punishment, but the general said that a crime against "our gallant American Allies deserved only the most severe penalty."

The sergeant was arrested, and there followed a trial that, though strange, was conducted under rules of law. A Soviet officer, some sort of political commissar, was judge. He and another English-speaking woman, who took notes as well as translated, sat at a table in the room. The accusers and the accused, under guard, waited on benches in the hallway outside. Each witness appeared alone, told his story privately, and was dismissed. Finally the accused was called in. A few minutes later he

248

came out with his guard and the two of them left. About fifteen minutes after that they returned carrying our pistols, watches, and money. The wristwatches were lacking bands and the pistols had been fired, but none of the money was missing.

After a word or two with these men, we four Americans went back to the commanding general's office to make a plea for clemency. The general saw us immediately. We explained that our belongings had been returned and that we hoped the sergeant's punishment would not be too harsh. The honor of the Red Army was at stake, the general said. The sentence was death, and it would be carried out the next morning. He dismissed our arguments impatiently.

Next morning when I left the hotel room I found the convicted sergeant in the hall outside. He shoved me against the wall with the point of his tommy gun and grinned. For the next few days, he stood regular guard duty outside our doors. The Soviets obviously wanted us to know that they hadn't punished the sergeant after all and that they didn't give a damn that he had robbed us. After I got back to OSS headquarters in Washington, D.C., I learned that OSS teams had had similar experiences with the Soviets in Europe and elsewhere.

Why did the Soviets embark on this policy of harassing OSS POW rescue teams worldwide? One motive probably was to intimidate us into staying close to the prison camps, so that we would not see that they were systematically looting the country and eliminating non-Communist political parties. But I think it also had to do with relations between the Soviets and the Allies at the very highest levels. The Allies hoped for democratic regimes in all the Eastern European countries and thought they had Stalin's agreement for free and fair elections. Stalin, for his part, wanted a belt of countries ruled by Communist parties that would be responsive to Soviet desires. Roosevelt believed that the League of Nations had failed to keep the peace between the wars because the smaller countries followed their narrow interests. The cure, Roosevelt thought, was the UN Security Council, which would give more power to the Great Powers. These, he hoped, would have a larger sense of responsibility to the peace of the world as a whole. In the summit conference at Teheran, Yalta, and Potsdam, the Soviet *nyet* became a familiar refrain. The cold war was beginning, the word was going out from Moscow, and we small OSS teams were among the first lower-level Americans to be in daily contact with the Soviets and so the first to feel the hostility.

. Soviet harassment increased over the next few days. Soviet patrols that encountered Americans would push them around. Twice, vehicles carrying Americans were run off the road by Soviet vehicles.

One night, just when we were about to go to bed, a Soviet patrol banged on our doors with their submachine guns. A Soviet delegation was coming in from Moscow, they said, and they needed our hotel rooms. We had fifteen minutes to vacate. They would take us to another hotel where they had made arrangements for us. We hotfooted it over to Soviet headquarters; the general was busy but his staff was obliging. Take an hour to vacate, they said.

The hotel they had booked was a third-rate one in the Japanese style, with sleeping mats and only one bathroom on each floor. Several times during the night Soviet patrols banged on our doors. "Just checking," they said. The next morning we decided that the better part of wisdom was to move out to the prison camp and stay there until the time came for our departure.

The city was also becoming dangerous for another reason. The basic population of Mukden is Chinese, but at the time most of the large stores were owned by Japanese. Each night Chinese would attack and loot a few of the Japanese-owned stores, the Soviets apparently making no effort to stop them. Some Russian soldiers even joined in. In the atmosphere of drinking and general carousing, fights frequently broke out between Russians and Chinese.

There was a fairly large number of rapes. When we left, a smaller OSS team arrived with the ostensible task of graves registration. Later I talked to one of the members of the team. He had witnessed a bizarre incident from his hotel window. A Chinese wedding party of about seventy-five people was wending its way along the street, with the bride in an enclosed sedan chair. The procession passed two drunken Russian soldiers who thought it a great joke to open the door to the sedan chair, perhaps with the intention of kissing the bride or to drink to her health. But the Chinese in the procession thought their intention was rape. They closed in on the two soldiers, who in turn opened fire with their tommy guns. When the melee cleared, a dozen Chinese wounded were being helped away by friends, five or six Chinese lay dead, and so did the two Russians, whom the Chinese had killed with their bare hands.

★ ★
Going Home

The Soviets finally got together a train to take the Hoten camp's American POWs to Mukden. Later, I heard that navy ships carrying the POWs were caught in a typhoon. The men had a rough passage to Okinawa, where they were put on planes for the United States. Most of them got home two or three weeks before my father and I did. One never made it at all. He was aboard an aircraft carrier that hit a loose mine during the storm. Damage to the ship was minor, but he was killed.

Those of us in the OSS team and a few other POWs whose circumstances were special saw them off on the train and went immediately to the airport. A B-24 flew us to Kunming, where we were debriefed on the Soviet takeover of Mukden. Then we continued on to Manila.

The huge plaza on Manila Bay, which had the Manila Hotel on one side and the Army and Navy Club on the other, was about the same as I had remembered it. So was what used to be called Dewey Boulevard, running along the shore of the bay from the Army and Navy Club. But the rest of Manila was a shambles. The city had been bombed and also fought for block by block with artillery fire. My family had lived in an apartment in a two-story, U-shaped building. I tried to find it, and I passed it six times before I realized that all that was left was one ground-floor apartment now temporarily roofed with tin.

Dealing with various claims, confirming the services that various Filipinos had performed, and certifying to the military service of others kept my father and Ed Mason occupied for a whole week. Then we caught a plane to San Francisco.

251

After I arrived at the POW camp, my father's attitude toward me began to change. Where before he used to say that someone he did not approve of "had no more idea of what is going on in the world than—than—young Roger Jr. here," now he would ask my opinion of what was happening in the world. Even when he was confronted with some personal decision, he would now turn to me for advice. As I saw his attitude change, some of the puzzlement that had hung over me during the war cleared up. I had managed to pass all the tests that my father would have set for himself. I had survived the battle of Myitkyina, been wounded, and returned to combat. I had commanded troops in battle. Not only that, the troops had been a battalion of guerrillas operating behind enemy's lines. And despite the odds, I had been on the POW rescue team that found his camp. He could longer think of me except as an equal.

I asked myself again why I had volunteered for Merrill's Marauders, a near-suicidal mission. Why I had sought a combat role after getting wounded. Why I had sought out the POW rescue mission to Mukden. The conclusion now seemed obvious. My behavior was compulsive. As a child I had fought my father to free myself from his domination. Since adulthood, I had been trying to free myself of the guilt of that rebellion and to win his respect. Now I was free from domination and free of guilt. I was also free to love him.

My mother met us at the airport in San Francisco along with my father's older sister and her daughter. It was a joyous reunion, but what stands out in my memory is my father's sister. She had been an extraordinary beauty when young, and she was self-centered. She talked steadily the whole ride from the airport to the hotel about the hardships of the war for the people at home, complaining about the rationing, the shortages, the lack of services, and so on and on. The rest of us fell silent. Finally her daughter said, "Please, Mother, these people have been through a war." She was right about that.

EPILOGUE I ★★★★★★★★★★★★★★
Burma Lessons for Vietnam

I never dreamed that my experiences as an American guerrilla leader would have any relevance to my future life and career. But I was profoundly wrong. When John F. Kennedy was elected president in 1960 he appointed me director of the State Department's Bureau of Intelligence and Research, and later I replaced W. Averell Harriman as assistant secretary of state for Far Eastern affairs, a position I held through the first few months of the Johnson administration. Both jobs carried major responsibility for policy toward Vietnam, to which my guerrilla experiences seemed obviously to apply. But for that story to make sense, some background on the intervening years is necessary.

★★★★★★★★★★★★★★★★★★★★★★★★
OSS Headquarters

My first assignment after the war was at OSS headquarters in Washington, D.C. Half of the people in OSS at the time were returning to civilian life. As people departed, those who remained were given greater and greater responsibility, floating to the top like corks. Since I was a regular officer and so slated to remain, I became one of the corks, principally as special assistant to the chief of Far East operations.

Some of our work consisted of winding down overseas operations or continuing those that were still needed, principally in China. Most of it, however, was taken up with the struggle to establish a peacetime secret intelligence service. I first became involved with a mission to preserve the capacity OSS had developed for fighting guerrilla wars. It was generally assumed throughout Washington that if there was to be a permanent intelligence service, it would be formed around the OSS branches responsible for espionage and counterespionage (SI and X-2), along with support services such as communications. So our task was to persuade the Pentagon that the knowledge of running guerrilla operations should be preserved, if not in the permanent intelligence service then in the military establishment.

Since I was one of the few people still around with field experience as a guerrilla leader, I was quickly coopted into this effort. We wrote endless memos, revised the appropriate sections of Field Manual 100-5, the how-to handbook for generals, and briefed a series of interdepartmental committees on the need for a unit specializing in guerrilla warfare. But the Joint Chiefs of Staff steadfastly refused to give a civilian agency responsibility for paramilitary activities or to accept the responsibility themselves. It was only six years later, in June 1952, that the Joint Chiefs decided that guerrilla warfare did indeed have a role and established the special forces with a training center at Fort Bragg, North Carolina. Even then, the special forces were given only token recognition and the lowest possible priority.

As the struggle for a permanent intelligence service continued, it was subsumed under a bigger struggle, the unification of the armed services, and little attention was paid to the place of intelligence. The National Security Act of 1947 was a compromise. It gave the air force equal status with the army and the navy but also established the Department of Defense, headed by a single secretary. Almost as an afterthought, the act created the Central Intelligence Agency. The CIA's functions were to coordinate intelligence activities, to produce "national intelligence" (making intelligence estimates and interpretations), "to perform services of common concern" (espionage and counterespionage), and "to perform such other functions and duties" as the National Security Council might from time to time direct. It was this latter umbrella clause that formed the legal basis for the order during the Eisenhower administration, NSC 54/12, that authorized the CIA to conduct covert action.

★ ★

Personal Affairs

While all this was happening, I was allowed at least some time for a private life. Immediately on returning from the war, I telephoned around in search of Eleanor Hoyt. I finally reached her at the University of Chicago, which she had just entered. Having deliberately put aside any thought of marriage until after the war, I had also put aside thoughts of Eleanor. She was the only girl I ever wrote a letter to from Burma, but I didn't write all that many, and of course I wasn't able to write any during the time I was behind enemy lines. Eleanor seemed to have put me out of mind as well and was surprised that I wanted to come see her. And she sounded annoyed that I didn't share her enthusiasm about Chicago, since this implied that I thought she should have been waiting for me, though I had never asked her to. However, she agreed to my visit.

After that poor start, we had a marvelous time together in Chicago. It was a short week, and when it ended I reported to OSS headquarters in Washington, D.C. For the rest of that spring I spent every weekend I could in Chicago. On 22 June 1946, Eleanor and I were married.

In the meantime, I had begun to think about what had happened to the army following World War I. After my heady experience as liaison officer to the Fourteenth Army and a guerrilla commander, as well as the year and a half being involved in the great bureaucratic and political struggle over postwar intelligence, I found the thought of running a PX—as my father had done after World War I—monstrous. But if intelligence were to play a bigger role in the future than it had between wars, I might be able to make a career specializing in it. About this time, the army announced that it had adopted a program to send officers for a master's degree in international relations. I applied and was accepted at Yale.

Another officer and I did well, and Yale asked the army to

255

let us stay a third year for the Ph.D. So near the end of the second year I had to start thinking about a topic for a dissertation. My first thought was to do something in the field of nuclear military strategy. I was, after all, a West Point graduate, a combat veteran, and a career army officer. And here I was at a university whose faculty had just published the first book about the atomic bomb and its military and political implications, *The Absolute Weapon*.[1] Bernard Brodie had edited the book and written the two chapters dealing with military and strategic implications. Until that time Brodie had written on sea power. When he came to work the morning after the atomic bomb devastated Hiroshima, a colleague, W. T. R. Fox, asked him, "Where does all this leave your battleships?"

Brodie abandoned his battleships and spent the rest of his life thinking and writing about nuclear warfare. In my search for a dissertation topic, I studied what he had written and took every course he offered. My personal interest was in military strategy. I thought I might be able to write a piece that argued with one or two of Brodie's propositions and perhaps even add to what he had to say. But a whole dissertation? In *The Absolute Weapon* Brodie had taken only two chapters to argue his points. Moreover, although two atomic bombs had been dropped, as yet no nuclear wars had been fought. What could I do in the way of solid research?

I decided to do a dissertation that would build on my experience in OSS, that is, on some aspect of strategic intelligence. I finished the research by June 1950, the end of my third year. The army's orders for my next assignment had arrived in spring. So it took me another year working nights and weekends to finish the dissertation, but it was accepted.[2]

The orders directed me to report to the American contingent of what would become the North Atlantic Treaty Organiza-

---

[1]Bernard S. Brodie, ed. (New York: Harcourt, Brace, 1946).

[2]In 1956 it was published as a book, *Strategic Intelligence and National Decisions* (Glencoe, Illinois: Free Press, 1956). The book was eventually one of those chosen for the permanent White House library. Much to my astonishment, and without my prior knowledge, it was republished in 1981 by Greenwood Press. The irony is that when Kennedy appointed me to head the State Department's Bureau of Intelligence and Research, I had to put my ideas into practice!

tion, at that time stationed in London. On 24 June 1950, a couple of weeks before Eleanor, our infant son Hoyt, and I boarded the ship, North Korea attacked South Korea.

★ ★
The Problem of NATO Strategy

Everyone assumed that the Soviets had ordered the North Koreans to attack—that having broken the West's monopoly of atomic bombs, the Soviets felt the time had come to test both its defenses and its will. Accordingly, the United States undertook to send four additional divisions to Europe. The other allies followed with increases of their own. Germany, they agreed, should be rearmed, although it wasn't until 1955 that the first German soldiers took to the field. And all the allies agreed to the establishment of NATO, the first international force with a unified command ever established in peacetime. In early 1951, Dwight D. Eisenhower became Supreme Allied Commander, Europe—SACEUR.

Half the American contingent stationed in London went to Supreme Headquarters, Allied Powers Europe (SHAPE), stationed in Paris, and half, of which I was one, went to the newly formed United States European Command (USEUCOM), stationed in Frankfurt. All of us concentrated on the problem of NATO strategy.

If a Soviet attack came, it would be without warning. The Soviets had twenty-two divisions in East Germany and another hundred and fifty in the Soviet Union itself. On their side of the line, the allies had no more than twelve divisions, of which two were American. The Soviet divisions could be secretly increased to thirty without much difficulty. These could hold maneuvers in East Germany and abruptly change direction, driving for the bridges over the Rhine. NATO intelligence estimated that if the Soviets did attack, they could reach the Pyrenees in six to eight weeks, about the time it would take an army to march the distance. A joke circulated among NATO staff officers: "What equipment will the Soviets need to reach the Pyrenees?" The answer: "Shoes."

What most frightened these officers, all of whom had served in World War II, was not the overwhelming numbers of Soviet divisions. The graver danger was revealed to newly arrived officers during a briefing in a large two-story room in which one huge wall was a display area for maps. At one stage, the briefing officer would pull back a curtain to reveal a gigantic blowup of an air photo of the World War II beachhead at Normandy. It had been taken a day or two before the Allied breakout from about ten thousand feet on a cloudless day, and every foxhole was clearly visible. Then the briefing officer would pull a cord and a transparency would drop down over the photo. It showed the area of destruction wrought by the atomic bomb that had been dropped on Hiroshima. That bomb had the explosive power of about fourteen thousand tons of TNT (by the time of these briefings, bombs had a yield of twenty *million* tons). Every foxhole would have been obliterated. Invariably, the response was a sharp intake of breath.

"Gentlemen," the briefing officer would say, "there will be no more Normandies. If we ever get kicked off the continent, we will never, ever get back."

The problem of what long-term strategy NATO should pursue seemed increasingly unsolvable. The basic assumption of the original strategy was that nuclear weapons would continue to be scarce and therefore unavailable for anything but attacking a beachhead or a few cities. But nuclear weapons were rapidly becoming plentiful, for both the allies and the Soviets. NATO planners had calculated that a force of ninety-six divisions, the Lisbon Force Goals, could hold in a conventional war like World War II. The nearer the allies got to the Lisbon Force Goals, the more likely it seemed that if the Soviets did attack, they would use battlefield nuclear weapons.

Few NATO staff officers thought anyone could win a nuclear war, but most still thought a nuclear war could be lost, in the sense that the loser would be occupied by enemy forces. Keeping the Soviets from occupying Europe was part of not losing a war. But if the Soviets launched an onslaught with conventional weapons, their troop deployment would make an enormously tempting target for battlefield nuclear weapons. The only way of keeping the Soviets out of Europe, the argument went, was to put a strong enough screen of troops along the border to compel them to concentrate their forces, and then to use nuclear weapons on those forces. But if the allies adopted that strategy, then the Soviets would be forced to use nuclear weapons to blast a way through allied defenses. More and more staff officers began to argue that both sides would resort to battlefield nuclear weapons at the very outset of war.

★ ★

A Personal Decision

From the time Eleanor, Hoyt, and I arrived in England in the summer of 1950, my career was foremost in my mind. It seemed increasingly obvious that I couldn't successfully continue as a career army officer and remain competent as a Ph.D. in international affairs. The army had tried hard to make sure that my first assignment was related to my postgraduate training, but it had its own needs. According to standard personnel procedures, my next assignment would be to the infantry school at Fort Benning for training as a battalion commander. I had already commanded a guerrilla battalion in combat, and the thought of repeating it all on paper was discouraging.

The Institute of International Affairs at Yale had moved to Princeton, and that university offered me a fellowship to turn my dissertation into a book. So early in 1953 I submitted my resignation from the army, effective as soon as the war in Korea ended. By June 1953, the peace talks at Panmunjon were making progress, and on 9 July I was notified that my resignation had been accepted.

I spent three years at Princeton. The first year I turned my dissertation into a book. The rest of the time my colleagues and I worked as a group on nuclear military strategy and published a book, *Military Policy and National Security*.[3] Gradually it be-

---

[3]William W. Kaufmann, ed., with Gordon A. Craig, Roger Hilsman, and Klaus Knorr (Princeton, New Jersey: Princeton University Press, 1956).

came clear that Princeton couldn't afford to maintain the institute as an independent body with its own staff, so we all began looking for jobs.

I became chief of the foreign affairs and defense division of the Legislative Reference Service, later renamed the Congressional Research Service. It was housed in the Library of Congress, and it did research for the members and committees of Congress. I was there from 1956 to 1961, working on foreign affairs and defense problems, and in the process I got to know John F. Kennedy, Hubert Humphrey, Henry "Scoop" Jackson, J. William Fulbright, Chester Bowles, Edmund Muskie, and almost all the other members of Congress who were interested in defense and foreign affairs. And, as I mentioned, when Kennedy was elected president he appointed me director of the Bureau of Intelligence and Research.

★ ★
Guerrilla Warfare—Again!

One of the first questions Kennedy asked after taking office was what was being done about Communist guerrilla insurgency. The American decision to fight in Korea seemed to have provided an effective deterrent against large-scale conventional wars. NATO and America's nuclear stockpile and bombers, and America's growing missile strength promised to deter an all-out attack by the Soviet Union itself. But in guerrilla insurgency the Communist world had apparently discovered a new tactic of aggression—what Kennedy called subterranean war.

In November 1957, following the Soviet Sputnik success, China's leader, Mao Zedong, declared on a visit to Moscow that the "east wind prevails over the west wind." The North Vietnamese reactivated the Communist cadres that had remained in South Vietnam after 1954 and began to use the old Ho Chi Minh trails through Laos to send them down. By mid-1961, the Viet Cong were estimated to have about twelve thousand mainline guerrilla troops in control of as much as a third of South Vietnam.

★ ★
The Taylor-Rostow Mission

President Ngo Dinh Diem called for help, and on 11 October 1961 President Kennedy sent General Maxwell D. Taylor and Walt W. Rostow to Vietnam to investigate. Their report recommended an increase in military and economic aid, including T-28 fighter-bombers with American instructors (who would covertly serve as pilots under an operation code-named Farmgate), more military advisers, and, finally, ten thousand combat troops, to be stationed along the border to deter the North Vietnamese from sending their ten regular divisions south to help the ex-southern guerrillas.

President Kennedy approved the recommendations to step up economic aid and to increase the number of American advisers (including the Farmgate pilots), but he turned down the recommendation for American combat troops.

★ ★
President Kennedy's View

In 1951, as a young congressman, Kennedy had visited Vietnam and been dismayed at the French military and strategic situation. As president, according to his brother Robert, he "determined early that we would never get into that position."[4]

---

[4]As reported by Daniel Ellsberg in an interview with Jann Wenner, *Rolling Stone*, 6 December 1973. The fullest account of President Kennedy's attitude toward Vietnam is given by Arthur M. Schlesinger, Jr., in *Robert F. Kennedy and His Times* (London: Andre Deutsch, 1978), chap. 31, "Vietnam Legacy." Here I have followed that account and added my own personal knowledge from the official positions that I held in the Kennedy administration. Documentation and additional details can be found in my *To Move A Nation: The Politics of Foreign Policy in the Administration of John F. Kennedy* (Garden City, New York: Doubleday, 1967); in my personal papers in the Kennedy library; and in my oral histories in the Kennedy library, the Lyndon B. Johnson library, the Columbia University oral history project, the Congressional Research Service, Library of Congress, and the historical office of the State Department. See also my article "Vietnam: The Decisions to Intervene," in J. R. Adelman, ed. *The Superpowers and Revolution* (New York: Praeger, 1986), from which this account is drawn.

He wavered several times in this determination. But a series of events gradually strengthened his conviction that U.S. assistance should be confined to aid and advisers rather than troops. These were the fiasco of the Bay of Pigs, the continued ineptness of the Diem regime, and finally the Buddhist crisis, in which Diem—the Catholic president of a Buddhist country—adopted anti-Buddhist policies.[5]

★ ★
The Search for a Strategic Concept

Although he refused to use American troops, President Kennedy continued to hammer away on the point that guerrilla warfare was different from any other kind and that it required new tactics and doctrines. In fact, one of the most important facts about guerrilla war, he believed, was that insurgents could be defeated only by their fellow countrymen, not by foreigners. Events underlined his point, and many of us in his administration, civilians as well as military, became engaged in searching for a strategic concept for dealing with "revolutionary" warfare.

One of the civilians was Walt Rostow, who became a spokesman for the "military" approach in both the Kennedy and Johnson administrations. Rostow was an economist specializing in the history of economic development, and he saw the modernization process as a true revolution containing its own dynamics. Like all revolutions, he argued, modernization was disruptive of old ways and during the transition produced extreme vulnerabilities on which Communists could prey. The Communists, Rostow said, were the "scavengers of the modernization process."[6]

Rostow saw the task for the United States as twofold—first, to hasten modernization past the vulnerable period of transition, and second, to protect a country and preserve its independence

---

[5]For a full account of Kennedy's changing attitude, see "Vietnam: the Decisions to Intervene."

[6]In addition to Rostow's various memos contained in *The Pentagon Papers*, see his speech on the subject reprinted in Franklin Mark Osanka, ed. *Modern Guerrilla Warfare* (New York: The Free Press, 1962), and in T. N. Greene, *The Guerrilla—and How to Fight Him* (New York: Praeger, 1962).

during that vulnerable period. And it was because transition was so uncertain that Rostow was led in the end to call for military means for dealing with a guerrilla war that had already begun. The "sending of men and arms across international boundaries and the direction of guerrilla war from outside a sovereign nation" was a new form of aggression, he maintained. This was "a fact which the whole international community must confront and whose consequent responsibilities it must accept. Without such international action those against whom aggression is mounted will be driven inevitably to seek out and engage the ultimate source of the aggression they confront."[7]

Applied to Vietnam this was, of course, an argument for bombing the north. Enough punishment of North Vietnam could theoretically make it cease its support for the guerrillas in the south and force it to order the fighting stopped.[8] As it developed in the Pentagon, however, the military approach was twofold—not only to punish and wear down the source of the aggression outside the country under attack, but also to seek out and destroy guerrilla units inside. The idea was to make maximum use of superior American technology. Helicopters could give counterguerrilla forces fantastic mobility; air power and artillery could give them overwhelming firepower.

---

[7] Ibid.

[8] On this point General Matthew Ridgway's criticism of both Rostow and me, delivered several years later, is one of the wiser things that has been said on Vietnam. The occasion was a conference in Bermuda sponsored by the Carnegie Endowment for International Peace in early 1968. I had been arguing against Rostow's theory that our higher technological and industrial development would permit us to escalate step by step until the North Vietnamese were finally forced to quit. The trouble with Rostow's theory, my argument went, was that the United States would run out of rungs in its ladder because of domestic and world opinion before North Vietnam would run out of rungs in its ladder. General Ridgway said that we were both wrong. The trouble with U.S. strategy in Vietnam was that it was trying to use military force to achieve goals that military force was incapable of achieving. Force could kill people, and the United States enjoyed a sufficient technical and industrial superiority that it could indeed kill all the Vietnamese in the world rather easily if it were immoral enough to do so. But military force could not change people's political attitudes—and that was what the United States was trying to do in Vietnam. It was a totally inappropriate use of military force.

★ ★
The Political Approach

As director of intelligence and research in the State Department, I put the Bureau of Intelligence and Research to work on the problem of guerrilla warfare. I also made a speech on the subject.[9]

I agreed that the United States should be prepared to become deeply involved, but differed with Rostow about the methods. Supported by work in the bureau, my basic premise was that a successful counterinsurgency program depended on winning the support of the mass of the people. This meant that military measures had to be carefully circumscribed. The danger of large-scale military operations was that their very destructiveness would alienate the people.

What is more, I argued, regular forces—although essential for the task of deterring conventional aggression—were unsuited because of training and equipment for the task of fighting guerrillas. Recalling how Japanese regulars had chased my guerrilla battalion in Burma with so little success, I argued that regular forces were roadbound, unwieldy, and cumbersome, inevitably telegraphing their movements to the elusive guerrilla. Pointing to America's historical experience—fighting Indians, using guerrilla tactics in Mindanao during the Philippine insurrection at the turn of the century, and using the OSS in World War II—I argued that the way to fight the guerrilla was to adopt the tactics of the guerrilla.

Suppose that instead of chasing my guerrilla battalion around the Burmese landscape with a regiment of three thousand men, the Japanese had put a grid of ten square miles on a map of the terrain and put a regular platoon into each square with instructions to behave like guerrillas, laying ambushes on all the trails in its square. A central reserve could be used to reinforce any platoon that made contact with our guerrillas and to lay ambushes on our escape trails leading

---

[9]My speech "Internal War: The New Communist Tactic," was also reproduced in Osanka, *Modern Guerrilla Warfare*, and in Greene, *The Guerrilla—and How to Fight Him*.

from the point of contact. If the Japanese had used this tactic against my battalion, within two or three weeks my poorly trained guerrillas would have thrown their weapons down, changed into civilian shirts and *longyis*, and made their way back home.

The Viet Cong might have been better trained and more highly motivated than my guerrillas, but if the South Vietnamese government adopted these guerrilla tactics to fight the guerrilla, the Viet Cong in any particular area would be slowly worn down. Then it would be possible to extend government control and the people could safely be given the means to protect themselves. And when one area was cleared and secured, the government's security forces could move on to the next.

★ ★

W. Averell Harriman as Assistant Secretary

In the meantime, W. Averell Harriman had been making progress in what eventually became known as the Geneva Accords of 1962, which neutralized Laos. Late in November 1961, President Kennedy made him assistant secretary of state for Far Eastern affairs. Harriman, in turn, persuaded Kennedy to put Michael V. Forrestal on the NSC staff to handle liaison on the Far East between the White House, the State and Defense departments, and the CIA.

When Harriman took over his new job, Walt Rostow, by now head of the policy planning staff in the State Department, wrote him a memo urging the bombing of North Vietnam. Harriman had recently been nicknamed The Crocodile because of his penchant for biting the head off anyone with whom he disagreed, and he immediately demonstrated how appropriate the nickname was. He read the memo, called in his staff, and told them he didn't want to see any more memos from Rostow. Then he telephoned me and said that from that point on, the Bureau of Intelligence and Research was the policy planning staff for the Bureau of Far Eastern Affairs.

265

★ ★
A Trip to Vietnam

On January 1962, *The Marine Corps Gazette* devoted its entire issue to guerrilla warfare and included my speech as well as one of Rostow's. President Kennedy wrote the editor that he had read the issue from cover to cover. He called me over to the White House and we discussed the problem of guerrilla warfare at some length. Then a few days later, General Taylor telephoned to say that the president wanted me to go with Secretary McNamara to Honolulu for the second of what was to become monthly meetings between top American officials dealing with Vietnam. When the meeting was finished, Taylor continued, the president wanted me to go on to Saigon with Ambassador Nolting, look the situation over, and report back to him on my findings.

★ ★
R. K. G. Thompson

The meeting in Honolulu was uneventful, but when I got to Saigon one of the first people I met was Robert K. G. Thompson, head of the British advisory mission. It turned out that Thompson had ideas for dealing with the guerrillas that were similar to ours in the bureau, but much more detailed and specific. Thompson was a career officer in the British colonial service who had spent most of his life in Malaya. He had played an important role in the defeat of Communist guerrilla terrorism there, where he had served as deputy secretary and then secretary for defense. At first, the British had dealt with the terrorism as if it were a purely military problem, relying on large-scale military operations, bombing jungle hideouts, and so on, but after two years they were worse off than when they started. It was then that the British developed the "new village" program that finally defeated the Communist guerrillas. Applying this experience to Vietnam, Thompson had come up with what he called the strategic hamlet plan.[10]

He pointed out that the Viet Cong's main effort was not fighting the government's regular troops—the Viet Cong could have done more of that than they were at the time. Instead, the Viet Cong was spending most of its time attempting to gain administrative control over the sixteen thousand hamlets in South Vietnam. The South Vietnamese government would only be wasting its time winning battles against regular Viet Cong units in the field; the effort wouldn't affect the struggle for control of Vietnam. If the government lost administrative control of the hamlets, the guerrillas would have a base for supplies, taxation, and recruits.

The only way to defeat a guerrilla force, Thompson believed, was systematically to cut it off from its true base of support—which was not a country far away, in this case North Vietnam, but the local people, in this case the villagers of South Vietnam. To cut guerrillas off from the people, you first had to give the people physical security. For if they weren't protected from marauding bands of guerrillas, they couldn't freely choose between the guerrillas and the government. What Thompson proposed as the instrument to provide this physical security was the strategic hamlet.

★ ★

Strategic Hamlets

The strategic hamlet program was a way of winning the allegiance of villagers and arming them so that they could defend themselves against marauding guerrillas and hold out until reinforcements came.

Setting up a strategic hamlet would require political skill,

---

[10]Thompson's ideas on strategic hamlets are more fully described in my book *To Move a Nation* and in his own books. Ironically, after the escalation of the war, Thompson also became an important adviser to the Johnson administration and a theoretician for the hawk strategy, which was the successor to the military approach.

care, and time. Civic-action teams would have to be trained to go into each village to provide simple government services, agricultural extension loans, schools, teachers, and effective police protection, as well as training in the use of weapons for self-defense. The role of the police, of course, would be vital, for they would have to win enough people over to the government side to identify Communist agents. Before that, it wouldn't be safe to distribute arms to a village militia. And during the weeks, months, or even years that this was going on, regular military forces would have to be stationed in the region to protect civic-action teams and villagers until the hamlet was ready to defend itself.

The essence of all this was that it had to be a *program*—one lone strategic hamlet couldn't effectively defend itself. There would be a hedgehog of hamlets spreading out like an oil blot toward the mountains and the jungle.

★ ★
A Government Attack at Bien Hoa

When I had my appointment with President Diem, he asked if I wanted to observe an action scheduled for 21 January 1962 against a Viet Cong battalion that had been located at a village called Bien Hoa. I told him yes.

The plan was prepared by the senior American adviser to the Vietnamese Third Corps. It called for pre-positioning four infantry battalions on boats in a river the night before the operation. They would be joined in the attack by parachute troops dropped in a field beside the village where the Viet Cong were reported to be encamped.

At 0755 the next day, B-26 bombers bombed and strafed what they thought was the village. However, the target was very near the Cambodian border, and through a tragic error in map-reading the B-26s in fact attacked a village in Cambodia, killing and wounding a number of villagers.

At 0800 more B-26s dropped 500-pound bombs on an installation near the drop zone suspected of manufacturing munitions, while T-28 fighter-bombers from the Farmgate squadron attacked huts bordering the drop zone with rockets. The explosion of the first bomb was the signal for the four battalions to disembark and set up blocking positions along the river and a canal, east and south of the area supposedly occupied by the Viet Cong battalion.

The bombing and strafing continued for forty-five minutes. A fifteen-minute lull ensued.

At 0900 an airborne battalion parachuted into the drop zone and immediately attacked the cluster of huts. Two of the four battalions in blocking positions also attacked, forming a pincers.

Except for the error that led to the bombing of the Cambodian village, the plan was well executed, but it was more appropriate to the European fronts of World War II than it was to guerrilla warfare. The pre-positioning of troops in boats on the river inevitably gave the guerrillas warning—and if they failed to heed that warning, the preparatory bombing gave them another. In any case, such elaborate traps rarely work against guerrillas; the only way to trap them is to make contact by blanketing an area with a large number of guerrilla-size patrols and then following up the contact with reinforcements and ambushes along escape routes. The greatest problem is that bombing huts and villages kills civilians and pushes them further toward active support for guerrilla insurgents.

And so it was at Bien Hoa on 21 January 1962. Villagers reported that there had in fact been about two hundred Viet Cong in the area, but that they moved out an hour before the air strike began. As a result, no contact was made with the Viet Cong that day. No one knows how many Cambodians were killed because of the map-reading error; it is known that the strafing and bombing around the drop zone, five civilians were killed and eleven wounded. A *Life* magazine photographer, Howard Sochurek, who followed the parachutists in by helicopter, reported that among the five civilians killed were two young boys and a girl.

In fairness, it should be said that guerrilla warfare was a new and radically different military experience that required servicemen to unlearn old lessons and learn new ones. It would be unreasonable to expect the military to abandon overnight principles it learned the hard way in bloody and honorable combat in World War II and Korea. And yet it is obvious that an operation like Bien Hoa was fruitless, and that it helped to recruit more Viet Cong than it could have killed.

★ ★

Report to the President

I had taken careful notes on Thompson's ideas, my conversations with president Diem, the briefings, and the Bien Hoa operation, and when I got back to Washington I organized them into an oral report to the president.

But first I went to General Maxwell Taylor, who was then special military representative to the president. After going through the whole briefing from start to finish, I suggested there might be portions of it that he would prefer to give the president himself in private. "No, sir!" Taylor exclaimed. "The president should get the full story straight from you, not secondhand. And don't pull any punches, either."

I delivered the report to the president with Taylor present. When I got to the Bien Hoa operation, Kennedy shook his head ruefully. "I've been president over a year, how can such things like this go on happening?" Turning to General Taylor, he asked him to find out why this was still going on and to have it corrected. At my anguished look, they both laughed. "And try to do it without making the author of the report too unpopular with the Joint Chiefs of Staff," the president added.

Kennedy was impressed with Thompson's ideas and thought that this was the direction we should go in developing a strategic concept for Vietnam. He told me to write the whole thing up as a formal report under that title, "A Strategic Concept for Vietnam." Over the next few weeks he kept me busy giving the oral version to different people—his brother Robert, the attorney general; the heads of the CIA and the Agency for International Development; and the vice president, Lyndon Johnson. Unfortunately, when I went to Johnson's office in the

Capitol to give him the briefing, he was in the midst of a political crisis that kept him preoccupied on the telephone much of the time. Later I wondered if U.S. policy toward Vietnam would have been different if he had been able to concentrate on the briefing. I doubt it. I think that even then his mind had already been made up about what course the United States should follow in Vietnam.

Then President Kennedy decided that I should also brief General Harkins—even though Harkins by that time had taken command of the American military advisory group in Saigon which meant that I had to make a special trip all the way to Saigon to give Harkins a two-hour briefing. His response was "Yes, I agree that all this is very important, and I have assigned two liaison officers to AID to make sure the AID people get what they need."

I said as politely as I could that implementing this kind of counterguerrilla strategy would take a bit more than two liaison officers. But General Harkins brushed the point aside and kept returning to the Ho Chi Minh Trail and the infiltration routes. He said he felt very strongly that these routes should be systematically bombed to cut off the supplies and recruits coming down them. I tried to argue from my experience in Burma that bombs could not stop guerrillas walking down jungle and mountain trails and that in any case the real source of supplies and recruits for the Viet Cong was the villagers of South Vietnam. If this judgment was correct, then our effort should be concentrated on protecting them and winning their allegiance. The whole military strategy and approach required drastic and fundamental rethinking. But it was as if I were talking to a brick wall.

When I reported back to President Kennedy about this, he made a remark that turned out to be painfully prophetic. First he recalled my experience infiltrating a guerrilla battalion past the Japanese in Lawksawk; that suggested that it would be impossible to cut off the infiltration routes completely, no matter what draconian measures were taken. But it was worse than that. Even if the flow could be choked to a trickle, he went on to say, we would still have the political burden. Every time things went badly in the future, there would be more reports

271

about an increased use of the trails and people in Saigon and Washington would clamor for action against them. "No matter what goes wrong or whose fault it really is, the argument will be made that the Communists have stepped up their infiltration and that we can't win unless we bomb the North. Those trails," he said, chopping the air with his right hand in a motion he often used when emphasizing a point, "are a built-in excuse for failure, and a built-in argument for escalation."

★ ★
A Follow-up Mission to Vietnam

Almost a year later, President Kennedy sent Mike Forrestal and me to Vietnam on another low-key mission to see how things were going. We arrived on 31 December 1962 and spent the evening at a New Year's Eve party at Robert Thompson's place. Then we got up early for a steady round of briefings. The briefers were optimistic, but underlying their optimism were things that Forrestal and I found disturbing. A memorandum for the record that I dictated at the time reads as follows:

> At this point, some 36 hours after having arrived in Saigon [January 2, 1963], I have the impression that things are going much better than they were a year ago, but that they are not going nearly so well as the people here in Saigon, both military and civilian, think they are. They have a sound concept in the strategic hamlet program; they have aid and they have lots of people. All this gives them a sense of movement and of progress. The trouble is, however, that the progress and movement is highly uneven. One would wish that this was the fault of the Vietnamese, and to a considerable extent, it is. But I am afraid, that a great share of the responsibility belongs to the Americans. We have the impression that any one of these programs, such as the strategic hamlet program . . . requires precise and efficient coordination of the activities of many different American agencies; and you also have the impression that this coordination is not really being accomplished. The failure to provide a police program that is even remotely phased in with the provision of barbed wire and radios for the strategic hamlets is one example. Thus you have strategic hamlets going up enclosing Communists inside their boundaries with no provision for winkling out those Communists.

Other things are similar. You have the impression that the military is still too heavily oriented toward "sweep"-type operations. There is also still the same emphasis on air power as there was before. Almost every operation, so far as I can tell, still begins with an air strike which inevitably kills innocent people and warns the Viet Cong that they should get moving, for the troops will be coming soon. I think all this indicates that the Americans are just as much to blame as the Vietnamese.

But the Vietnamese—or at least Brother Nhu—deserved a great deal of blame. Nhu had taken command of the strategic hamlet program and turned it to his own narrow political purposes, making a sham of it. He was using it as a tool for disseminating his ideology of "personalism" as a way of government. His strategic hamlets offered little if any protection for the villagers. And rather than establishing them slowly at the edges of secure areas—the oil-blot approach—he was trying to convert some of the most remote villages along the Cambodian border, villages to which the Viet Cong had easy access and in which they had long since entrenched their sympathizers.

Forrestal and I wrote a balanced report that tried to give the positive as well as negative side of what was happening in Vietnam. But we added an "eyes-only" annex for the president that gave the unvarnished and gloomy truth.

★ ★
Promotion to Assistant Secretary

In March 1963, Averell Harriman was promoted to the number-three slot in the State Department, the job of under secretary for political affairs, and I was given his former job as assistant secretary for Far Eastern affairs. And in April 1963 I found myself once again at the monthly Honolulu meeting, with Secretary of Defense McNamara, General Earle Wheeler, then–Chief of Staff of the Army, Ambassador Nolting, and General Harkins. General Harkins gave us the facts and figures—the number of strategic hamlets established, the number of Viet Cong killed, operations initiated by government forces, and so on. He said that of course he could not give any guarantees, but that by Christmas it would probably all be over.

273

Secretary McNamara was elated. He recalled that early meeting I had attended, when the prospects looked so black, commenting that that had been only a year and a half before. A moment later, a State Department aide passed me a note, which I wordlessly passed on to Ambassador Nolting. It contained two words, an attempt at Latin: *cave statisticus.*

It was statistics that had painted such a rosy picture of the situation in Vietnam. As a Vietnamese general once put it to an American friend of mine, "Ah, *les statistiques!* Your secretary of defense loves statistics. We Vietnamese can give him all he wants. If you want them to go up, they will go up. If you want them to go down, they will go down."

The truth of the matter was that the Pentagon's strategy, derived from U.S. military experience in World Wars I and II, was crafted around an encounter with Soviet forces on the north German plain. American equipment had been designed for that purpose, American forces had been organized for it, and men had been trained for the kind of fighting it would require. The Soviet threat in Europe was the only one that threatened the survival of the United States, and it was right and proper that the military prepare for this threat.

The fact that the United States military was not trained or equipped for meeting a guerrilla war in the jungles and mountains of Vietnam was crucial. The person who saw this most clearly was General Matthew B. Ridgway. Ridgway was the one who had brought the United States back from the brink of disaster in Korea after MacArthur's mistake of splitting our forces, which had permitted the Chinese to drive a wedge between them. And it was Ridgway, as chief of staff of the army in 1954, who almost single-handedly prevented the United States from intervening in Vietnam with American bombers and troops at the time of Dienbienphu.[11]

Ridgway's basic argument against intervention was twofold: the United States was prepared, equipped, and trained for an entirely different kind of war, and Vietnam was strategically and politically peripheral to the security of the United States.

---

[11] See Melvin Gurtov, *The First Vietnam Crisis,* (New York: Columbia University Press, 1967).

One of the tragic aspects of Vietnam is that at that time there were no general-statesmen in the high command like General Ridgway or General Marshall, who in 1949 kept us from intervening in the greatest quagmire of all, Communist China.

As it was, the Pentagon was determined to use Vietnam to test, polish, and perfect the strategy devised for meeting Soviet forces in Europe. Fittingly, the book that most effectively spells out why this strategy was so inappropriate to Vietnam was written by a West Point graduate and career army officer, Colonel Andrew F. Krepinevich, Jr., while he was teaching national security affairs at West Point.[12] It is worth quoting what Krepinevich has to say on the subject:

> Ironically, such "experts" as the administration had were not at the center of the policy process but on the periphery. Roger Hilsman, initially director of intelligence and research at the State Department, had fought with guerrillas in Burma during World War II. He was a West Point graduate and had a close relationship with R. K. G. Thompson, the noted British expert on guerrilla warfare. Despite these credentials, Hilsman was never given a major role in the administration's counterinsurgency program. The same fate befell Air Force Brig. Gen. Edward Lansdale, who had worked with Magsaysay in the Philippines and in the special military mission in Saigon. Lansdale, not a favorite of Taylor's, quickly found himself relegated to a minor role in the policy process. Furthermore the administration, while upgrading the status of the Special Forces, did not see fit to challenge the Army's designation of MAAG chiefs or, later, the commander of MACV, yet the officers assigned were quite ill-suited for supervising counterinsurgency operations. General officers with training in the field, such as Major General Rosson and Brigadier General Yarborough, remained on the sidelines.

As Krepinevich goes on to say, Kennedy's emphasis on counterinsurgency shook the army brass. The notion that a group of civilians should require the army to deemphasize its strong suits (heavy units, massed firepower, and high technology) in favor of stripped-down light infantry units encountered strong resistance. General Lemnitzer, chairman of the Joint Chiefs of Staff from 1960 to 1962, said that the administration

---

[12]*The Army and Vietnam* (Baltimore: The Johns Hopkins University Press, 1986). The quotes that follow are from pages 36 and 37.

was "oversold" on guerrilla warfare. General Earle Wheeler, chief of staff of the army from 1962 to 1964, said that "the essence of the problem in Vietnam is military." General Taylor felt that counterinsurgency was "just a form of small war" and that "all this cloud of dust that's coming out of the White House really isn't necessary." Taylor later recalled the army's reaction to Kennedy's program: it was "something we have to satisfy. But not much heart went into [the] work."

★ ★
The Buddhist Crisis and the Coup Against Diem

Then came the Buddhist crisis, which culminated in the coup against President Diem. It began as a march on Buddha's birthday to protest certain government regulations that the Buddhists regarded as discriminatory. Government troops brought in to keep order fired on the crowd and nine people were killed.

Militant Buddhists staged demonstrations throughout Vietnam. World opinion was outraged. The Buddhists had bitten on an issue not so much of religious persecution as political discrimination, and when they bit they tasted political blood. Then they pushed even harder. For a time they became the rallying point for all kinds of discontent in what was already a discontented society.

Very soon the Buddhists hit on a form of protest that was as dramatically effective, especially on TV, as it was gruesome. After notifying American TV crews to be at a certain place at a certain time, a Buddhist *bonze* (monk) would appear at the place, sit down in the lotus position, drench himself with gasoline, and immolate himself in a towering column of fire.

As the Buddhist crisis continued, President Diem became increasingly isolated and came more and more under the influence of his brother Nhu and his wife. Nhu's neo-Fascist philosophy led him to harsh policies, and he was known to have begun using opium regularly. Madame Nhu, whose views earned her

276

the nickname Dragon Lady, was if anything more hard-line. She scornfully described the immolations as Buddhist barbecues and offered to donate gasoline to any *bonzes* who wanted to follow the example.

The culmination of the Buddhist crisis came on 21 August 1963. Units of the Vietnamese Special Forces, which were under the command of Nhu, disguised themselves in army uniforms and attacked Buddhist pagodas in all the major cities of South Vietnam, killing and mutilating priests and nuns and desecrating religious relics. The U.S. government publicly condemned the action. Although Washington realized that condemnation would encourage plotting, neither hawks nor doves believed that the United States could honorably remain silent.

Plotting coups had been a way of life in South Vietnam for some time. In the months after the attack on the pagodas, however, it seemed to proliferate. Various groups of Vietnamese generals became convinced that Diem would have to be removed—to preserve their own lives as well as the future of South Vietnam—and on two occasions plotters approached the American embassy to ask what the attitude of the U.S. government would be if they staged a coup.

In both Saigon and Washington, American officials were divided. The advocates of a political approach had become convinced that Diem could no longer successfully lead the country. How could a president who ordered an attack on Buddhist pagodas win the political support of the people, they asked, in a country that was 95 percent Buddhist? The advocates of a military approach admitted that Diem had seriously damaged his chances but saw no successor of needed ability and prestige.

The U.S. government never actually plotted a coup with the generals. However, no effort was made to hide American disapproval of Diem's policies, and this undoubtedly encouraged the generals who eventually did engineer one.

The U.S. government had no advance knowledge of the coup, and many individuals, both hawks and doves, doubted that the generals would in the end do anything. Getting Vietnamese generals to move, one Washington wit remarked, was like trying to push a piece of cooked spaghetti. But because there had been so much plotting, when Diem was finally overthrown on 1 November 1963, most Washington officials were surprised only by the timing.

Inevitably, the Buddhist crisis affected President Kennedy's attitude toward Vietnam. At the beginning of his administration he told a number of aides that he thought the United States was overcommitted in Southeast Asia, but that since we were already there, he was willing to send aid and advisers if the South Vietnamese government could rally its own people and use the aid effectively.[13] The Geneva agreements of 1954 had authorized 685 American military advisers to South Vietnam to train its army. The first increase Kennedy approved added another 500. There were repeated requests for additional advisers, but Kennedy authorized only a few—the total when he was killed was 16,500. And on each occasion he expressed his reluctance more sharply. As Roswell Gilpatric, McNamara's deputy, said, "Resistance was encountered from the President at every stage as this total amount of U.S. personnel deployment increased."[14]

In fact, it was crucial in President Kennedy's view that no matter what strategy was followed, the central role had to be played by the Vietnamese. And he reiterated this on every occasion. Americans could not win the war for them: "In the final analysis, it is their war. They are the ones who have to win it or lose it. We can help them, we can give them equipment, we can send our men out there as advisers, but they have to win it, the people of Viet-Nam, against the Communists."[15]

Schlesinger believes that Kennedy "was vaguely searching for a nonmilitary solution—vaguely because Vietnam was still a sideshow."[16] As he reports, Kennedy was disturbed at any statement by an administration official that appeared to increase U.S. commitment in Southeast Asia or obstruct a political settlement. In fact, as early as July 1962 Kennedy ordered McNamara to start planning for the phased withdrawal of

---

[13]Again the fullest account of Kennedy's attitude is in Schlesinger's *Robert Kennedy and His Times*, on which I draw here.

[14]Roswell Gilpatric, in an interview by D. J. O'Brien, 12 August 1970, 1, RFK Oral History Program, Kennedy Library, Boston, Mass.

[15]CBS interview with Walter Cronkite, 2 September 1963.

[16]Schlesinger, *Robert Kennedy and His Times*, p. 709.

American military personnel from Vietnam, although it was not until May 1963 that the Pentagon produced a plan that was satisfactory.[17]

As the Buddhist crisis progressed Kennedy became more and more convinced that the Vietnamese could not win the struggle against the Viet Cong. On several occasions he telephoned me—I was by that time the action officer for Vietnam—to make sure that everything possible was being done to keep the U.S. profile low. "Remember Laos," was his most frequent admonition. He wanted to avoid creating an obstacle to any opportunity, such as a negotiated settlement, that would permit an American withdrawal.[18]

On one occasion when the South Vietnamese forces lost an engagement, *The New York Times,* clearly with a purpose of its own, ran the opening paragraph of the story in one half of a little box in the middle of page 1. In the other half of the box it ran the opening paragraph of a story about an American general who had just arrived in Saigon for an inspection visit. The president called me at home before breakfast and turned the air blue with his anger. "Don't you understand that this general's visit inevitably increases U.S. commitment, contrary to my repeated orders to you?" When he paused for breath and I finally got a word in, I pointed out that I hadn't been informed of the general's visit and that I had no authority to prevent a general from going to Vietnam even if I had been informed. That very afternoon, Kennedy issued a national security action memorandum saying that no officer of general or flag rank would visit Vietnam without the written permission of the assistant secretary of state for Far Eastern affairs.

As the opening step in the plan he had forced the Joint Chiefs to prepare, Kennedy ordered the first 1,000 American advisers of the 16,500 stationed in Vietnam withdrawn.

Within a few days of issuing that order, President Kennedy was assassinated in Dallas.

---

[17]*Pentagon Papers,* vol. 2, pp. 670–71.

[18]Author, in a recorded interview with D. J. O'Brien, 14 August 1970, 20; letter to *The New York Times,* 8 August 1970; *To Move a Nation,* p. 536; and Hilsman Papers, Kennedy Library, Boston, Mass.

Shortly after Kennedey's death, Walt Rostow again sub-mitted a memo raising the question of bombing North Viet-nam.[19] The memo also proposed bombing infiltration routes in Laos and removing many of the restrictions on bombing and other military measures in South Vietnam.

I immediately wrote a memo in response opposing all three proposals. Extensive bombing of the south, I argued, violated the principle of the strategic-hamlet concept and would erode the al-legiance of the people. As for infiltration routes, I doubted that bombing would have much effect and cited my own experiences in Burma. The routes were jungle trails. The men coming down them were on foot. The supplies were carried by reinforced bicy-cles. How could bombing stop this kind of infiltration? In any case, most of the Viet Cong's supplies and recruits came not down trails from North Vietnam but from villages inside South Viet-nam. Cutting off infiltration routes, even if bombing could in fact accomplish that, would have only a marginal effect.

Furthermore, I pointed out, so far the men coming down the trails were southerners who had gone north in 1952. If the United States raised the ante by bombing infiltration routes, the North Vietnamese would undoubtedly respond by including northerners. The United States and South Vietnam would be no better off than before and perhaps worse. They would be paying the international political cost of escalating the war for nothing.

As for bombing the north, I argued that although the United States and North Vietnam had never actually communicated with each other on the question, they were in fact both adhering to a tacit agreement.[20] So far the Viet Cong consisted solely of southerners, as we had established beyond doubt. By refraining from sending northerners south, the north was trying to main-tain the fiction that the struggle was purely internal to the south, not an international war or even a civil war between north and south. North Vietnam had ten regular divisions that it had re-frained from sending south. The tacit agreement was that if these divisions were committed, the United States would be justified

---

[19]For a fuller description of these events, see author, *To Move a Nation*, p. 527ff.

[20]Ibid., p. 534ff., and Hilsman Papers.

in bombing North Vietnam. By the same token, if the United States bombed North Vietnam, the north would send regular divisions south.

President Johnson responded to these two memos by deciding to postpone a decision. In the meantime, he appointed a committee to study just what northern targets might be bombed and what the effects would be.

★ ★
The Political Groundwork for Escalation

The final decision to bomb North Vietnam came in February 1965, but President Johnson had laid the political groundwork for the decision much earlier. As vice president, Johnson had become familiar with the individuals and organizations involved in decisionmaking on Vietnam. Kennedy's decision to negotiate the neutralization of Laos indicated his position. The White House staff, principally McGeorge Bundy, the national security adviser, and Michael V. Forrestal, his staff specialist on Asia, were skeptical about military intervention. In the State Department, Dean Rusk was hawkish, while George W. Ball, the under secretary, W. Averell Harriman, and I were decidedly dovish. Secretary of Defense McNamara was hawkish, as was the director of the CIA, John A. McCone. The attorney general, Robert F. Kennedy, was very dovish.

The members of the Joint Chiefs of Staff were a special case. After the Korean War, the military generally felt that they should never again be required to fight a limited land war in Asia. Their feelings were so strong that around Washington they were jokingly dubbed the Never-Again Club. In its extreme form, their position was that before being sent into an Asian war, they should be guaranteed permission to do whatever was necessary to win, including using nuclear weapons.

In both the Senate and the House, the members of committees dealing with foreign affairs tended to align with the doves, while the members of armed-services committees generally aligned with the hawks.

Undoubtedly President Johnson didn't plan in advance to escalate the war, but he also seemed determined to win the war, even if winning required escalation. Given his conviction, the clever course for Johnson would be to remove any opposition in advance, and this he proceeded to do with consummate political skill. His first target was the assistant secretary for Far Eastern affairs—me.

President Johnson was probably the cleverest politician of his generation. At one point, for example, he wanted to remove John Gronouski as postmaster general, but he didn't want Gronouski to find a position outside the government from which he could criticize the administration. As the president put it, "I would rather have him inside the tent peeing out than outside the tent peeing in." So Johnson offered him the ambassadorship to Poland. Sure enough, Gronouski found the prospect of being the first Polish-American ambassador to Poland irresistible. In my case, the president found that I had spent part of my childhood in the Philippines and offered me the post of ambassador there. It was tempting to return to the Philippines as ambassador, but the purpose was so obviously to shut me up that I preferred to resign.

In the case of W. Averell Harriman, the president shifted him from under secretary to roving ambassador with particular responsibility for African affairs. Harriman told me privately that if he had been twenty years younger, he too would have resigned. He went on to predict that Johnson would escalate the Vietnam war, that the escalation would fail, that the United States would have to negotiate, and that the president would have to choose him, Harriman, to be the negotiator because of his record of negotiating with the Soviets—remarkably prescient commentary.

As for George Ball, the president made him feel as if he were the only spokesperson for the opposition that would be permitted to remain. For almost two years Ball was content playing the "house dove," but then he came to feel that he was being used and left for private life.

Members of the White House staff couldn't exercise independent power, and therefore Michael V. Forrestal wasn't a serious problem. He was encouraged to stay on, but eventually returned to private life. However, McGeorge Bundy's position as national security adviser was problematic for Johnson. For reasons known only to himself, the president seems to have felt that Bundy could be tempted to go along with a policy of escalation in Vietnam, perhaps because of the possibility of eventually replacing Rusk as secretary of state. In any event, after Johnson had tentatively decided to bomb North Vietnam, he persuaded Bundy to go to Vietnam for a final check and recommendation. Bundy was reluctant but he did go, in fact he acquiesced in the decision, which effectively accomplished Johnson's purpose.

Robert F. Kennedy was a much more formidable political problem. To take care of him, President Johnson first announced to the public that for the election of 1964 he would not choose a vice presidential running mate from his present cabinet, which was a roundabout way of saying that he would not choose Kennedy. Nor, as attorney general, would Kennedy be allowed to play an important role in the administration. Privately Johnson suggested that the wisest course for Kennedy would be to resign and run for the governorship of Massachusetts. In the end, Kennedy decided to run not for governor, which would have kept him out of foreign affairs, but for the United States Senate from New York.

The most formidable problem of all, however, was the Joint Chiefs of Staff. Johnson removed this obstacle by dividing them. Between the two world wars, the doctrine of air power had been developed. The theory was that strategic bombing alone could win wars without the bloody attrition of battlefield combat. Bombing factories would destroy an enemy's capacity to build weapons and war materiel. Bombing cities, including workers' housing, would destroy civilian morale and therefore support for the war. Interdiction bombing—striking road and rail networks leading from home areas to the war zone—would prevent any supplies produced from getting to the front. It was this strategy that the United States had followed against Germany and Japan in World War II.

Following the war the United States mounted a huge research effort to assess the effectiveness of the bombing. To the despair of the air force this report, *The Strategic Bombing Survey*, concluded that such bombing was not decisive and that the resources that went into it would have been better spent in close air support for ground forces.

The Korean War gave the doctrine of air power a second chance. The U.S. Air Force gained almost total air superiority over Korea and bombed the factories and towns of North Korea and the road and rail networks virtually at will. But again, after the war the conclusion was that strategic bombing was not in fact decisive. There was no doubt that bombing had slowed down the enemy's offensive buildup. Bombing also made it more costly. In effect, the enemy had to put three tons of supplies into the logistical pipeline to get one through to the front. But eventually the enemy succeeded in amassing the supplies for an offensive, and once again it was clear that bombing could not win wars by itself.

In effect what President Johnson did was to hold out to the air force the prospect of one more chance to prove that strategic bombing was effective, that it could by itself win wars.

But all this came later. I submitted my resignation in January 1964, knowing if I didn't that President Johnson would fire me. He asked me to stay on until 15 March to give him time to find a successor. (The man he chose was William P. Bundy, McGeorge Bundy's older brother.) For the few weeks that I remained, the strategic argument continued. Indeed, it continued for a whole year before the decision to escalate was finally made.

★ ★

The Hawks' Strategic Rationale

The hawks conceded that although local, purely Vietnamese issues, such as the need for land reform, were at work, the Viet Cong movement was ultimately inspired by Moscow and Peking and that a Communist victory would redound to the benefit of China and the Soviet Union strategically, economically, and politically.

Their first argument was that Vietnam constituted a strategic route and base for the penetration and domination of all of Southeast Asia. By the same token, Vietnam itself constituted an avenue into Southeast Asia for the Communist Chinese.

The second argument was President Dwight D. Eisenhower's falling-domino theory, enunciated at a press conference in 1954. The idea was that if Indochina fell to a native Communist insurgency, then Communist parties in all the other Southeast Asian states would be encouraged to rebel and the Soviet Union and China would be encouraged to aid them. Implicit in the domino theory was the assumption that Southeast Asia was strategically crucial if the United States was to maintain its position in Asia and hence protect its own security.

One of the most sophisticated geopolitical arguments for American intervention was offered by President Johnson himself in a reflective mood at a meeting of the National Security Council.[21] He said that the fabric of what international peace and stability the world had was made up of sets of expectations by all nations—enemies, allies, and neutrals—about how each of the others would behave in a crisis. If the United States let South Vietnam "go down the drain," then every country in the world would have to go back to the drawing board, every nation would have to reexamine its assumptions about security. Japan would have to ask itself whether or not it was a wise decision to place itself under the American nuclear shield and become an ally of the United States. Germany would have to rethink its position about the NATO alliance. All of our friends and allies would have to think hard about their friendship with the United States. One thing was certain, he went on to say, and that was if we let Vietnam go down the drain, many more nations would feel compelled to build their own nuclear weapons. Nuclear proliferation would become rampant.

The policy implications flowing from this analysis were twofold. The first conclusion was that Communist aggression could be met successfully only by military force. The second conclusion was that it *must* be met if the vital interests of the United States were to be preserved. Even failure, as Secretary of State Rusk said, would at least teach the Communist world that such aggression would be costly.

---

[21]Notes on NSC meetings, Hilsman Papers.

★ ★

The Doves' Rationale

The rival view that Kennedy, Harriman, Ball, and I pushed did not deny that the leaders of the insurgency were bona fide Communists and that Moscow and Peking gave them full support. But we argued that the insurgency was more accurately described as an anticolonialist and essentially nationalist movement, feeding on social discontent in South Vietnam, whose leaders happened to be members of the Communist party through an accident of history. The leaders of the insurgency, we argued, were nationalists first and Communists only second. We conceded that a Communist Vietnam would be troublesome politically to American interests in Southeast Asia, but that it would be no more than troublesome. The economic implications were minuscule. Strategically, Vietnam was of little intrinsic importance. The Soviets would undoubtedly be given permission to use the port facilities of Cam Ranh Bay as a base, but, we argued, Hanoi's demonstrated determination to remain independent of Moscow and Peking assured that the use would be limited.

Concerning strategic issues, we reached the opposite conclusion on every point. Consider a topographical map of Southeast Asia. The border between Laos and Vietnam is the spine of a mountain range, with subsidiary ridges coming off that at perpendicular angles. Road and rail networks from China to Vietnam must at places pass within a few miles of the sea, which makes them extraordinarily vulnerable to interdiction by air and naval power. Thus Vietnam seemed to have little strategic value as an invasion route from China into Southeast Asia. It was worth noting, we argued, that the Eisenhower administration implicitly acknowledged that Vietnam had little strategic importance by its refusal to intervene in what was then Indochina at the time of Dienbienphu.

The only feasible route for a strategic entree from China into Southeast Asia was through Laos. The route would be well inland, screened by many miles of mountain ranges, and it would end up in Thailand, the very heart of Southeast Asia, where it could connect with road and rail networks. Thus we insisted that if any country had any strategic importance as a route into Southeast Asia, it was Laos and not Vietnam. The Chinese actually built such a road—from China across Laos, linking up to the roads to Thailand—as part of their aid program to Laos during the latter part of Eisenhower's administration and the early part of Kennedy's. The Eisenhower administration did in fact consider intervening in Laos in 1960, partly because of the road building and partly because of Soviet support to the Communist guerrillas in Laos and Vietnam, but finally decided against it. The Kennedy administration also decided against intervention in favor of negotiating the neutralization of Laos, which was accomplished by the Geneva accords of 1962. If Laos was strategically more important than Vietnam, our argument concluded, then why should the United States fight for Vietnam and not Laos?

As for the domino theory, we conceded that if the Communists controlled all of Vietnam, Cambodia and Laos had only a small chance of maintaining a neutral status and would probably come under the domination of Vietnam. The population of Laos was about two million and the population of Cambodia no more than six, while the populations of North and South Vietnam together amounted to about thirty-eight million. But the probability that Laos and Cambodia would come under the domination of Vietnam would make Thailand, Burma, Malaysia, and Indonesia more determined to deal swiftly and ruthlessly with any foreign-stimulated insurgency. Thus the probability that Laos and Cambodia would become dominoes made it much less likely that the rest of Southeast Asia would.

In answer to President Johnson's argument that if the United States permitted Vietnam to go down the drain, the fabric of international politics would unravel, we argued that on the contrary if anything unraveled the fabric of international politics, it would be U.S. intervention in Vietnam. None of the other nations of the world, we pointed out, could see any strategic, political, or economic importance to Vietnam. If the United States turned the struggle in Vietnam into a major war, the rest of the world would think it had gone mad. It is bad enough for your friends to think you mad; if your enemies do, the world will become a much more dangerous place.

287

Thus those of us against escalating the struggle in Vietnam reached exactly the opposite conclusion: that the mistake would not be letting Vietnam go down the drain but for the United States to intervene.

And the policy that flowed from this analysis was fundamentally different. If the insurgency was a nationalist, anti-colonialist movement, then sending foreign troops of any kind would be self-defeating. Foreign troops would recruit more peasants for the Viet Cong than they could possibly kill. And Americans would probably recruit more than those of almost any other nation. In Korea, the hated colonialists were Japanese, and when the peasants looked up at Americans marching by they saw the liberators. But American troops in Vietnam—white men and black men, like the earlier French and Senegalese colonial forces—would look quite different to the peasants.

★ ★
Departure

I left the government on 15 March 1964. For the rest of that year President Johnson was mainly preoccupied with the upcoming election. In the meantime, the situation in Vietnam steadily deteriorated.

Immediately after the election, Johnson fixed his attention on Vietnam and decided something drastic had to be done. His initial proposal was not to make the struggle an American war but only to bomb North Vietnam. Code-named Rolling Thunder, it divided the Joint Chiefs and nullified their resistance to anything that seemed likely to lead to another limited war in Asia.

Thus in February 1965, the United States began bombing North Vietnam and the supply routes leading to South Vietnam. A few weeks later regular combat ground forces were introduced to defend the airfields. The situation continued to deteriorate in spite of the bombing of North Vietnam, and in July the United States introduced ground forces on a large scale, with the total eventually reaching over half a million men. Clearly the lessons of guerrilla warfare the OSS learned in Burma were not applied in Vietnam.

288

EPILOGUE II ★★★★★★★★★★★★★
Thoughts on Guerrilla Warfare

The struggle over U.S. policy toward Vietnam made me think hard about my experiences as a guerrilla in Burma and what lessons it held not just for Vietnam but for policy toward guerrilla warfare in general.

Headquarters of Detachment 101 had credited our guerrilla battalion with having killed over three hundred Japanese, including one hundred and four in the ambush after we blew up the bridge near Ponywa, and wounding another two hundred. Our own casualties were fewer than half a dozen. We blew up several bridges and ambushed and destroyed several truck convoys. Probably more important was our intelligence gathering. The air corps had commended us for having supplied over 90 percent of the information for their bombing operations in the area. The British had commended us for our intelligence work. Colonel Peers added that equally important was the fact that guerrilla groups operating behind enemy lines forced the Japanese to use troops to protect their rear areas, troops they badly needed at the front. The constant threat of ambush, Peers went on, increased the psychological stress the Japanese were under.

In terms of cost-effectiveness, it cannot be doubted that the guerrilla efforts of OSS Detachment 101 were a resounding success. For our battalion, the cost had been the commitment of three Americans and one Englishman, pay and supplies for three hundred guerrillas, C-47s and crews to supply us, and radio and administrative personnel at headquarters. The intelligence we gathered alone would have justified such small costs many times over.

In individual terms, I found being a guerrilla behind enemy lines considerably better than being a platoon leader in Merrill's Marauders at Myitkyina, where I was told to lead my men straight into dug-in machine guns. Your only hope was that one or two men would still be on their feet when they got close enough to the pillbox to throw a grenade. In such circumstances, an infantry platoon leader could do almost nothing to influence the situation. His brains and skill were essentially irrelevant. The only thing that counted was his luck.

A guerrilla leader, on the other hand, could match his wits against the enemy's. If he was careful about gathering intelligence, perceptive in analyzing it, and knowledgeable about the tactics and strategy of guerrilla operations, he could do a great deal of damage to the enemy and at the same time minimize the risk to his own men.

A guerrilla leader can be successful only in very special circumstances. For us, the circumstances had not been perfect, but they had certainly been good.

First and foremost is terrain. Guerrillas need cover to operate effectively—mountains, forest, or jungle. Guerrillas can operate in an urban or suburban setting—an example is the Irish Republican Army in Ulster—but they have to have superb training, organization, and communications in order to come together briefly for an operation and then disperse. Detachment 101 had both mountains and jungle. The terrain was sparsely populated and had few roads. On mountain and jungle trails, guerrillas on foot are as mobile as a motorized enemy. It was the terrain that made it possible for us to find safety in constant movement, rarely spending two nights in the same place.

The second essential is the sympathy of the population. Mao Zedong used to say that guerrillas are fish swimming in the sea of the people. The French *maquis*, who fought a German army of occupation, had a sympathetic population. That was our battalion's greatest lack. When Detachment 101 was operating with Kachin guerrillas in Kachin territory, the situation was close to ideal. The Kachins' traditional enemies were the

Shans, the Burmese, and the Chinese, and the British colonial authorities were their friends and allies. The Americans had the additional good will earned by missionaries. But our battalion was operating in Shan country with Karen and Chinese forces. Here the population had little love for the British. But by this stage of the war they had even less love for the Japanese. So they were essentially neutral, wishing that both sides would go away and leave them alone. Our battalion had no way of winning the active support of the population. The only thing we could do was try to keep them neutral by being scrupulous in our relations with them—paying generously for what we took from them, repaying them in kind two or three times over for scarce commodities such as rice and tobacco, and making sure that no villager, male or female, was ever molested by our men.

A third essential is a logistical system. And the logistical system has to be able to handle not only supplies but also the wounded. That is vital for morale. In Vietnam, the Communists built a superb logistical system, the so-called Ho Chi Minh trails, from North Vietnam down the mountain and jungle trails of Laos and Cambodia into all parts of South Vietnam. Supplies were carried on men's backs or wheeled along the trails on reinforced bicycles (in the final stages of the Vietnam war, the trails were improved to take trucks part of the way). The wounded were evacuated not to North Vietnam but to thousands of villages where they were concealed and cared for by sympathizers.

The system by which we were supplied in Burma was, of course, even better. By the time of our operations, the Allies had established almost total air superiority over Burma. Airdrops delivered all our supplies and light planes evacuated the wounded. If we had had helicopters of the kind available to Americans in Vietnam, we would have been even better off, in terms not only of evacuations and deliveries but also of close-in fire support.

But although I found being a guerrilla safer than being an infantryman, and although the OSS guerrilla effort in Burma was outstandingly cost-effective, in most wars guerrillas are useful only at the margin. In most instances, even with all the advantages described above, guerrillas cannot be effective unless the main body of the enemy is fully engaged by regular forces.

Again consider the French *maquis*. Their terrain was not

ideal, except in some of the mountain areas of the *massif central*. But the population was totally sympathetic and united against the Germans. Supplies of food and support for the wounded came from the people. Ammunition and special weapons and equipment such as radios came by airdrop from the Allies. Still, the *maquis* were largely ineffective until after the landings in Normandy. Before that time, the Germans could easily concentrate one, two, or even three divisions against any *maquis* unit that tried to become active. As a result, during this period the *maquis* pretty much confined their effort to the odd bit of sabotage and the assassination of French quislings.

On the other hand, after Normandy it was only at extraordinary risk that the Germans could withdraw divisions from the front to chase guerrillas, and the *maquis* came into their own. Following the breakout from Normandy and throughout the great sweep of Allied armies to the Rhine, the *maquis* ambushed, blew bridges, disrupted German communications, and also provided the main screen for the Allied right flank, a job that otherwise would have required several divisions.

Guerrillas, then, can never be more than a supplement. Guerrilla warfare is the principal weapon only of the weak. And with this as their principal weapon, the weak can never prevail in a war between states. They can, however, sometimes prevail in a civil war. The circumstances have to be even more special for that. The experience of Mao Zedong and the Chinese is instructive. The Chinese Communists attempted to seize power in 1927 and failed. They were driven into the mountains and later undertook the Long March to Shensi and Yenan. Their defeat forced them to depend on the peasants and the countryside rather than on the workers and the cities. Thus they turned Marx and Lenin upside down. These experiences were what focused Mao's thought on guerrilla warfare and led the Chinese Communists to develop the doctrine and strategy of "people's" or "revolutionary" warfare.

In 1948, local Communist parties launched revolts throughout Southeast Asia—in the Philippines, Malaya, Indochina, Indonesia, and Burma. Initially, their techniques were unsophisticated, little more than campaigns of indiscriminate terrorism. But after the Chinese Communist victory on the mainland in 1949, the influence of Chinese doctrine on both tactics and strategy began to be felt. As it happened, only the Vietminh revolt against the French in Indochina achieved any success, but it could be argued that in the Philippines and Malaya, at least, the indiscriminate use of terrorism had already alienated so many of the peasantry that it was too late for a change in strategy to do much good.

The Chinese Communist doctrine of revolutionary warfare is laid out in Mao's various works. The combination of what Mao was saying and what the Chinese were doing added up to more than a call from the Chinese to other peoples to follow their revolutionary example. Mao's first principle was the phrase already quoted: "Guerrillas are fish," Mao said, "and the people are the water in which they swim. If the temperature of the water is right, the fish will thrive and multiply." Mao's revolutionary warfare was guerrilla tactics plus political action.

Mao had a great deal to say about tactics, but there was a difference between mere tactics and revolutionary warfare itself. Mao's revolutionary war progressed through three phases. The first was almost purely political, with activist cadres building support among the people, propagandizing, and recruiting. The second was active guerrilla warfare, with bands of guerrillas ambushing government forces and raiding and harassing, but avoiding pitched battles. Their terrorism was highly discriminating—the assassination of government officials, especially unpopular ones, and sabotage.

This second stage was a systematic effort to destroy the people's confidence in the government's ability to function and protect them, and to make the government suspicious of the people. Power could be seized in the turmoil that followed this stage, especially if government leaders lost their nerve.

If not, the revolutionaries resorted to the third and final stage. This was to establish "liberated areas"—base areas, that is, where supplies and recruits could be obtained and where the efforts of the people could be directed to the support of the struggle. Here guerrillas would be transformed into regular forces and would turn their terrorism and harassment into a civil war, engaging government troops in conventional combat and destroying them.

In the first stage—if the temperature of the people was right—all that was needed were trained and dedicated cadres and a doctrine to guide their efforts. Food, money, and supplies could be obtained from the people; their contribution committed them to the cause. Even in the second stage, outside help was not really essential. Money and supplies came from the people; weapons and ammunition could be taken from government forces through ambush or surprise attack. Building the political base was still the first priority, and too many arms too soon from outside might interfere with that task. (In most guerrilla movements, the most useful outside help at this stage has been the contribution of highly specialized equipment—radios, codes, and medical supplies.) It was only in the third and final stage that outside help might make a decisive difference, after the struggle had been transformed into a regular civil war. At that time, two conventional armies are locked in sustained combat and the need for ammunition, weapons, and supplies assumes large-scale proportions. But even at this stage, outside help might not be crucial if the liberated areas were large enough to form an adequate economic base and if no substantial outside assistance was going to the government side.

These special circumstances prevailed in China after World War II, when the Communists were finally successful. They prevailed in Cuba when Castro came to power; the government in Cuba, in fact, collapsed before the third stage had even begun. They also prevailed in Vietnam, although Communist forces had to fight almost continuously for thirty years, from 1945 to 1975.

To repeat, guerrillas operating against a *foreign* invader cannot be successful unless the main body of the enemy is fully engaged by regular forces—illustrated by the fact that the *maquis* did not become effective until after the Normandy invasion. But what if the guerrillas are operating not against a foreign invader, but their own government?

Most guerrilla movements depend on a sympathetic population for food, for recruits, and for silence about their whereabouts. At the very least, as happened in the case of the American-led guerrillas in Burma, the population has to be neutral. As Mao said, guerrillas are fish that swim in the sea of the people. If the government is ruthless enough to dry up the sea, guerrillas cannot survive.

But most governments find it politically and morally impossible to be totally ruthless toward their own people in responding to a guerrilla revolution. The Chinese government's repression of students in Tiananmen Square in 1989—ruthless though it was by civilized standards—was actually sharply circumscribed in many ways. A government that is a foreign power in occupation feels fewer moral and political restraints, especially if it is totalitarian and can conceal the truth from its own people. The Nazis in World War II were under no such restraints in occupied territories. On one occasion Czech partisans assassinated the Nazi boss of Czechoslovakia just outside the village of Lidice. The villagers had nothing to do with the assassination, but the Nazis killed all the males of the village over ten years old and scattered the females and children over Eastern Europe. Some survivors are still looking for their relatives. On another occasion, the Nazis followed the same procedure in the village of Oradour-sur-Glane in France, except they killed the women and children as well as the men. If a government is that ruthless, a guerrilla movement cannot succeed; but neither can such a government ever win the support of the people. The Nazis, of course, did not care. They had no hope of ever winning the Czech or French people, but by being totally ruthless they could paralyze the guerrillas so long as their own regular forces were not engaged by the Allied armies.

But if a government fighting guerrillas among its own people is so ruthless that it alienates the people, it will lose. This was the fate of the Batista regime fighting Castro's guerrillas in Cuba. To defeat guerrillas, the government must put its first priority on winning the support of the people. Once that is achieved—once the sea of the people has been dried up—the guerrillas will be easy to deal with. The problem of the Diem government in South Vietnam was that most of its members were Catholics and the people were Buddhists; the members of the government were largely ex-northerners, and the people were southerners; the members of the government were Frenchified, and the people were not. So the government really did not trust the people, and its attempts to win their loyalty were half-

295

hearted. It ended up accepting the American military's advice to chase the guerrillas in the jungles and mountains—giving the Viet Cong civilian cadres a relatively free hand to win converts in the villages.

Guerrilla warfare indeed is the weapon of the weak. But in some circumstances the strong will find it a powerful adjunct to their more orthodox efforts. And in other, admittedly special circumstances—when a government is alien or so arbitrary, tyrannical, and repressive as to become the equivalent of alien—guerrilla warfare may eventually be successful, even if the government's resistance continues for decades or generations.

APPENDIX ★ ★ ★ ★ ★ ★ ★ ★ ★ ★ ★ ★ ★ ★ ★ ★

Summary of Detachment 101's Accomplishments

DETACHMENT 101
OFFICE OF STRATEGIC SERVICES
Burma—April 14, 1942 to July 12, 1945

"THE AMERICAN-KACHIN RANGERS"

The first United States unit to form an intelligence screen and organize and employ a large guerrilla army deep in enemy territory.

They pioneered the unique art of unconventional warfare, later incorporated as fundamental combat skills for our Army Special Forces (Green Berets). They have been credited with the highest "kill/loss ratio" for any infantry-type unit in American military history.

The Presidential Distinguished Unit Citation awarded to Detachment 101 says in part, "The courage and fighting spirit displayed by its officers and men in offensive action against overwhelming enemy strength reflect the highest tradition of the armed forces of the United States," signed Dwight D. Eisenhower, Chief of Staff, January 17, 1946. He was of the opinion that Detachment 101 performed in an outstanding manner, one of the most difficult and hazardous assignments that any military unit had ever been called upon to perform.

Total 101 personnel—Officers	250
Enlisted men	750
Highest guerrilla strength	10,800
Espionage agents with radios	162
U.S. personnel killed, all causes	27
Native personnel killed	338
Espionage agents lost	40
Japanese killed	5,400
Additional Japanese estimated killed or wounded	10,000
Japanese captured	78
Bridges demolished	57
Trains derailed	9
Vehicles destroyed—captured	272
Supplies destroyed—captured—tons	15,000
Allied airmen rescued	425
Intelligence furnished to Northern Combat Command (NCAC)	85%
Targets designated for 10th U.S. Air Force	75%

Source: OSS/101 Association.

Index

Van Arsdale, Albert (*cont.*)
    background of, 159
    after WWII, 159
V-E (Victory in Europe) Day, 194,
    221, 247
Venereal disease, 57, 61–62, 109
Viet Cong, 265–70, 280, 284
Vietnam, (map) 34–35, 253
    lessons for, learned in Burma,
        253–88
    battle at Bien Hoa, 268–70
    Buddhist crisis in, 276–77
    escalation of war in, 281
    bombing of North, 288
Vietnamese Special Forces, attack
    on pagodas, 277
Villagers, 168, 170, 189
Vinegar Joe. *See* Stillwell, General
Visayan Island commanders, 44–
    45

Wainwright, General Jonathan
    M., 233, 244
    decision to surrender, 42
    memoirs, 46
War colleges, 13n, 86
Wedemeyer, General Albert C.,
    230
Weller, George, 213, 223–24

West Point (U.S. Military
    Academy), 2–12
    casualty rate of class of June,
        1943, 50, 52
    courses and mock exercises, 8
    early graduation, 50
Wheeler, General Earle, 273, 276
Wingate, General Orde C., 65, 75
World War I, 5, 8
World War II, 1, 5, 15, 295
Wu, Major Cheng-shi, 232

Y, the Marauders' defense
    perimeter at Myitkyina, (map)
    68, 79, 83, 87, 159
Yamato Hotel (Mukden), 233, 243
Yarborough, General William P.,
    275
Yaws (tropical disease), 124

Zeros, Japanese, 82, 150, 156
    downed by C-47, 84–85
    at Heho airfield, 202
Ziino, Joseph, 133, 141, 147,
    background of, 130–31
Zombro, Dr. Fred, 101–102
"Zone of the Interior" (United
    States), 96

About the Author

After the war, Roger Hilsman continued to serve with the Office of Strategic Services as deputy chief of Far East operations (1946–47). He earned his master's and doctorate in international politics at Yale (1947–50) and then served in NATO planning (1950–53). Dr. Hilsman taught at Princeton (1953–56), after which he worked in the Congressional Research Service, first as chief of the foreign affairs and defense division (1956–58), then as CRS deputy director for research (1958–61). President Kennedy appointed him the State Department's director of intelligence and research (1961–63); he later served as assistant secretary of state for Far Eastern affairs (1963–64). Following Kennedy's assassination, Dr. Hilsman returned to academic life at Columbia, where he is professor of government and international politics. His previous books include *Strategic Intelligence* (1956) and *To Move a Nation: The Politics of Foreign Policy in the Administration of John F. Kennedy* (1967). He and his wife live in Lyme, Connecticut.